THE COINS OF THE ANCIENT CELTS

by D.F. ALLEN

edited by DAPHNE NASH

at the University Press

EDINBURGH

Edinburgh University Press
22 George Square, Edinburgh

ISBN 0 85224 371 5

Printed in Great Britain by
The Scolar Press
Ilkley, Yorks

€12-50

[1st Edn 1980]

The Coins of the Ancient Celts

Contents

Preface

DEREK ALLEN delivered the Rhind Lectures in Edinburgh in 1964 on the subject of the coins of the Ancient Celts. It was his intention to write a book based on these lectures, but his untimely death in 1975 prevented the completion of the task. Since I agreed to prepare the existing material for publication, I would like to give some account of what the text of the present book represents.

At the time when Allen gave the lectures the study of Celtic coinage was very much less advanced than it is today, and there were many subjects, such as the silver cross coinages of the Garonne basin, the gold coinages of Belgic and Central Gaul and of the Rhineland, and the silver coinages of Cisalpine Gaul and of the Danube basin, which he had to describe in the lectures as virtually unexamined. It is a tribute to his powers as a scholar of Celtic coinage that very little of what he wrote in 1964 on these subjects has been seriously undermined by recent research. There are still many uncharted areas, but in the last fourteen years a number of important studies – not least by Allen himself – have transformed our understanding of the Continental Celtic coinages. It remains true, however, that little has been written on the subject in English except by Allen, and this book therefore supplies the need, which he clearly recognised, for a substantial treatment of Celtic coins in the English language.

It was certainly Allen's intention to take account of recent studies in his book – this is evident from the revised first chapter and the bibliography – and after 1964 he himself contributed major studies on previously ill-researched topics such as monnaies-à-la-croix (1969), potin coins (1971, 1976), and coins of the Treveri (1971), Cisalpine Gaul (1971), eastern Gaul (1973, 1976, 1978) and the Rhineland (1974), the results of which would undoubtedly have been incorporated into the final redaction of the book. At his death, the material for this book consisted of an annotated set of the six original lectures, together with over 200 slides used to illustrate them; an enlarged and revised version of the first lecture which was to be the introduction to the book;

and a select bibliography which had been kept up to date until 1971.

It was evident from the revised first chapter that the final book would have differed somewhat in arrangement and length of discussion from the original lectures, but there were insufficient indications of the changes Allen had intended to make for me to rearrange most of the lectures to any significant extent. Chapter 1 is therefore Allen's own revised text into which I have incorporated, where relevant, material from Rhind Lecture 1 which it replaces; the other six chapters are the remaining five lectures very much as they were delivered, but with Spain and southern Gaul detached from the treatment of bronze coinage, and instead made into a separate chapter, as it was clear from his bibliography that Allen intended to do himself. I have worked into the text the many additions to the lectures that Allen had written onto his spare copy, and I have made minor changes to the wording of sections on some subjects on which he published subsequent work, in order to take into account his most fully considered opinions on them.

My principal alterations have been to the bibliography. Allen stated that the bibliography was to take the place of footnotes in justification of the text, and I have therefore taken the opportunity to include details of the recent literature on subjects covered in the lectures, including some works that offer alternative views to those expressed in the book. I considered this preferable to making alterations to the lectures in matters where I could not know what opinion Derek Allen might have come to hold.

It was Allen's explicit wish that the coins used for the half-tone illustrations should come as far as possible from British collections. I have endeavoured to observe this rubric, only turning to foreign collections when I could find no adequate examples in British museums to illustrate a point made in the text. Several coins illustrated are from Allen's own collection, which now belongs to the Heberden Coin Room at the Ashmolean Museum in Oxford. The maps, drawings and diagrams are all derived from slides used for the Rhind Lectures; the maps and diagrams have been re-drawn, but I have reproduced Allen's drawings of coin types exactly as they originally appeared.

I could not have revised the bibliography on Central Europe without the advice and suggestions of Dr Karel Castelin, and I take this opportunity to thank him for his generous help with it. My thanks are also due to the British Academy for a grant to prepare this book and for providing a slide projector; to Mr C.C. Haselgrove for help with the bibliography on British coins; to the Bibliothèque Nationale in Paris for providing casts; to the British Museum for allowing me to make impressions of hundreds of coins and to Miss O. Rennie at the Ashmolean for making casts from them. Derek Allen's own closing words to the sixth and final Rhind Lecture are fitting in conclusion : 'It only remains for me to thank the Society of Antiquaries of Scotland for their kindness in arranging this series of lectures, which have compelled me to arrange the disorganised thoughts of many years' standing, also to thank many museum curators and others who have contributed to the gathering of the material, and at the same time to thank you for your courtesy in listening so attentively to this exposition of an abstract subject which makes as many demands on the audience as it does on the lecturer.'

Daphne Nash
Ashmolean Museum, Oxford, February 1979

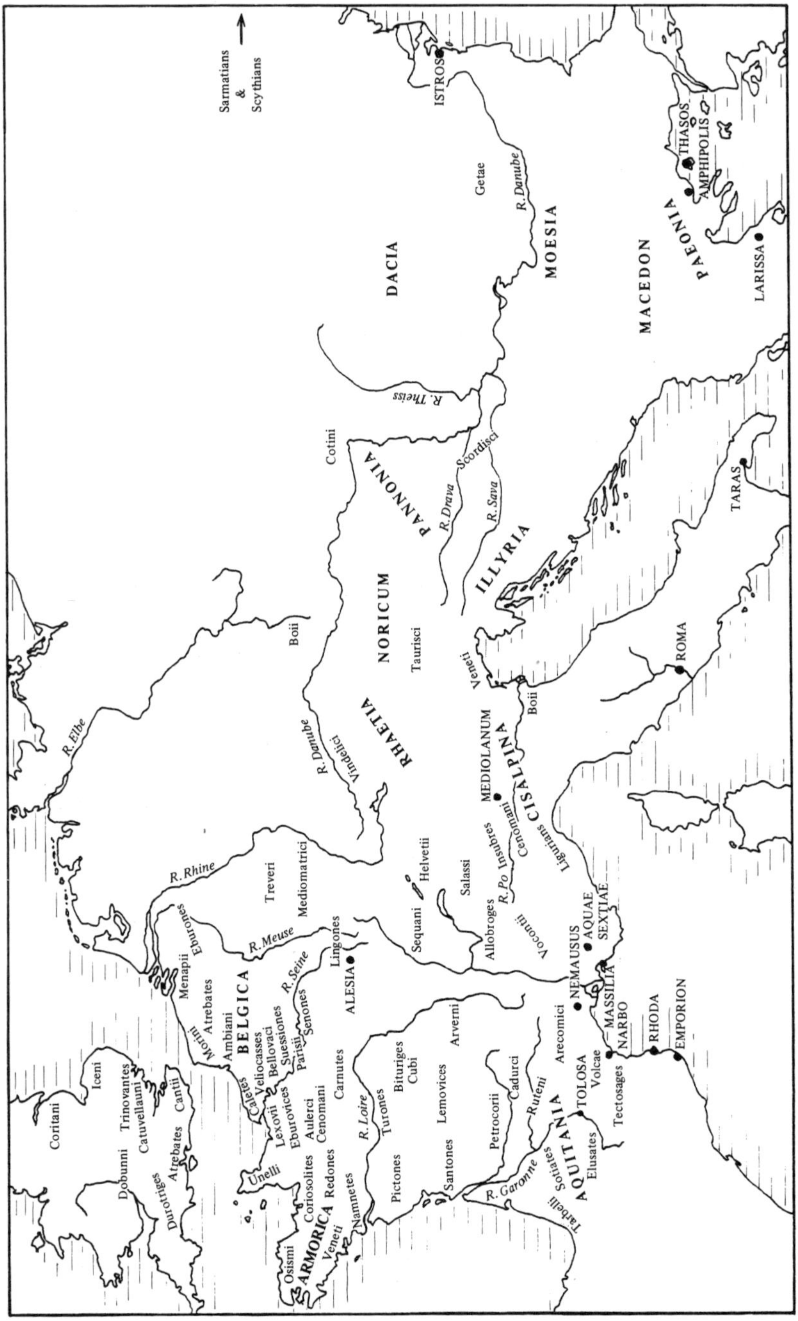

Map 1. Celtic Europe

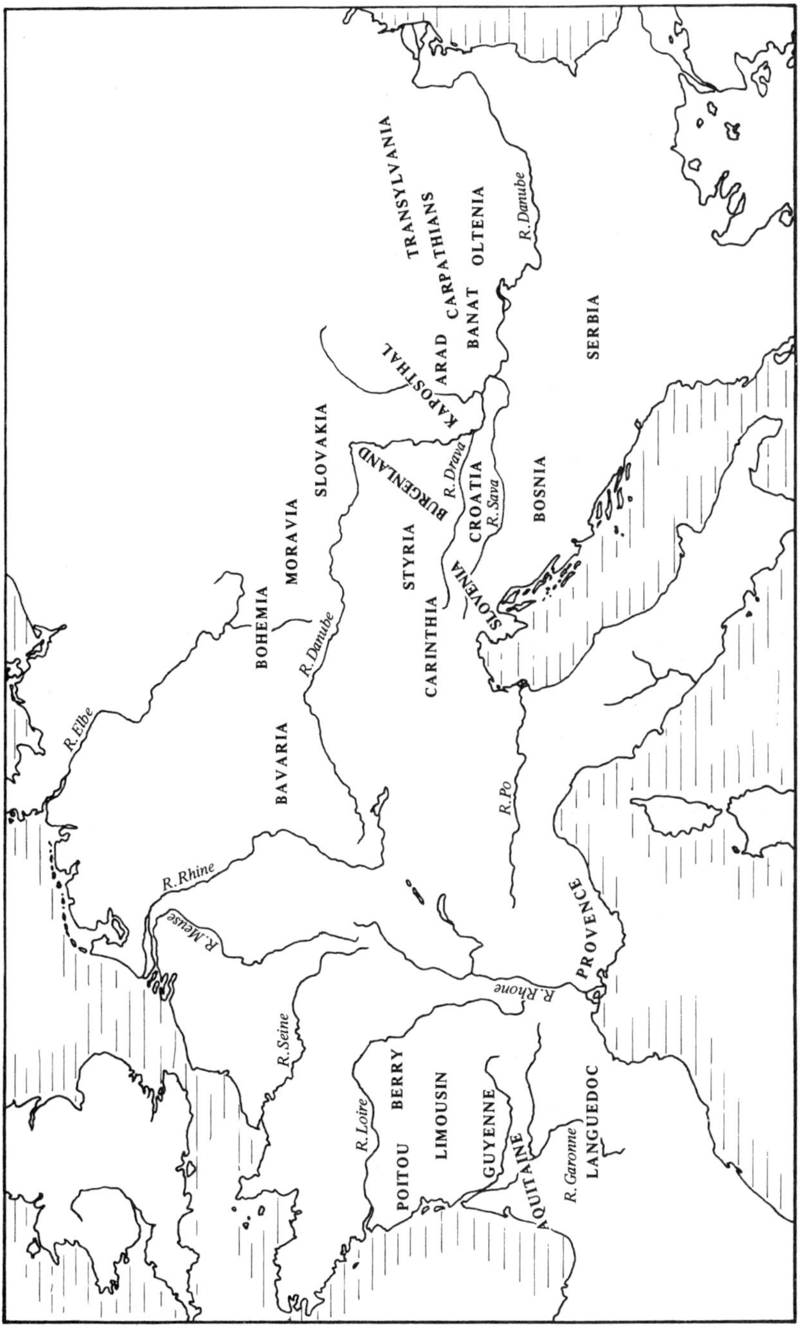

Map 2. European regions

I

Prolegomena to the Study of Celtic Coinage

The Nature of Celtic Coinage, its Origins and Function

It is over a hundred years since Sir John Evans started a new epoch in the study of Celtic coins in Britain by the publication of his book on *The Coins of the Ancient Britons*. There is still no truly comparable foundation for the study of the coins of the Celts in Europe. In this book I shall try to describe to you, as simply as I can, the current state of knowledge about this wide, obscure, but archaeologically essential, subject. Celtic coinage in Britain, both in time and place, can only be understood properly if it is seen in its European context.

Coinage was an invention of the Greeks of Asia Minor during the seventh century B.C. The concept rapidly spread, mainly by the activity of the Greeks themselves, throughout the Mediterranean, but for several centuries it scarcely penetrated beyond the coastal belt. It was not until well into the fourth century B.C. that the fiercely independent peoples of the European interior, who to Greek eyes were no more than barbarians, began to adopt this Greek practice. Growth at first was slow, but by the second century B.C. some form of coinage had spread over most of Europe from the Atlantic to the Black Sea. In the following century the expanding Roman Empire, with its powerful monetary economy, quickly rendered native coinage, then at its peak, anomalous and obsolete. Its ultimate home was in Britain, where vestiges outlived the first century A.D.

The present book provides a short introduction to the native coinages of Europe during this period, and more particularly to those that can properly be called Celtic. Nearly all the territory where the coins were made was occupied in antiquity by people known to the Greeks and Romans as *Galatai*, *Galli* or *Keltoi*, whose main common characteristic was that they spoke some form of the Celtic language, which still survives in Wales, Ireland and Brittany. In terms of archaeology they belonged generally to the la Tène civilisation in its middle and late phases. These Celts, as we may call them, were subdivided into numerous tribes and clans; and at the margins it is hard to distinguish them from Iberians, Ligurians, Germans, Illyrians, Thracians and Dacians. Basically they were all farmers, but in addition to open agricultural settlements each tribe had its strongholds, often on hilltops, known to the Romans as *oppida*, which sometimes grew into veritable cities. Society was stratified into classes, ranging from war-loving chieftains through priests and smiths to peasants. The leaders were quarrelsome, expansionist and migratory; tribes and oppida, as well as their rulers, came and went. But the Celts were also imaginative and artistic in an individual, largely non-representational style, which bears little resemblance to its distant origins in classical art. These characteristics are reflected in the coinage.

All the native coinages of Europe began as imitations of Greek or Roman coins. The models were those that in any area appealed to the inhabitants, whether by reason of familiarity or because there was something appropriate in their types. It is common misconception to identify ancient coins too closely with trade. In antiquity significant trade was conducted by barter. With the partial exception of the hinterland of Macedon, exploited by the Greeks for its silver ores, very few Greek or Roman coins found their way to the heartlands of Europe before these regions were submerged in the Roman Empire. Native coins were made to satisfy local needs and few ever travelled far from their point of origin.

We can only surmise what those needs were. Vast quantities of coins survive, numbered in hundreds, rather than tens, of thousands, and on the Continent a single hoard has contained more than ten thousand coins. The coins in each area were, from the start, made of consistent weight and metallic composition and certainly represented standardised currency values. The likelihood is that coinage was first required for such purposes as tribute, taxes, fines, dowries and offerings, rather than for transactions in the market place. The coins were always hoarded and soon, too, forged. The only occasion when they are mentioned in our historical sources is during the second century B.C, when we are told that Luernius, King of the Arverni (in Auvergne), scattered gold and silver pieces from a chariot as largesse at a ceremony and rewarded a eulogistic bard with a purseful of gold (Strabo 4.2.3). During Caesar's campaigns some of the later types of coin were probably, in substitution for the Roman denarius, used to pay soldiers. It is only in the oppida, where, in the first century B.C, the embryo of an urban economy was emerging, that we have clear evidence for the use of coinage for small scale commerce or bazaar shopping.

Origins. There can now be no doubt that the practice of imitating familiar Greek and Roman coins was adopted by some Celts in or before the latter part of the third century B.C. This was some three centuries after the concept of coinage had become widespread in the Mediterranean. Within a century at most the use of a local style of coinage had been introduced in at least half a dozen basic areas, to which others were soon added. No doubt the Celtic peoples were by then already cognisant of coinage from their contact with Macedonia, Etruria or Massalia and its colonies; but today there survives little direct evidence from finds of Greek coins in Celtic territory for the early trade routes. If Greek coins penetrated the land beyond the advanced civilisations of the Mediterranean, it was in small numbers and they were soon melted down. Roman coins did not circulate regularly in Gaul until after the Roman conquest.

The earliest coins tend to be outright imitations, and it is often difficult to pinpoint their place of origin. They are followed by others that diverge greatly, often no doubt unconsciously, from the originals. These lead in turn to deliberately differentiated local varieties, sometimes wildly different from the first archetype, but nevertheless in direct descent. This is the stage when legends appear. Traditional types were most persistent, even through several centuries, but finally we may meet with true innovations within the contemporary idiom. The early stages tended to develop slowly and were geographically isolated; later on development was rapid and few inhabited areas are without their extensive or even prolific coinages.

Distribution Areas. Because of the local and regional differences in conventions of weight and fineness, there were obvious practical difficulties in the way of free and easy interchange of coins between neighbouring Celtic areas; in general coins did not circulate outside very narrow distributions, and, when they did, their pricing was subject to test or assay. It was no part of the function of Celtic coins to be readily exchangeable with the established major currencies of the ancient world. In fact, most types of Celtic coin are, in the absence of special circumstances, confined to a distribution that may be described in England as the area of a couple of counties, and on the Continent as generally not much larger (say, a circle with a diameter of anything from fifty to one hundred miles). Within it there is a marked tendency for distributions to follow the course of rivers. For establishing these distributions, single finds are more significant than hoards. Hoards, which could be as large as between thirty and forty thousand coins, reflect exceptional circumstances; they may have been lost by adven-

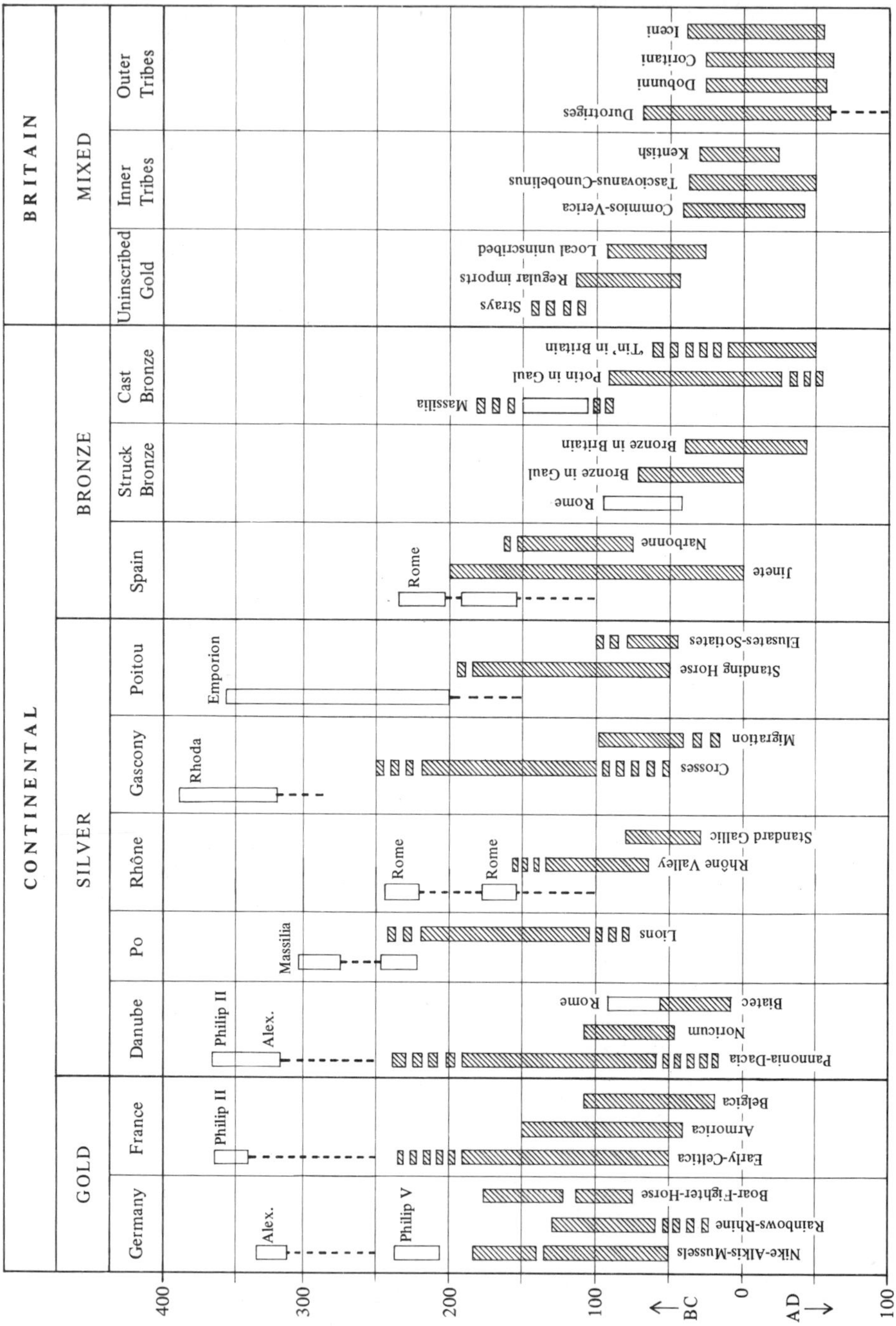

Figure 1. Synoptic time chart

turers, merchants or refugees, or even by a defeated tribe in transit. The great value of hoards is that they help to establish the relative chronology of the coinages.

Attribution. We do not know who issued coins before the stage when names appear. Although coin types or die groups are nearly always confined to particular regions, we have generally no sound reason to suppose that the issuer was a tribe as such. Indeed, the stronger probability is often that they were issued by individual chieftains, since (outside Spain) every early name we have is, so far as we can tell, a personal, not a tribal, name. Even where an issue can be safely identified with a tribe, let us say one well located by Caesar's commentaries on the Gallic war, the coinage is still normally in the name of the individual ruler. Our task is to identify, locate and date the groups; it will often be more or less fortuitous whether we can also attach tribal names to the resulting pattern. Much misunderstanding has been caused in the past by the over-free use for purposes of convenience of tribal names to describe any and every coin, irrespective of the evidence. What we know of the tribal names of Gaul and other Celtic areas mostly dates from the time of Julius Caesar and early Imperial writers. It is most unsafe, during an age of migrations, to argue back in detail from the tribal pattern as stabilised by the Roman Empire to the position a century or more before.

When the copying started, there is no need to assume that coinage was the prerogative of any central authority; the smiths, whose prominent role in the hierarchic Celtic society is attested in all its literature, may simply have made them. But, as the coinage evolved, it early acquired local and institutional characteristics, which suggest its issue by or for some central tribal authority. Consistent standards could not otherwise have been maintained, even for short periods. By the time that inscriptions, particularly in the west, regularly appear on coins, this authority was personified in an individual. Most of the names are certainly those of the responsible issuer, a magistrate or chieftain, and what are presumably magistrates' names are often linked in pairs. Tribal names occur but rarely, and may describe the nationality of the magistrate, not the coin. Of the many chieftains mentioned by Julius Caesar in the commentaries in which he describes his conquest of Gaul (that is of the Celts who lived between the Rhine and the Pyrenees), only some dozen can be identified with names on coins. Amongst them Vercingetorix, leader of the Gauls in their final struggle against Caesar in 52–1 B.C, issued gold coins (coins no. **203**, **204**). In Britain, where the existence of a coinage in these metals is attested by Caesar (*BG.*

5.12.4–5), there must have been a monetary convention during the last fifty years before the Roman conquest, possibly Roman-imposed, since the weights of gold and silver coins, related to the Roman aureus and denarius, remain constant in different tribes, even when they were at war, and in successive reigns. Five of the issuers call themselves kings, and there can be no doubt that in Britain they were, in their respective areas, the central authority for the issue of coinage. There are many varieties of coin with the name of the king Cunobelin, whose death it was led to Claudius' decision to invade and conquer the country.

Nevertheless, it would be illusory to imagine that we can arrange the surviving coinage of the Celts, of which several thousand types are on record, in an orderly tribal pattern, ruler by ruler, spreading consistently across the face of Europe according to some chronological system. If one thing is certain about the Celts, who in this respect differed little from some of their neighbours, it is that they were fickle and changeable, constantly at war or on the move and with never-ending internal feuds and factions. Our information is partial, even fragmentary, both in regard to Celtic history and geography. Archaeology and coinage often tell different stories, coinage representing one section of society, the richer. The most we can hope to do is to determine the general pattern of the coinage, and the broad sweep of the story. The insoluble and the inconsistent will always remain, even when the main outlines have been established.

The Geographical Distribution of Celtic Coinage

The areas within which Celtic and other native coins are found is very large. Spain had an extensive native coinage of silver and bronze, and some of it was issued by Celtic-speaking or Celtic-influenced people, but the whole Spanish coinage, employing a local Spanish script, hangs together and is best studied as a provincial offshoot of Roman coinage. Celtic traces, other than in the language underlying names, are few, and confined to such details as the form of weapons or insignia carried by horsemen. Celtic coinage, therefore, for the purposes of this introduction, has been taken to begin at the Pyrenees. At the other extreme, although Celtic-speaking people roamed the length of the Danube, and some became established in Anatolian Galatia, the main Celtic thrust ended in the Carpathians, and there is little or nothing to connect the native coins found in the Thracian territories beyond them with the Celts. Similarly to the south, the coins found in the hinterland of Venice are indistinguishable in character from those of Cisalpine Gaul, north of the Po; yet it is a fact of history that the Veneti did not

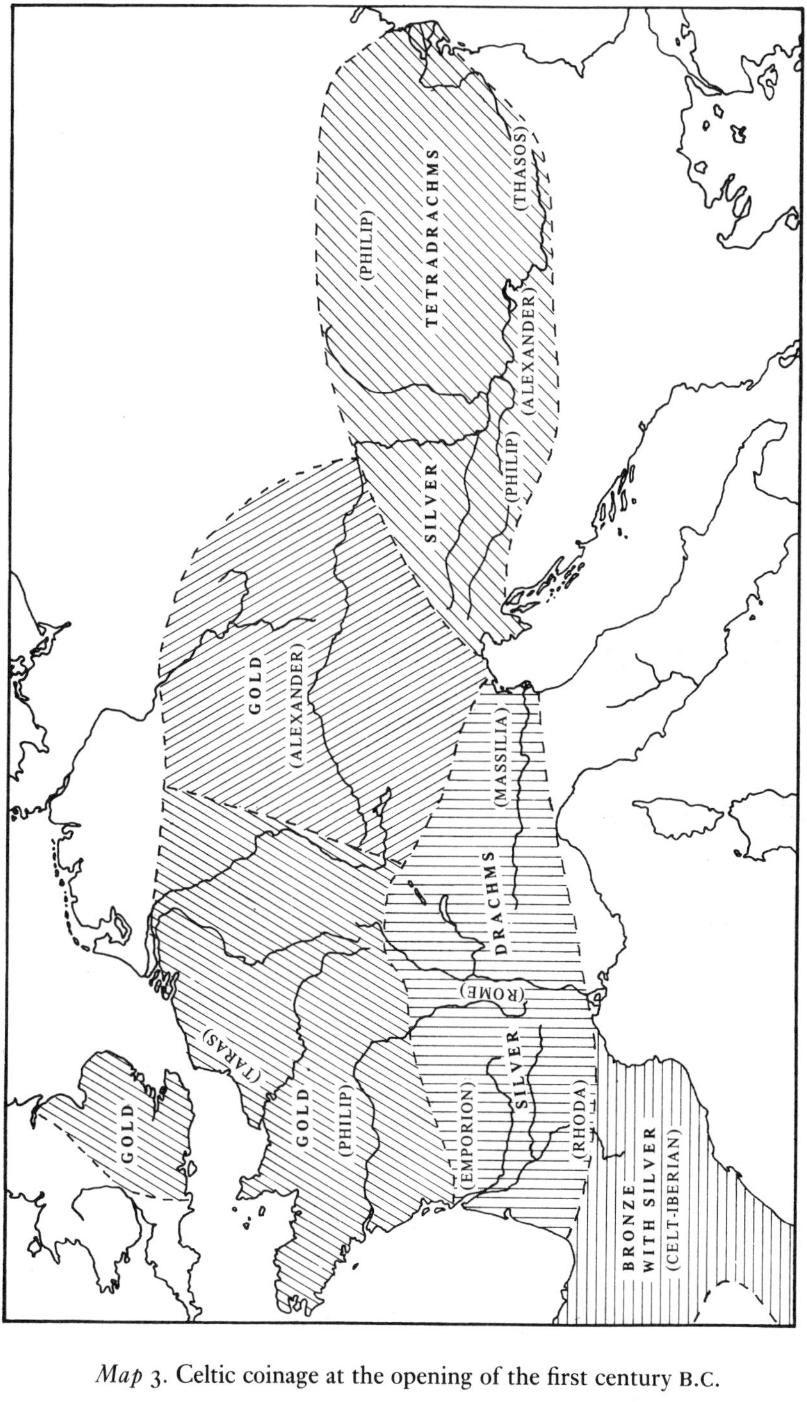

Map 3. Celtic coinage at the opening of the first century B.C.

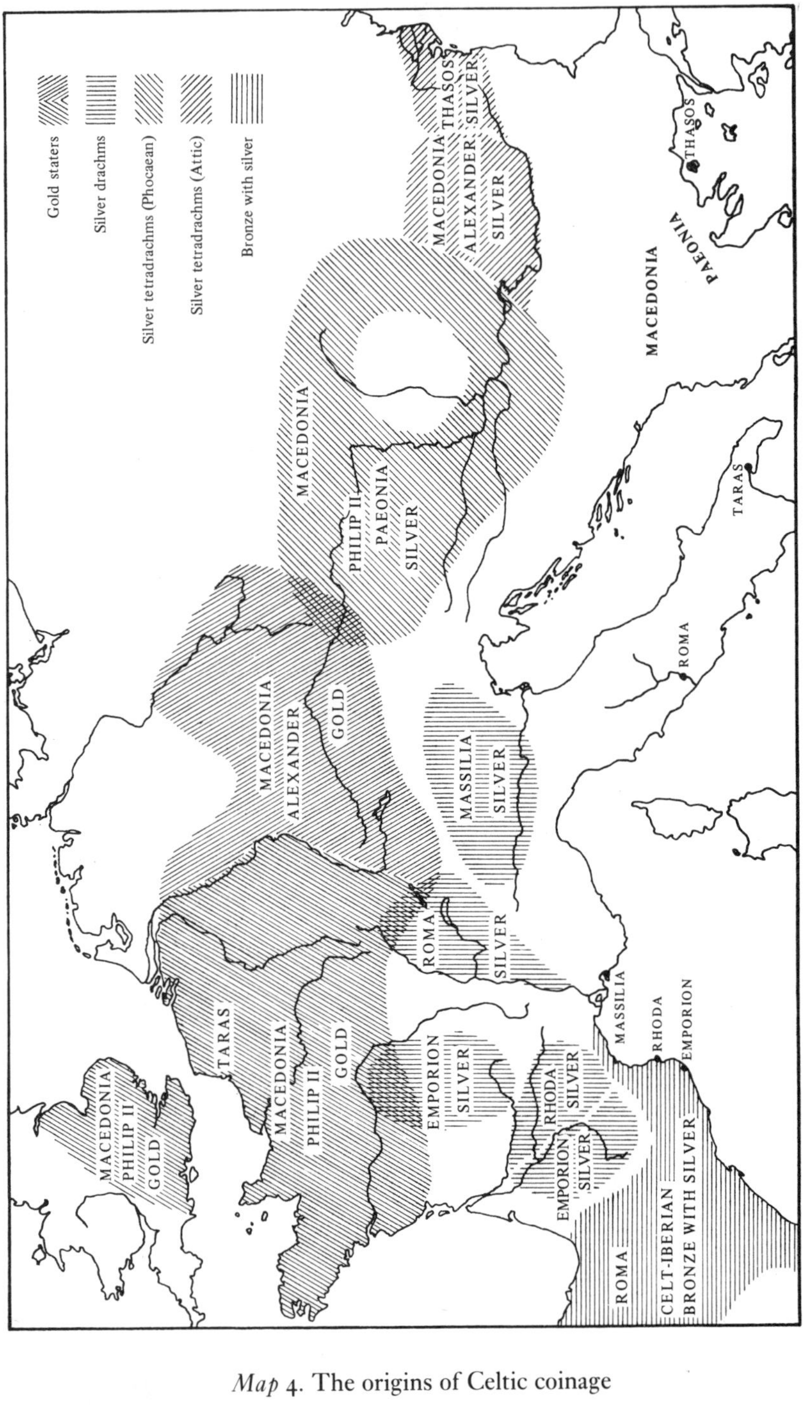

Map 4. The origins of Celtic coinage

speak a Celtic language. The coins do nothing to solve the inveterate (and in many contexts meaningless) question of where the Celts ceased and the Germans began. Coinage is absent in the forests of central and northern Germany, and further peters out north of the Carpathians. Otherwise, some form of native coinage, which for simplicity's sake we will generally call Celtic, occurs pretty well throughout continental Europe of the middle and late la Tène periods, starting where the classical coins of the Mediterranean belt cease.

Celtic coinage is of gold, silver and bronze, and the gold and silver are always, like ordinary Greek and Roman coins, hammered between dies. Bronze coins may either be struck in this way or cast in moulds. The coinages in each metal are of distinct origins and start in widely separated areas. As time went on complexities and cross-currents intervene, but the origins remain fundamental to any comprehension of the subject. For this reason some over-simplification in the account that follows is inevitable if the story is to be intelligibly presented.

In principle, Europe may be divided into three zones according to the metal of the basic currency. One zone, a very small one, is no more than an extension into the Mediterranean coast of France of the essentially bronze coinage of north-east Spain, dominated by the coinage of the former Greek colony of Emporion. The second zone, a vast one, stretching continuously from the Atlantic coast south of the Loire to the mouth of the Danube, used silver coins. North of this, in a zone comprising northern France, Belgium and Britain, in western and southern Germany, in northern Switzerland and in western Czechoslovakia or Bohemia, the basic coinage was of gold. This banding was only to some degree consequential on the location of mines and minerals; like the types of coins, it was fundamentally a matter of choice. All subsequent developments must be seen as overlaid on this basic pattern.

The brief summary will be expanded in the sections that follow. It is now time to turn to the coins themselves and to describe them, zone by zone, in terms of the prototypes or models out of which they grew. Evidence for dating is given, wherever possible, but the interpretation is often controversial. For any particular subject or area there is no real alternative to going back to the original and widely scattered sources, to which pointers are given in the bibliography. There is no easy route to the truth.

The Silver Belt : Eastern Sector

Celtic coinage began in the silver belt (see chapter 2). The earliest coinage of which we know are imitations of tetradrachms of Macedon in the middle Danube area, imitations of drachms of Massilia north of the Po, and imitations of the didrachms of Rhoda in the Garonne basin. All these go back to the third century B.C. or earlier; if others are of the same date, we have as yet no proof.

Philip II of Macedon.
The Danube Basin: Pannonia and Dacia
(Romania, Hungary, North Yugoslavia)

The Danubian coins were probably the first. Close imitations of tetradrachms of Philip II of Macedon (359–336 B.C.), with a bearded head of Zeus and a horseman reverse, have been found in a hoard from Scărişoara, Oltenia, in Romania, with Greek coins of Istros that are datable to the late fourth century B.C. The long series of Danubian imitations must have begun about 300 B.C. At first they remained faithful to their models, and many are found with cuts to test the metal; others were countermarked to assert their authenticity. Later, no doubt in the second century B.C, many divergent varieties appear in different localities. They spread from a centre in Banat or Oltenia, both round the half-circle of the Carpathian mountains in modern Romania, the ancient Dacia (or Geto-Dacia), and westwards up the Danube into Hungary, the ancient Pannonia. Some of the changes represent the evolution of a single traditional coin type, but others reflect new influences, for instance from the coins of Patraos (340–315 B.C.) or Audoleon of Paeonia (315–286 B.C.), or from the autonomous coins of the Greek cities of Amphipolis or Larissa. There are occasional borrowings, too, from the Heracles head on the coins of Alexander III of Macedon (336–323 B.C.), which continued to be issued after his death. A hoard from Zemun, near Belgrade, Yugoslavia, dated by Greek coins to about 220 B.C, shows developed imitations of Philip, Alexander and Larissa coins to have been in existence by that date.

It is not yet possible in most cases to assign the many varieties of Danubian tetradrachms to particular tribes; nearly all are anonymous, and it is not yet certain that the issue of the main types was tribal. Types seem to travel back and forth in a pattern that is less easy to disentangle than in the west. Relative date can be determined to some extent by weight and fineness. The most striking types at first belong to Transylvania, whose more stereotyped and decadent successors belong to Oltenia and Muntenia, the home of the Getae. But as time went on, a large base cup-shaped variety displaced the others in Transylvania and Banat. From an early date in Serbia the coins were formed in thick and narrow lumps. In Eastern Hungary, in Dúnantúl, there are vigorous types, some with antecedents in Transylvania, which display a certain

Celtic wildness and stylisation. It is in this area that small silver coins were first introduced, a sign of the local use of coin other than for hoarding, and in a few areas we have traces of experiments with a bronze coinage.

Developments on the Sava and Drava : Noricum (Austria)

From Hungary a version of the same coinage spread down the rivers Sava and Drava into Austrian Styria and Carinthia, the ancient Noricum. The heads are beardless, a style derived perhaps from the drachms of Philip II on which Apollo is beardless; and before long the horse on the reverse has become a lively spearman, reflecting the influence of Roman proximity. Almost alone amongst the coins of the Danube basin, the later types bore the names of Celtic chieftains, such as *Adnamati* or *Svicca*, in good Roman characters. This coinage, supplemented by small silver change with an origin in the coins of Massilia, appears to have survived until the Roman conquest or shortly before it (Noricum in 16 B.C, Pannonia in 9 B.C.); the last ruler, *Atta*, uses a head based on that of Augustus. In Dacia, by contrast, although not conquered until the reign of Trajan, the coinage cannot have survived the establishment there of the alien kingdom of Burebista (*c*.44 B.C.), and its demise probably occurred in the first twenty years of the century, since the coins are not found at certain excavated sites, such as Costeşti.

Philip III of Macedon.
South of the Danube, near its mouth : Moesia (Bulgaria)

In the east, three important tetradrachm coinages were based on a heavier tetradrachm than that of Philip II. The first of these, found in Bulgaria and eastern Romania, for which the name Moesian might be appropriate, imitates the earlier tetradrachms of Philip III of Macedon (323–316 B.C.) or the posthumous coins of Alexander III, which resemble one another, having a Heracles head on the obverse and a seated Zeus on the reverse. In addition to tetradrachms, there are coins of smaller denomination.

It is difficult as yet to say much more than that the bulk of this coinage appears to be of the mid second century B.C. in date. In hoards the tetradrachms are sometimes associated with the following group, both of which usually show crude craftsmanship, readily distinguished from the sometimes highly sophisticated products of western Romania and Hungary.

Thasos Imitations : The Black Sea Hinterland

Again in Bulgaria and eastern Romania there are found vast numbers of crude imitations of the tetradrachms of the autonomous Greek island of

Thasos. This prolific series began in 146 B.C. after the Roman conquest of Macedonia, and some of the post-Roman coins of Macedonia, too, are copied. The Thasos imitations lasted well into the first century B.C. and probably throughout most of it. Though widely distributed, their home was in the Thracian hinterland; the implication is that they followed and replaced the Philip III group. It does not seem that these imitations fall into the distinctive regional classes that are usual in such coinages, but they have not been adequately studied. In later versions the effeminate wine god on the obverse and the standing Heracles on the reverse vanish into a barbarous and unsystematic confusion, whose appearance has nothing Celtic about it.

The 'Biatec' Series : Southern Slovakia

In contrast the third group of heavy tetradrachms, confined to southern Slovakia, is both the most organised and the most dramatically Celtic of all these coinages. In time as well as place it is confined to a small span, in the middle of the first century B.C, since the Roman model of some varieties can be dated to 67 B.C. in one case and 60–46 B.C. in another. Although examples occurred in the Gerlitzen Alps hoard buried in or after 43 B.C, the coinage probably continued until Pannonia was overrun by the Romans in 12–9 B.C. The bearer of the first name in the series, *Biatec*, can also be shown to have struck gold coins, which will be met later in their proper place at the end of the series in the gold belt to the north. Hoards, too, associate the coins with the tetradrachms of Noricum that bear Celtic names. Both Biatec and a long row of successors whose names are on the coins used sub-classical mythological subjects: gryphons, harpies, centaurs and so forth, beautifully engraved. After *Biatec*, and *Nonnos*, his successor, each name usually had only one die and sometimes the name on the die was changed (*Titto* to *Ainorix* to *Fariorix*). These remarkable coins, of which the winged centaur of *Busu(maros)* is perhaps the most striking, have an important place in art history, but stand apart from the common run of Celtic coins in other countries. Why the Boii, first heard of in Italy and later displaced from Bohemia, who apparently issued them, chose at this late date to adopt the obsolete weight of the Thasos imitations, remains a mystery.

Imitations of Roman Denarii : Hungary

In and near Hungary, there is found a series of crude direct imitations of Roman denarii, which clearly belong to the later part of the first century B.C. Some bear names; the inscription *Ravis* may refer to the tribe of the Eravisci in Dúnantúl, while other names are probably personal. The types are as varied as their models, but it is hard to detect much Celtic influence in their style. They are never found mixed with the Biatec series of coins, nor with Philip imitations, and it seems likely that they only came into being after that series had ceased. This practice of copying Roman denarii was widespread in eastern Europe during the late first century, starting after about 30 B.C, and a hoard of dies for the purpose has been found at Tilişca in Dacia.

The Silver Belt : Central Sector

Massilia Imitations of the Po Valley: Gallia Cisalpina (Italy north of the Po)

Imitations of silver drachms of Massilia (now Marseilles), the Greek colony near the mouth of the Rhône, began not long after the tetradrachm series had started on the Danube. A hoard from the Capitol in Rome, buried before 212 B.C. (according to the latest interpretation of the disputed chronology of early Roman coins) contained worn imitations of the lighter type of Massilia drachm; they were brought to Rome, no doubt, after the defeat of the Celts at Telamon in 224 B.C. Imitations are known, too, of the heavier drachms that precede the Capitol type. Though the starting date is less precise than in the Danubian region, we can be sure that imitations had begun towards the middle of the third century B.C. Since none have been found in the territory of the Celtic Senones south of the Po, who were annihilated by the Romans in 282 B.C, that date may provide the starting point. The types remained uniform throughout, the head of a nymph accompanied by a lion or other wild beast on the reverse.

Distinct series are found amonst the Insubres around Milan, the Cenomani in the Ticino and the non-Celtic Veneti towards the Adriatic. Several hoards of uninscribed coins are dated by the presence of Roman coins to the late third or early second century B.C. (e.g. the Biandrate hoard in Cenomani territory, the San Zeno, Gambolo or Padua hoards amongst the Veneti). The latest coins bear inscriptions of Celtic names in an Italiot script, and these are found in hoards down to the first quarter of the first century B.C. (e.g. the Gerenzago, Ornavasso and Treviglio hoards). Even if the act of coinage ended with the grant of Roman citizenship to the Cisalpine Gauls in 89 B.C, there is evidence for the latest of the inscribed coins, with the legend *Rikoi*, remaining in use down to Augustan times, for instance from burials at Como and Ornavasso.

A Ligurian group? : The Maritime Alps

Some obols (and rare di- and tri-obols), on which the Massilia lion has been transformed into a wild beast beyond recognition, also belong to the final phase. The obols are best known from a hoard dated by a fragment of a Roman denarius to after 82 B.C. (the Serra Riccò hoard). It is possible that these coins are Ligurian rather than Celtic, belonging to the hinterland of Genoa. Neither the drachms nor the obols of Massilia are copied in the Rhône valley, where the originals circulated, while these imitations are found only in Cisalpine Gaul, where the originals are virtually absent; this is typical of the whole of Celtic coinage.

The Silver Belt : Western Sector

Rhoda Imitations : The Garonne Basin (South-west France)

Imitations of the didrachms of Rhoda followed a similar course to the imitations of Massilia in the Po valley. They are not, so far as we know, found in the hinterland of this Greek colony on the Bay of Ampurias in Spain, but only across the Pyrenees, mainly in the large areas of south-west France that drain into the Garonne. This is the area dominated in antiquity by the Volcae, of whom there were two branches, the Tectosages (including the Tolosates of Toulouse) and the Arecomici (around Nîmes). The starting date of the coinage may be deduced from the presence in two hoards from central Spain (the Drieves and Valera hoards), which may now be dated to *c.*210 B.C, of worn examples of types that are far from the earliest. Some forms of the coinage continued down to the time of Caesar, though the capture by the Romans of Tolosa, the capital of the Tectosages, in 106 B.C. no doubt marks a turning point. The most marked characteristic of the coins is the cross on the reverse, ultimately derived from an underneath view of the rose on the coins of Rhoda, shown with four petals, though in some cases there are mixed influences from the coinage of Massilia. The angles of the cross are generally filled with symbols, the commonest being a ceremonial axe. Different varieties of these 'monnaies-à-la-croix' can sometimes be linked with known tribal areas, the Tolosates, the Tectosages, the Cadurci, the Petrocorii, and later the Ruteni. Only a few bear legends, and some of these are in Iberian script. A peculiarity of the monnaies-à-la-croix is that many of them were struck on chopped flans.

Emporion Imitations : Towards the Loire (West-central France)

Imitations of the didrachms of Emporion, the Greek colony facing Rhoda across the Bay of Ampurias, Spain, went step by step with the monnaies-à-la-croix and may well have begun at about the same early or mid third-century date. An early monnaie-à-la-croix is found overstruck on an early imitation of Emporion. The types derived from Emporion are found between the Garonne and the Loire, principally along the valley of the Vienne, in the region of the Pictones (Poitou). On the obverse is a nymph's head, at first related to those on monnaies-à-la-croix, but later differing radically; the reverses are based on a pegasus or horse. This silver tradition, too, survived in modified form until the time of Caesar.

The Impact of Rome : The Rhône Valley (South-east France)

Between the Rhoda-derived monnaies-à-la-croix in Languedoc and Guienne and the Massilia-derived lion drachms of Cisalpine Gaul is found another extensive series of small silver coins. These coins occur first on the left bank of the Rhône, and their ramifications spread later into east-central Gaul and ultimately far beyond. The coinage is of mixed, but mainly Roman, origin. Hoards should one day provide evidence of starting date, but have not yet done so. The first and heavier coins, whose types probably derived from Carthaginian Spain, could precede the first Massilian invocation of Roman aid in 154 B.C. against raiders from Liguria; the alternative derivation from earlier Roman coins is less probable. Some of them have legends in Italiot characters, but others in Roman lettering.

The heavier coins are followed by others, somewhat lighter, where the Roman derivation becomes obvious. In weight they were clearly intended to pass as the equivalent of a Roman quinarius. The main series, with a head of Roma on one side and a spearsman (derived from one of the Dioscuri) on the other, probably follow the establishment of a Roman colony at Aquae Sextiae (Aix-en-Provence) in 124 B.C, but their distribution mainly in the Rhône valley is confined to the eastern part of the Roman Provincia. Legends on the coins are numerous and the series had a very long life, remaining in circulation down to Caesar's war and after.

In Central Gaul there soon began a very large development of silver quinarii under Roman influence. An important and relatively early series was that which bears the name in Greek characters, ΚΑΛΕΤΕΔΟΥ. This was soon copied and corrupted, perhaps because Greek was ceasing to be the local script as Rome replaced Massilia as the dominant influence. The coinage began in the first quarter of the first century B.C. and flourished down to just before the campaigns of Caesar. It was probably made by the Aedui, but circulated not only there but amongst the Sequani and Lingones also. In due course it was overtaken in the same home area by other coinages of generally similar type with Latin legends, which continued to be made until well after Caesar's wars. All these coins, which survive in vast numbers, are likely to have been made largely to pay soldiers in an area of constant warfare; but some may also represent taxes on the traffic of the Rhône.

The end of the story of silver coinage in Gaul will emerge at a later point in this narrative. It is time now to turn to the gold belt, into which the coins last described have for the first time begun to intrude.

The Gold Belt : Eastern Sector

Imitative coinages of gold are found in a separate belt to the north of the silver belt so far described (see chapter 3). It starts on the Atlantic coast of France north of the Massif Central and it spreads across Europe as far east as the western or Bohemian part of Czechoslovakia; the occurrence of gold coins elsewhere is sporadic and relatively unimportant. The area falls into two sectors, an eastern and a western. It seems probable that the eastern was the later to start, although there is no direct evidence. Weights go through a parallel development, but production in the east was from the first on a much smaller scale.

Alexander III of Macedon : The Bohemian Coinages

On the upper waters of the Elbe and spreading east along the north bank of the Danube towards Switzerland, the coins are essentially based on the gold stater of Alexander III of Macedon (336–323 B.C.), with a helmeted head of Athena and a winged figure of Victory, but there are other influences. Of these the most important is the later coinage of Philip V of Macedon (220–178 B.C.), on which the reverse shows a standing figure of Athena brandishing a shield and spear, but Roman influence also enters in. As works of art most of the coins of this series are poor things, though there are exceptions. The coins of the Boii in Bohemia are important for the light they throw on primitive monetary systems, for the full weight coins divide not into quarters (or halves and quarters) as is almost universal amongst the Celts elsewhere, but into thirds, thirds, and thirds again (i.e. ninths and twenty-sevenths).

In the Bohemian series the basic coin is an imitation of a stater of Alexander III, but it is accompanied from an early date by a third combining an obverse derived perhaps from Rome, and a reverse obviously drawn from Philip V. Both undergo radical changes, losing weight and standard in the process. The beginning can be placed about 200 B.C; the end is marked by 'mussel' coins, the final degradation of the stater, a few of which bear the name of Biatec, already encountered on the heavy silver coins of Slovakia. There is every reason to believe that the issuer was one and the same, even if the silver coins followed the gold, in the mid first century B.C, after he was driven out of Bohemia proper.

Derivatives of the Bohemian Coinages

North, West and South-west. In parallel with the regular Bohemian series, and datable relatively by weight and standard, there is an interesting series of gold coins, extending into Prussia, with original Celtic types, owing very little to Macedonian prototypes. Horse, boar, cow, weapons and figures appear. A most impressive coin is one with a Scythian curled dragon on it. A series not yet well studied, probably from the vicinity of Lake Constance, consists of staters and half staters with a style all their own, on which the winged figure on the reverse wears a peaked helmet and carries a spear (figure 2). On another variety a headless figure is being consumed by a giant bird.

Figure 2. Lake Constance figure

Although the main currency of Switzerland follows an entirely different pattern, the Alexander III type turns up again in the Alpine route across the Great St Bernard pass to the gold producing region of the Salassi at Aosta. The type, a rare one, is uninscribed north of the Alps, but inscribed in Italiot characters in Italy. This attests a tribe, of which there is other evidence, between the Boii and north Italy.

The 'Rainbow Cup' Series of Vindelicia (*Bavaria*). To the west of the Bohemian area, in the ancient Vindelicia (Bavaria), there are found a great many coins that have for centuries been called in Germany 'rainbow cups' (*Regenbogenschüsselchen*); they were believed to have magical properties. The types start with a curled dragon derived apparently from the Bohemian type, and therefore subsequent to it. Many varieties exist, with different forms of serpent, bird head, torques, globules, crosses and the like. A few are literally smooth on both sides. They have not been exhaustively studied as a group, but their metrological system is related to the Gallic rather than the Bohemian coinages. The coins remained in use, at least in a debased form, until the Roman conquest of Bavaria, as is shown by those discovered at the famous oppidum of Manching.

The Gold Belt : Western Sector

The western sector comprehends all France north of the Massif Central, and parts of Belgium, Switzerland, the Rhineland and Britain. Here the coins are essentially based on the gold stater of Philip II of Macedon (359–336 B.C.), though there were occasional minor influences from the Macedonian coins of Alexander III (336–323 B.C.) and Lysimachus of Thrace (306–281 B.C.), and the mid third-century B.C. coins of the Greek city state of Tarentum in south Italy. This prodigious Celtic coinage offers a vast range of variations on a single theme, the beardless head of Apollo on one side and a horse-drawn charioteer on the other. Some, mainly in Gallia Comata (central and north-western Gaul), are of strange originality and beauty; others, especially in Gallia Belgica or north-eastern Gaul, spreading ultimately to Britain, are reduced to meaningless and repetitive formulae, constructed from stock-in-trade elements intelligible only in earlier phases. There is little reliable evidence as to when the coinage began. Several silver coinages had begun in the third century B.C. and there is a strong presumption of this date for the western gold, especially coins based on types of Tarentum, though any coinage in the interior is likely to be later than coinages nearer to the Mediterranean.

It has been a constant subject of debate why the eastern and western sectors are derived from different models. Gold staters of Philip and Alexander circulated in enormous numbers side by side long after the coins were struck, and coins of Lysimachus and Tarentum with them. It is inconceivable that any area familiar with the one was not equally at home with the other. The choice of model was, therefore, deliberate. What we may call the German Celts preferred armed standing figures, while the French Celts were demonstrably enamoured of horses. It is unnecessary to ask by what route the originals reached the lands in which they were copied; there is no evidence that they ever reached them in quantity, either by trade or as booty, and, had they done so, native substitutes would hardly have been required. It is more to the point to enquire, though there is no ready answer, why gold was preferred in the north and silver in the south, since both metals were equally accessible in either zone.

The First Phase

The earliest phase of the coinage is represented by copies of gold staters of Philip II of Macedon, soon accompanied by quarter staters, a denomination of local invention. It is attractive but unsafe to link these coins with the tradition, recorded by Strabo (4.2.3), of an Arvernian

Empire stretching from the Atlantic to the Rhône, in the late third or early second century B.C, an empire which, if it ever existed, had collapsed long before the Romans defeated the Arverni under Bituitus (Luernius' son) in 121 B.C. Imitated staters are found in most parts of France, including the Auvergne and Berry, but early ones are especially frequent in the Rhineland. At this stage it is unlikely that the phenomenon was national or territorial. The coins, however, soon acquired local characteristics, especially in the quarter staters, and the next phase of somewhat lighter coins (weighing less than eight grams) is essentially regional. It is impossible yet to say precisely when it began, but the evidence is plain that the differentiation was deliberate and self-conscious. It is defensible to treat these coinages as tribal issues, even if we are not always certain of the tribes.

Regional Developments

The Arvernian Group. The comparative evolution of local coinages in different parts of Gaul has not been fully worked out, even though some of them have been individually well studied. They can generally be approximately located, even if they cannot be dated. The fulcrum of distribution by the first century B.C. is the Massif Central, and the gold staters of the Arverni and some of their neighbours, the Bituriges Cubi in Berry and the Lemovices in Limousin, can only be identified at this relatively late date. Their end, however, is easily established, since there are gold coins in the name of the Arvernian Vercingetorix, who was captured after the fall of Alesia in 52 B.C.

The Rhineland Group. At a much earlier date, probably in the second century B.C, we can isolate various Swiss and Rhineland coinages, whose derivation from the Philip II stater is more obvious. The coins of the component tribes of the Helvetii may be amongst the earliest but so too are coins of the Treveri around Trier. These are competent and practical coins of no outstanding artistic merit, and in this region legends are scarcely found.

The Armorican Group. By contrast the Armorican region of north-western Gaul from the Cherbourg peninsula to Finistère produced a wealth of coins of outstanding artistic merit. The earliest phase consists of versions of the stater where the horse has acquired a rider, usually female and in ecstasy; they are found amongst the Redones around Rennes. Later the Veneti, followed by the Osismii, the Unelli and other tribes, produced some astonishing *tours de force* in gold in an unmistakable style. Particularly characteristic are the small heads on strings displayed on some obverse and reverse types (figure 3). In a final phase the same or similar types were made in billon or base silver, and in

Figure 3. Osismian billon stater

enormous numbers. These may be dated to the period immediately preceding and during Caesar's campaigns, especially through a series of hoards found in Jersey that were dominated by coins of the Coriosolites around Corseul (figure 4). Some quarters and fractions, however, probably continued to be struck for some years afterwards. It is only in this post-conquest stage that legends began to appear.

Figure 4. Coriosolites billon stater

The Belgic Group. The coins of Belgic Gaul, that is from the Rhine mouth to the Seine and the Marne, form a regionally distinct group. They start with half staters imitated from coins of Tarentum but very soon the Tarentum tradition becomes utterly confused with the Macedonian. An important coin, which had a very long life, is a broad flat stater with a head and horse in a characteristically wild style (**199**; figure 5). This type is now attributed to the Ambiani on the Somme. In due course deterioration set in, perhaps following the invasions of the Cimbri and Teutones, whom the Belgae succeeded in turning back, and the coins became smaller and thicker while the elements of the types disintegrated to a point of near or absolute incomprehensibility. At this

Figure 5. Gallo-Belgic A (Ambiani) stater

stage the coins, which are generally very common, can be assigned to a variety of different tribes in the area, Ambiani, Suessiones, Atrebates, and Nervii amongst others. A few bear legends at the end. From Belgic Gaul actual coins, and, more importantly, the idea of coinage was transported to Britain. Belgic gold coinage appears to have ceased soon after the Roman conquest in 51 B.C.

Figure 6. Parisian gold stater

The Parisian Group. Parallel with the coins of Belgic Gaul, and equally on broad flat flans, are the beautiful coins of the Parisii (figure 6). Tribes adjacent to the Belgae to the north, and the Eburovices, the Lexovii and the Baiocasses in the region dividing the Armorican from the Belgic tribes, all had their own characteristic coins, but these are not well sorted out.

Other Groups. It is impossible in this survey to do more than illustrate examples of the enormous range of gold coinage in Gaul. Not every tribe or ruler appears to have issued gold coinage, but at its peak, in the late second or early first century B.C, different local coinages of similar standard and derivation existed in most of the northern part of Gaul from the Atlantic to the Rhine, and even across it. The internal chronology of Celtic coinage in the West is obscure but is more easily established than its beginnings. The pillage in Gaul during Caesar's campaigns of 58–52 B.C. drove an already declining gold currency completely out of circulation, unless perhaps its vestiges were suffered to survive on the Belgic frontiers with Germany. It is only in Britain, where the first coinage was not even imported until the end of the second century B.C, that the floruit of the gold stater lasts from the time of Caesar to the Claudian conquest of 43 A.D, and in outlying districts even later.

The Bronze Belt : The Mediterranean Coast

We may notice in passing here a small belt of bronze coinage in Provence and Languedoc in the south-west of France, scarcely overlapping with the silver monnaies-à-la-croix (see chapter 4). Though issued by and for a Celtic population the large bronze pieces found here belong in principle to the Iberian system, itself derived from the Roman system of the second century B.C. Although the coins of Narbo, the present Narbonne, have the town and tribal name in Iberian characters, other coins have Celtic chieftains' names in Greek letters, sometimes accompanied by the Greek title *Basileus* (king). A number also bear the name of the tribe of the Longostaletes, unlocated and otherwise unrecorded. The types follow models from Carthaginian Spain or Roman Emporion. They must have begun in the second century B.C, but they did not disappear from use when the Romans formed the province of Narbonensis in 118 B.C. They occur mainly on first-century B.C. sites, and their end is likely to have come during Pompey's reorganisation of Spanish affairs after the Sertorian war in 71 B.C.

The Overlay of Subsidiary Coinage

Up to this point the early coinages of Europe present an intelligible pattern – the traditional use in each area of an established type in one metal. It was usually a type of Greek origin, which, as time went on, suffered a variety of changes, some due to the operation of Gresham's law, others to the self-conscious adoption of local characteristics in each tribal or economic area. These can be isolated and identified.

In the first century B.C, the picture was greatly complicated by the superimposition on this basic pattern, especially in the west, of enormous quantities of subsidiary coins in silver and bronze, deriving in the main from Roman rather than Greek traditions (see chapter 5). It was the custom of the Romans constantly to change their coin types, as new money magistrates were elected, and this inconsistency is duly reflected. The relationship of the subsidiary coins to the main series is often obscure; in Gaul it is rarely possible to present the two as a coherent system, although in this respect regions differ. Britain stands apart; gold staters and quarter staters, silver and bronze coins of consistent weights were all issued in the same names; the few anomalies are negligible or explicable. But in Gaul it is the exception to find a full set of gold, silver and bronze coins in a single name, and often the authorities issuing gold and subsidiary coinages in any one area were different.

Bronze Counterparts of Gold

There is some reason to think that in Gaul a need for small change had begun to be felt before the full impact of the new Roman concepts arrived. Thus some gold currencies appear, from a relatively early date, to be accompanied by a bronze (rather than a silver) counterpart. This may have started with the Arverni, early in contact with Rome. Likewise amongst the Bituriges Cubi we have a series of bronze coins with names, but with one exception not the same names as on the gold coins. A bronze series is, again, obviously related to the Belgic-influenced coins of the Veliocasses, near the mouth of the Seine. In the Belgic area there is an almost total absence of early silver coins, but a very large and varied issue of bronze coins, some of which found their way to Britain; a few imitate gold coins. Silver coinage, as a hanger-on or subsidiary to a recognised gold coinage, is rare; a few Arvernian silver coins of this kind exist, but the practice never became widespread.

The Development of Silver

In the years before the Roman conquest, a number of Gallic authorities, inspired by the highly successful coinage of the Aedui in Côte-d'Or and their neighbours, whose Roman-based silver coinage has already been mentioned, began to produce comparable silver coins. In most cases the issuers appear to have been magistrates rather than tribes and the coins frequently bear names. One goes so far as to mention a *S(enatus) C(onsultum)*. In essence this new phenomenon reflects the need, in a money economy, for locally produced small change, on the Roman model. A great many may have been required as pay for troops. The date of these pieces can be determined approximately by the presence of many of a cross-section of them, as well as some of the bronze, in the nineteenth-century excavation of a mass grave of those who died in 52 B.C. in the defence of Alesia, the last stronghold of the Gauls under Vercingetorix.

The Duration of Subsidiary Silver or Bronze

A very high proportion of the surviving small change of Gaul and Germany was, however, issued after the Roman conquest, presumably with the blessing of the Roman masters. Although in some cases we can only guess on grounds of style, there is a strong presumption that certain types absent from the Alesia grave deposits were not then in existence. Although dated hoards before the conquest are extremely rare (coins of the Roman Republic did not circulate widely in Gaul before then, any more than did the coins of the Greeks other than those of Massilia), a wave of hoards, mainly of small silver coins of standard size, often with inscriptions, quickly followed it. Although many of the coins in these are of the type in existence before the conquest, others were certainly struck during the subsequent phase down to about 30 B.C, when under Roman influence a money economy was developing. There is some reason to think that the reorganisation of the currency in Gaul, including the erection of a prolific Roman mint at Nemausus, later replaced by Lugdunum, took place in Augustus' visit to Gaul in 27–26 B.C. In a few cases silver and bronze coins in Gaul copy post-conquest prototypes. In others, e.g. the Meilleraie-Tilly (Vendée) hoard, hoard evidence shows that these coins circulated as late as *c.*10 B.C. Whereas up to the war period, as we have seen, the distribution of coins is confined to very narrow limits, no doubt in the main tribal, during and after the war the whole population of Gaul was so displaced that tribal frontiers were weakened and coin distributions lose previous meaning. It is rarely possible to locate the approved local magistrates whose names appear on these pieces.

Unattributed Coins

If we set aside the subsidiary bronze and silver coins, and the pre- and post-conquest coins with magistrates' names (mentioned in the last three sub-sections), there still remain a very large series of unattached and unattributable coins, often with legends. Even when it is not clear from the find-spots, it is often a reasonable presumption that the coins belong to particular oppida and were not made for the use of a tribe as a whole.

Potin or Cast Bronze Coins : Another Overlay

One particular type of late coin deserves special mention, the strange cast bronze or 'potin' coins of central and eastern Gaul. This method of making coins in cast strips was a Gaulish invention, simple and inexpensive. It seems to have started by imitating struck bronze coins of Massilia, presumed to be of the second century B.C, which have an Apollo head and butting bull. Before the end, the coins were by no means confined to this Massilia pattern, and adventurous new types were attempted. More than one variety of the coins existed before the *débâcle* at Alesia, but the full development did not take place, it seems, until later; potin coins were still in use in Germany early in the first century A.D. and in Britain the local Kentish version lasted down to the Claudian conquest. Potin coins seem to have had an existence largely independent of the regular coinages in other metals; very few can be closely linked by legends or otherwise with struck coins either before or after the conquest. The likelihood is that, as token coins with a conventional value, their often primitive appearance belies their utility. They were issued by anyone who had the metallurgical skills to make them and make a profit out of doing so. The enormous surviving quantities prove their contemporary importance, but even so they remain somewhat of an enigma.

The Confluence of the Streams in Britain

It is in Britain that all the streams of Western Celtic coinage converge. Before the conquest of Gaul coinage in Britain amounted to an extension across a narrow strip of water of the coinage of northern Gallia Belgica. After the conquest the coinage, of a Britain politically isolated from the continent, developed its own personality.

The First Phase : Importation and Imitation

A few isolated gold staters, halves and quarters, reached Britain probably in the mid second century B.C. from the mainland.

Despite isolated finds of early Philip II imitations and the import to the west country of a few Armorican gold coins, the first significant appearance of coinage in this country was the importation of very large numbers of the broad flat staters and quarter staters of the Ambiani, which we have already met in Belgic Gaul, in particular on the Somme. The date probably lies at the end of the second century B.C, but proof is lacking. The area of importation was Kent and Essex, the parts of Britain most accessible to the continent. Simultaneously another type from much the same area was reaching the London district.

Direct importation from Belgic Gaul of various types of stater and quarter stater, most notably uniface staters, continued over a growing area of southern Britain down to Caesar's incursions in 55 and 54 B.C. Five distinct types can be traced, each following a different path. To what extent these separate importations represent common rule on both sides of the Channel, for which there is historical evidence, or a trace of the wealth of invading chieftains and their hordes, for which there is also textual warrant, is controversial.

For much of the first century B.C. the currency of Britain consisted of a mixture of the imported coins with locally made versions, derived from a disintegrating version of the Somme staters. As on the continent, these soon became regionalised, with distinct versions in Kent, the West Country, Lincolnshire and East Anglia. There are hoards of the coins scattered along the east coast, as far as Scotland, and the south coast to Penzance and Carn Brae in Cornwall, but the regular use of gold coinage never crossed the line from the Humber to the Severn. Local developments of these uninscribed gold staters reached their peak numerically and in artistic development in the Home Counties.

The Dynasty of Commius : South of the Thames

In the aftermath of Caesar's conquest of Gaul a Gallic chieftain of the Atrebates named Commius, with whom Caesar had maintained a love-hate relationship, escaped to Britain. A form of stater, found exclusively in Britain, but modelled on a type attributable to the Suessiones, is occasionally found bearing the name of Commius, and appears to record this event. It is found on the south coast and is followed there and in Kent by coins bearing the names of a series of rulers each calling himself the son of Commius (*Commi Filius*) : *Tincommius*, *Eppillus* and *Verica*. The types of these coins are Roman influenced. Tincommius is named in Augustus' *Res Gestae*; Verica, eventually exiled, sought the aid of Claudius and was instrumental in causing Claudius to conquer Britain. Eppillus, at first in evidence at Calleva (Silchester), later transferred to Kent, and probably displaced Dubnovellaunos, who is also mentioned in the *Res Gestae*. This presents the approximate timetable of these rulers of a single dynasty. Before their arrival there is little or no firm evidence of the presence of small silver and bronze coins. The coinage of this group on the south coast consists of staters, quarter staters and related silver coins, including minims; in Kent, as elsewhere in south-eastern Britain, bronze coins replace the silver minims as the smallest denomination.

After Claudius' conquest of Britain Celtic coinage disappears; the area was under the sway of Cogidubnus, *Rex et Legatus Augusti*, and all we find thereafter are home-made versions of the standard imperial coinage of Claudius and his successors.

The Dynasty of Tasciovanus : North of the Thames

While events took this course south of the Thames, a rival development was taking place to the north. In the Home Counties, based on Verulamium, another dynasty was formed under a ruler named Tasciovanus, not otherwise known to history; he is presumed to be the successor of Cassivellaunus, the adversary of Caesar. Starting from the uninscribed coins of the region, we find an extensive series of coins in the name of Tasciovanus and his various associates, in gold and later silver and bronze. All have legends and many borrow types from Rome; the Celtic element is, however, much stronger here than in the south. The evidence of distribution and of a rare legend is that the rule of this king (he called himself *Rigoni* or Great King) extended over Essex, that is the tribe of the Trinovantes.

In succession to Tasciovanus, whose types show him to have been contemporary with Augustus, there is a very extensive coinage at Camulodunum of the son of Tasciovanus, Cunobelin. It seems certain that those coins on which he declares himself the son of Tasciovanus were issued at Verulamium. The gold coins are all of Camulodunum; the silver and bronze are of both mints, and there is evidence from the types that they were contemporary with Tiberius. Cunobelin's death in 40 A.D. was another of the factors leading to Claudius' conquest of Britain. Cunobelin consolidated the kingdom and added Kent to it. He was certainly in rivalry with Verica to the south.

In addition to Cunobelin, there are coins of another son of Tasciovanus, Epaticcus, whose sphere of activity appears to have lain in the southern area. He is not known to history, but there are coins, almost identical with his in silver, bearing the name of Caratacus, Cunobelin's son and one of his heirs, who led the resistance to Claudius.

The Outlyers

In addition to the kingdoms north and south of the Thames and in Kent, where the story is confused by much coming and going, there developed after Caesar's incursions a number of peripheral states making and using coins. Each had a distinct regional style, and coins are only rarely found outside them.

The Durotriges in Dorset and parts of Hampshire and Somerset remained true to tradition. Their coins follow the model of the first British imitations of Continental gold: the metal deteriorates through silver to bronze and eventually cast bronze (figure 7). A smaller denomination follows a similar course, but ceases at the stage of base silver. There is hoard and site evidence that the coins continued in use into the second century A.D, though their manufacture must have ceased long before that.

The Dobunni, with their centre in Gloucestershire, first adopted the model of the coins from the south coast, the same model as was used by Commius; coins of this kind had travelled the length of the Thames. To these they attached a silver coinage of local vintage. In the first century A.D. names appear, and there is evidence that these inscribed coins were

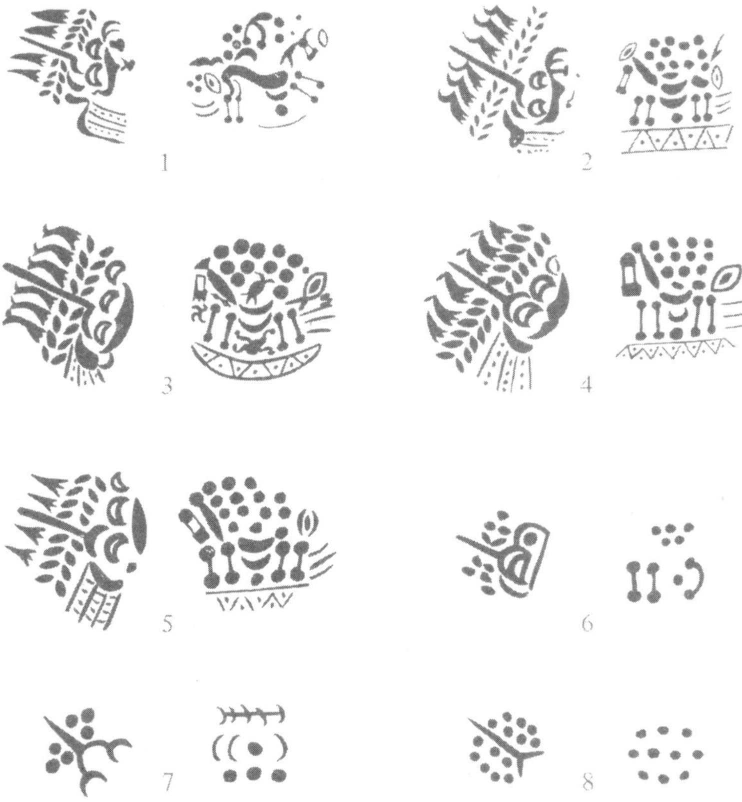

Figure 7. Development of the Durotrigian coinage
1 Gallo-Belgic C (AV); 2 British A (AV); 3 British B (AV)
4 Durotriges (AR); 5 struck Durotriges (AE); 6–8 cast Durotriges (AE)

current at the time of Claudius' invasion and were allowed to continue for some years after: the Dobunni, or part of them, surrendered early to Rome.

In Lincolnshire and Leicestershire the Coritani had an extensive coinage in gold and silver from a relatively early date. The silver pieces were of two denominations. Names appear, usually in pairs, and here again there is positive evidence from hoards that the coins continued in use, at least in one isolated area, until well after the Roman conquest of the south.

The commonest coinage of all is that found amongst the Iceni of Norfolk and Suffolk (figure 8). Here an early gold coinage appears to have expired; the area was a poor one. But in its place we find a vast silver coinage, preserved in very large quantities by the discovery of at least a dozen hoards. There is little doubt that these were buried on the occasion of Boudicca's rising against the Romans, to whom the Iceni were allied, but not fully subjected, in 61 A.D. There are at all times three distinct streams of Icenian silver coins, implying at least three constituent elements. The later coins all bear the tribal name *Ecen* . . . .

Figure 8. Coin types of the Iceni

A fact of great significance is that from the time of the establishment of the two dynasties onwards, there appears to have been a common monetary convention in Britain. Gold staters are all of consistent weight and of a fineness which is not unduly far from consistency. Likewise, silver coins aimed at a uniform weight. There is a greater variety in the weight of bronze coins, but their value must always have been conventional. From all this only the Durotriges stood out as independent.

Cast Potin in Britain

The potin coinage of the Continent reached Britain in an attenuated form. The models came from central Gaul, and the date suggested by the British evidence, the hoards from Snettisham and along the Thames, is earlier than is welcome to French scholars, and suggests the earlier part of the first century B.C. In Britain the coins had a very extended life, changing little with time. At one stage the technique of manufacture involved, very surprisingly, the use of papyrus. The home of these strange pieces is Kent, and they were still in use here when the first Roman villas were being built.

This, in rapid summary, is the story of Celtic coinage, its span in time and space. It can be studied from many points of view, historical, geographical, economic, metrological, metallurgical, linguistic, artistic, religious; it has attracted more than its share of uninformed speculation. There is space here only to draw attention to a few facets of interest.

History and geography go together. Where consecutive written history is lacking and the geographers are late, there is no source more important than the coins for the history or geography of Europe during the centuries of half-light transition from prehistory into the Greco-Roman world, or in archaeological terms the civilisation of middle and late la Tène. Numismatics are no substitute for field archaeology, but an intelligent combination of the two can go some way towards replacing the missing written word.

Technical Aspects of Celtic Coinage

Metrology and Metallurgy

The history of all ancient coinage is one of decline in weight and metal standard, followed by a drastic reform, when the process starts again. By studying the progressive decline in the weight and metal standard of Celtic coins, we have the surest available means of arranging them in historical order even though we cannot be sure that events kept in step in all areas. The chart (figure 9) shows the comparative weights of some key gold Celtic coins. It will be seen that, starting with the philippus coinage of Gallia Celtica, there is a steady decline in weight through the coinage of Gallia Armorica and Gallia Belgica to Britain. There is an exactly parallel decline in weight in Germany and the East.

The story of the silver coins is more difficult to illustrate because of the variety in the weights of the coins from which the traditions stemmed, but the picture is again one of steady decline (figure 10). In the Danube area weights fall to half the original weight. In Gaul the smaller silver coins derived from Rhoda and Emporion models follow a different pattern from those depending on Massilia or Rome.

Although the process of decline is as clear in Gaul as elsewhere, at

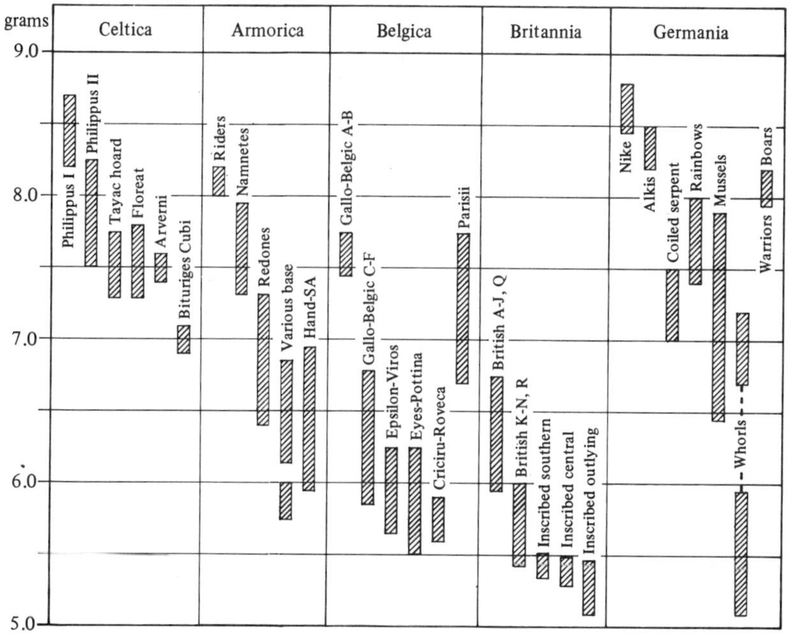

Figure 9. Gold coinage weights

the time of the Gallic wars the vast majority of silver coins were, irrespective of tribe, of a uniform denomination, reduced from, but clearly related to, the Roman quinarius. This implies some measure of deliberate common policy over a large area, adopted, perhaps, under the economic compulsion of the Roman threat. Similarly, throughout Britain, after the invasions of Julius Caesar, the standard gold stater and silver coin had a common weight (about two-thirds of their Gaulish counterparts), which remained constant to the end; but the fineness of the metal, as revealed by specific gravities, declined, and ultimately, perhaps because the supply of gold had given out, we have strikings in base silver and even bronze. There is an exact parallel for this in the Rhineland.

On metrology and metallurgy we should be on surer ground. At most times and places it is possible to deduce with some precision what was the intended weight of coins. In the early stages this was closely related to the weight and fineness of the models, but other standards of weight and fineness always supervened. It should be possible with time to relate the metrological facts to actual or intended weight systems. That such existed, locally or over large areas, is unquestionable, but the margins of error are usually too large at present for satisfactory proof. It

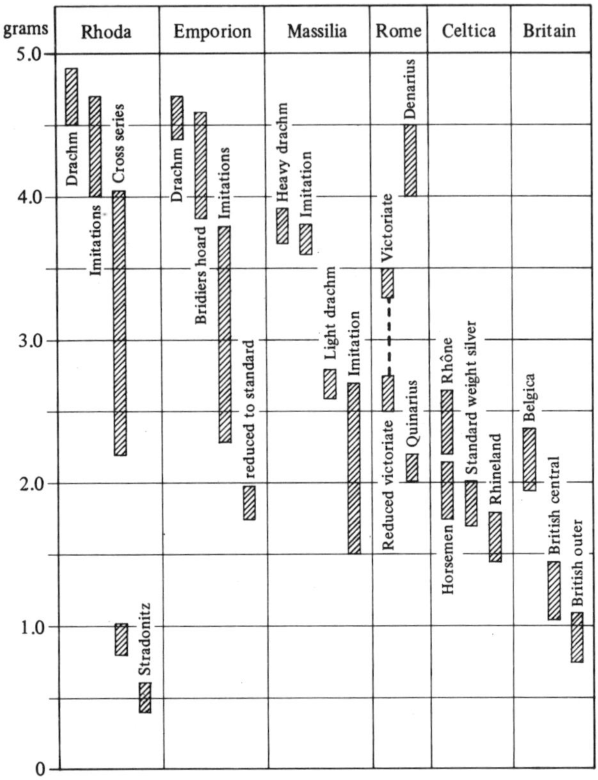

Figure 10. Silver coinage weights

seems likely, however, that in the Rhineland and Britain there was a Celtic pound of 309.1 g.

Beside these signs of the use of a common Celtic pound, one must set some clear evidence for the essentially local nature of Celtic measures. Thus the gold coins of the east divide on the principle of thirds and those of the west on the principle of quarters. But even so, consistency is lacking. In Bohemia and Moravia division is into thirds, ninths and twenty-sevenths, that is thirds, thirds and thirds again, but both in south Germany and on the Rhine the associated coins instead divide into quarters. Similarly, while the pattern in Gaul was division into halves and quarters, or (later) quarters only, there is, nevertheless, a comparatively small area in central Gaul (the Bituriges Cubi of Berry) where, even down to the end, division was into thirds and sixths.

In Britain, in the absence of any certainty as to the ratio of gold to silver and silver to bronze, the quadratic equations that should demonstrate the British system of weights and measures remain elusive; but there is some reason to think that the British gold coin was intended to weigh two-thirds of the Roman aureus and the British silver coin one-third of the Roman denarius, or 1/240 of the same Celtic pound.

There is in fact one very clear case where a relationship with the known Celtic pound can be established. The Tayac-Libourne hoard from the Gironde consisted of about 325 late second-century B.C. gold coins from several parts of Gaul, some minor goldsmith's leavings and a large gold torque, broken but with no missing parts. The average weight of the coins was 7.60 g, or exactly one-fortieth of the Celtic pound, while the torque weighed exactly two-and-a-half of these Celtic pounds. Thus the total weight of the hoard was, within .02 per cent, the equivalent of five hundred coins or twelve-and-a-half Celtic pounds. This is the perfect example, but so few hoards are fully recorded that such results are usually impossible.

Dies. Initially the techniques for making Celtic coins cannot have differed from those of the Greek and Roman coins copied. The vast majority were struck from dies, of which there must have been enormous numbers. In the case of the British tribe of the Iceni, the surviving coins number between twelve and fifteen hundred in gold and silver, and there were employed in making them something in the order of three hundred obverse dies and about double that number of reverse dies. This is certainly no more than average and implies an output of, say, between two and three million coins at least. No British dies have survived, but I know of a number from the Continent; three from Switzerland, four from France (**579–81**), three pairs from Hungary, while a hoard containing dies for making denarius imitations was found at Tilişca in Romania (Forrer II, pls 19, 20). The typical die is of bronze, conical, globular or bullet-shaped; in one instance it is set in an iron shaft. The dies were partly punched, partly engraved, while the metal was soft, and they were subsequently hardened. The minuteness and precision of Celtic engraving, even when the types were outlandish or primitive, could be remarkable, but standards varied. Dies could be resoftened and touched up or altered. For instance, we have an example from Slovakia of a reverse die in three states, with a different legend on each (*Titto*, *Ainorix*, *Fariorix*) – the Harpy is identical and only the legend changed.

There is a feature occasionally found on Greek coins that is common on silver coins of central and south-western Gaul, and occurs also on bronze coins in Belgic Gaul, but not in Britain. More than one obverse die was sunk into the same block of metal, so that a carelessly placed blank after being struck, shows parts of more than one obverse, but only one reverse, die (**272**, **287**). The purpose of this economy is obscure, as the dies seem all to be similar and contemporary.

There is a tendency in struck Celtic coins for the obverse or lower die, which normally bore the head side, to become cup-shaped, and for the reverse to reflect the contour, as may be seen in the gold staters (**154–61**, **224**). This helped to keep a globular blank in place for striking. We find examples of cup-shaped coins as far apart as Bulgaria and Belgic Gaul, from whence the practice reached Britain.

In general, Celtic coins, particularly in Gaul, are narrower than the dies from which they were struck. Only part of the pattern is shown, as may be seen for instance on **293** or **324**; several coins are thus needed to obtain the full design or legend. In theory, no doubt the blanks for the coins should have been hammered thinner than they were.

Blanks. Except in Aquitaine, the blanks on which the coins were struck were cast. Traces of the casting are often revealed in the shape of the coins or in the splitting or other marks on the edge, even after striking. For, instance, the shape of the silver coins of Limousin or of bronze coins from the border of Belgium and France show that these blanks were cast moulds, a series of little cup-shaped holes in a clay plate. The plate moulds have been found at eight or nine sites in Britain, on several sites in Czechoslovakia including Okluky and Stradonitz, and occasionally in France and Germany. Fragments are sometimes found in fantastic numbers; two years' excavations at Old Sleaford produced more than two thousand five hundred. Their metallurgical use has been fully demonstrated: it seems to have been to permit the division, by eye, of accurately weighed amounts of metal into smaller lumps of the right size to produce a blank. Each hole in a plate (fifty at Verulamium, pl.40, twenty-five at Mount Beuvray in France) was filled with these lumps, and the plates were heated in a charcoal furnace. Each individual globule was then used as a blank for striking into a coin. The process was employed for gold, silver or bronze coins. In Aquitaine, by contrast, the blanks for silver coins were made by chopping pieces the right size from hammered-out plates of metal (**22**, **104**). This is closer to the mediaeval than to the usual ancient technique.

The blanks for many Gaulish bronze coins were also cast, but by a different technique. The metal came from the clay (or stone) mould in trees or strips, with each blank joined to its neighbour by a tongue or neck of metal that had to be cut before a blank was ready for striking (**1**). This technique is never used for silver coins. Most of the moulds, if not all, were one-sided, and the blank often has a bevelled edge in consequence. No such mould has come to light. The technique is rare in Belgic Gaul and unknown in British coins. It certainly began before Julius Caesar's Gallic wars, but its widest use is in Gaul after the Roman conquest.

Potin. A similar method was employed for casting the whitish potin or tin coins, both before and after the conquest (**398–400**, **404**, **409**). Two-sided moulds were certainly used in Gaul; the junction on the rim is plainly visible on most specimens. A few such clay moulds were found at the Celtic site of Boviolles (Meuse) in France. Examples of coins still joined by the connecting tongue have also been found, sometimes not of identical type. Some of the moulds seem to have been engraved or drawn individually, so that no two coins from them are identical. Others have probably been made by impressing in the mould an existing coin, which is then reproduced exactly.

In contrast with Gaulish, British tin coins were individually drawn; no two have ever been found identical. It has been noted that many British tin coins show traces of graining, most clearly seen on **399**. Evans suggested that the explanation lay in the use of wooden moulds, but this is certainly wrong. It is now sure from this and other examples that the graining must be traced to the use of a fibrous or textile base, almost certainly papyrus, for impressing the coin shape into the mould; the design was then scratched on with a stylus. I have never noted similar graining on any continental coins.

Sources of Metal. Taken as a whole, Celtic coinage does not, in any direct sense, represent the conversion of metals mined in Celtic areas into coinage. In some regions, however, this did occur, for instance in Bohemia and in the Caucasus, where the tetradrachm coinage must certainly have been struck from locally mined silver ore. The gold coinage of the Salassi in Haute-Savoie will have come from the ore panned in the Alpine mountain torrents. But by contrast the well-known gold mines of the Tolosates and Tarbelli in Aquitaine lie in a region where the coinage is exclusively of silver.

While metals from any convenient source may have been used, many Celtic coins were probably made from melting down Greek, Roman or earlier Celtic coins of greater weight and often better metal. Analysis of a silver coin from east Gaul with the legend *Kaletedou* establishes that it is of exactly the same composition as a contemporary Roman denarius, even to the traces of impurities; while the coins of Poitou with the legend *Contoutos* and similar coins are on analysis clearly shown to be of orichalcum, the composition of copper and zinc first introduced for coins by Julius Caesar and extensively used by his successors. The Celtic coins were certainly made from melting down Roman coins of this metal.

Banking and Testing. We have clear evidence that the Celts took the weight and varied composition of their coins seriously. We have from Stradonitz and elsewhere coin balances used by the bankers in the markets. From an early date it became common to cut or bend coins to ensure that the metal on the surface ran through (**2, 15, 21**). Cutting is found widely in Gaul and on the Danube, bending in Central and north-west Gaul. Also in Gaul are found many coins that show signs of having been wiped on a touchstone.

Countermarks, no doubt to distinguish the quality of the coin marked, appear at an early date, certainly in the second century B.C. They are fairly common on Danubian silver, and occur also on early (but not later) gold staters in Gaul (**3, 4**). In one important case there is a double countermark, the second, a sea serpent to left, being imposed on the first, a rosette.

Particularly intriguing are coins that have not been countermarked, but have been made in the original die to look as if they had, presumably on the theory that a countermarked coin was more acceptable than a plain one.

Plating. Some of the precautions that cutting and countermarking imply were necessitated by the prevalence of plated coins, that is, coins with a core of bronze and an outer coating of good gold or silver. After the earliest days there is scarcely a type in the west – it is less common in the east – of which there are not plated examples, barely distinguishable, when in good condition, from the regular coins they resemble. The art of plating coins became very widespread in the Greek world in the third century B.C. It is found on Celtic coins from the early second century B.C. to the end of the coinage. Plated coins were being issued in Britain as late as the Claudian period. Even though they may have been issued from official mints (if such phraseology applies at all to the coins of the Celts), there is no doubt that plated coins were intended to deceive by their appearance, and were often successful in doing so.

Values and Denominations

Paradoxically, the coins tell us little about the several economies they were, amongst other purposes, intended to serve. One can, perhaps, distinguish a rich from a poor country; one can say whether gold or silver was scarce. We know, for instance, that Cunobelin must have issued more than a million gold staters, equivalent to over sixteen thousand Roman pounds of gold. The size of the smallest denomination and its metal may be revealing, less perhaps of wealth or poverty than of the depth to which a monetary economy had penetrated. As to the actual value of coins and their purchasing power, we have almost nothing to go on save, perhaps, the implications of some penalties in ancient laws. The size of buried treasures might sometimes be correlated with known or deducible circumstances, for instance the amount of tribute paid, if we could be sure of their intended purpose. We have already referred to soldiers' pay. The only sums whose purpose is unmistakable are the occasional Charon's fee in burials (if for simplicity one may borrow the Classical counterpart); in one British instance at Verulamium the fee was ten bronze coins. But the simple reasoning that a horse or a boar shown on a coin means that this was the price of such a beast is certainly fallacious.

Although for convenience coins are usually described by the Greek or Roman names of the denominations that were imitated, we do not in fact know the true names for the coins. There is a single exception, a heavy bronze coinage of post-conquest date of the Lexovii (Lisieux), which has an inscription giving the denomination as *semissos publicos*; this is a Celtic version of the Latin *semis*, half an *as* in the Roman system (**453**, **454**). The occasional presence of an S on other bronze coins, all of much lighter weight, may warrant the assumption that the semis (marked with S on Republican Roman coins) was the normal name of the small bronze used in Gaul. Silver coins of several parts of Gaul sometimes bear an X behind the head, the mark that on early Roman coins indicated the denarius, but this does not prove that they bore the same name. No other legends give any clue, and there are on the coins plenty of abbreviated words that we simply do not understand.

Legends

The coin legends are, in fact, very largely confined to personal names, and, when complete, are nearly always in the nominative; only a handful are in the genitive (see chapter 6). When a second name is present, its relationship with the first is open to more than one interpretation. If it is followed by F (for *filius*), this proves a father and son relationship, from which, in Britain, dynastic sequences can be constructed (though we must remember the frequency of adoption amongst the Celts). But in other cases we can only guess whether the second name was a father's or that of a parallel magistrate, or in some cases an ethnic description.

The proper style for a Celt was to name either his parentage or his tribe or both; his tribe more particularly when he was out of his own territory. Where a tribal name occurs, it is not necessarily a description of the tribe issuing the coin; the single example in Britain is the Iceni, whose name is used on coins probably of the time of Prasutagus, after the Roman conquest of the South. It is even more rare for coins to name the mint town; the three British examples, Verulamium, Camulodunum and Calleva, are exceptional and the usage is scarcely met again this side of Spain. Titles are occasionally used; of those we can identify, *Basileus* (king) occurs on the Mediterranean coast, *Rex* (king) several times in Gaul as well as in Britain, *Vergobret* (elected magistrate) once at least and *Arcantodan* (moneyer) two or three times also. All coin legends appear to have been thought of as composed in Greek or Latin, the languages of business, not in the local Celtic tongue. One can at the end trace the slow elimination of the Celtic termination –OS (often given as –O), in favour of the Latinised –VS, as well as the occasional adoption of Latin names out of deference to new masters, Iulius, Gaius, or Quintus, always in combination with a more homely Celtic name. There is something to be learned about Celtic pronunciation from the use of doubled letters, exceptional letters (such as Θ), and alternative spellings of the same names. One has the impression that the engravers or their masters were fumbling with alien tools when they tried to spell Celtic names in Latin (or sometimes mixed Greek and Latin) or other scripts.

Subjects

The subjects depicted on the coins, superficially a monotonous sequence of heads, horses and boars, contain in fact an astonishing diversity of material and treatment (see chapter 7). Being always in some sense derivative, there is an element of tradition throughout, seen most strongly in the basic coinage of each area. One of the problems is to distinguish the traditional and imitative from the original and representational. When we can put our fingers on the latter, we have again to consider whether we are dealing with the routine bric-à-brac or ingrained habits of an engraver's workshop, or with genuine conceptions that demand interpretation in Celtic terms. Despite such ambiguities and the inherent inadequacies of their small scale, Celtic coins at their best give an unrivalled insight into the visual conceptions of their makers.

Obverses. True to tradition, the great majority of Celtic coins have on one side a head, male or female; if beardless, the sex is generally indeterminate, for torques and ear-rings do not necessarily imply a woman. Moustaches without beard are a rarity, despite Classical texts to prove that Celts wore moustaches. There are no portraits as such. Most heads must have been thought of as gods or goddesses, or other superhuman beings; the Celtic pantheon lacked the definition and clear personifications of the Greco-Roman and we can only class the individuals generically. Often a symbol accompanies the head, presumably to give it a personality. We have heads with boars, suns, lyres, wheels or sea-serpents in the hair. Another has a boar on the neck, while several have tattoo marks on the cheek, three circles or a lyre. Once a horse seems to go in at one ear and come out at another. Many areas knew a broken-nosed god. In some cases the numismatic cliché of the truncation at the neck has been interpreted as a severed head, an object of awe and reverence amongst all the Celts. One fascinating group of heads from Armorican Brittany, probably thought of as severed and erected for exultation, has the principal head accompanied by four miniature heads, echoing it and each attached by a cord. It is common for strings, indicative perhaps of power, to issue from the mouths of gods, goddesses, or heroes. There are examples of every conceivable hair style. This is how the Celts thought of the human form, translated into the superhuman dimensions of the magical world around.

Reverses. Likewise, on the other side, tradition generally required an animal type, most typically a horse or horseman. But from the very early days it was customary, perhaps even obligatory, for the main type to be accompanied by subsidiary types or symbols. The relationship of parts to the whole varies. A human-headed horse may have beneath it a lyre, sun, triquetra, flower, hand, head, kneeling or uprising manikin, boar, dog or other wild beast; above, it may have a charioteer, flying manikin, or a wide range of animals or birds. These are examples only, and there are often other decorative gap-filling ornaments scattered around.

It is impossible to be certain to what extent these gathered elements hang together to make a story with a meaning; the unity need be no more than artistic, yet very often one wonders if there is not implied some fanciful tale in the manner of Irish legends of the Ulster cycle. Some compositions were probably created only to be recognisable and acceptable in a particular locality. Although natural animals are regularly shown – we have spirited horses, boars, bulls, bears, dogs, eagles, ravens, snakes and lizards – often the preferred beast was a monster somehow diversified from nature, some in the orientalising manner, such as the pegasus, hippocamp, gryphon, harpy; others are such essentially Celtic inventions as the man-headed horse and the goat-headed snake; but many were meant as no more than ferocious and unidentifiable monsters on the most pedestrian level, conceivably to scare off the forger. Natural beasts were often depicted not as themselves but as images erected on a standard for war or worship: this is indicated by the framework on which they stand, and in some cases we see them held in the hand. The human figure is most often seen either on a horse, and then armed, or standing winged; amongst the Celts a winged man was as regular as a female Victory.

Objects. Objects too are shown; weapons predominate, such as axes, swords, spears and shields. There are many representations of the carnyx, the dolphin-headed Celtic war trumpet. We have a few temples and temple columns, thrones for priests, chieftains or gods (the Celts in the ordinary way had no chairs), and altars of different forms. Of particular interest is a wooden image (**335**, **336**), touched by a Gallic Heracles, closely resembling those found in France at the source of the Seine and Chamalières. On a late gold stater a traditional and meaningless element, the arms of a charioteer, are converted into an excellent representation of a Celtic collar fibula. Many devices cannot yet be interpreted.

The Sources for the Study

The material for this study is mainly derived from the standard works of Blanchet, Forrer, Paulsen and Pink (see bibliography). Of these Blanchet and Pink are by far the most important. The latter's *Einführung in die Keltische Münzkunde* of 1950 provides the best existing general summary of the subject. The greatest contribution of recent years has been made by Dr J-B. Colbert de Beaulieu of Paris, to whose vital work I am greatly indebted; most of it, however, is published in local French periodicals, which are not readily accessible. Valuable work has also been done by Dr Karl Christ in Germany, Dr Karel Castelin in Czechoslovakia, Constantin Preda in Romania, Dr Simone Scheers in Belgium and Carl-Axel Moberg in Sweden. There has been little serious study of this subject in English except in the field of the British coinages, although the public collections available in Great Britain are in most respects excellent.

The most important collections of Celtic coins are abroad; of these Paris is pre-eminent, but there are important collections in most international cabinets, of which perhaps Vienne, Munich, Mainz, Zurich and Berlin may be singled out. In Great Britain, the collection of the British Museum is the largest, and with the Universities of Oxford, Cambridge, Manchester, Leeds and Glasgow together gives an almost complete coverage of the Celtic coinage of the British Isles. In regard to Continental Celtic coins, again the largest and finest collection in Britain is at the British Museum, though it is not much more than illustrative, but the University museums each add something, and useful examples are to be found in some public museums such as Cardiff or Colchester. Put together, the public collections in this country cover the subject pretty well, each to some extent filling the gaps of the others, but the process of collecting has been haphazard and coincidental. To some extent there has been in the past an understandable prejudice against Celtic coins on the grounds that they are little more than a barbarous reflection of the real thing, travesties of the cultivated products of the advanced civilisations of Greece and Rome. The disintegrative tendencies of modern art and the cult of the primitive have provided an ambience within which the balance can be restored. Barbarous or not, the history of early Europe is written in these coins, and no other surviving Celtic remains illustrate more vividly the life and thoughts of our insufferably quarrelsome but superbly imaginative forebears, farming and fighting while Theocritus and Vergil were describing the Mediterranean peasant's life in vastly different terms.

There is no really good book on Celtic coins, especially in the English language. The subject is hard to study because the material is so scattered, and any attempt to master it involves reading critically books of differing quality in a variety of languages. Owing to the scale of the study no one individual can hope to master all the literature. Some further reading is recommended in the bibliography, but there can be no real substitute for seeing and handling the coins themselves, which exist in extraordinary numbers.

2

The Silver Belt

The Central Sector : The Po Valley

I start my description of the great belt of silver coins, which stretched across southern Europe from the Atlantic to the Black Sea, with the Celts of Cisalpine Gaul in the central sector, because their coins set the time scale for the rest. Celts from the north west settled in the Po valley, mostly on the north bank, shortly before the sack of Rome in 390 B.C, having dispelled Etruscans from the area. Throughout the third century B.C. these Celts provided a constant threat to Rome and to the other peoples of Central Italy. They were decisively defeated by the Romans at Telamon in 225 B.C, when the Romans captured Mediolanum. Nevertheless, despite the founding of Roman colonies amongst them at Placentia and Cremona in 218 B.C, they were still able to provide Hannibal with much help and they were not finally reduced until 191 B.C, when those who lived south of the Po (including the Boii) were forced to cede half their territory and migrated northwards towards the Danube. By the time of the invasion of the Cimbri and Teutones in 102 B.C, they were sufficiently assimilated to Rome not to support the invaders, and in 81 B.C. Sulla reorganised Cisalpine Gaul into the frontier province of Northern Italy.

Compared with the splendours of Celtic art elsewhere, the Celts of Cisalpine Gaul make a poor showing, but from an early stage they used coins imitated from the silver drachms of the Greek colony of Massilia with the head of Persephone on one side and a lion on the other (5; figure 11). The first are plain copies, but with a corrupt legend, of the drachms of heavy standard, struck in Massilia in the fourth century B.C. There is also a heavy drachm of good style bearing in Italiot characters the name *Anarekartoi*. This initial phase presumably falls in the first half of the third century B.C.

Subsequently we have a long series of imitations in Celtic style of the similar light drachms of Massilia, which had begun to replace the heavy ones before the middle of the third century B.C. There are three

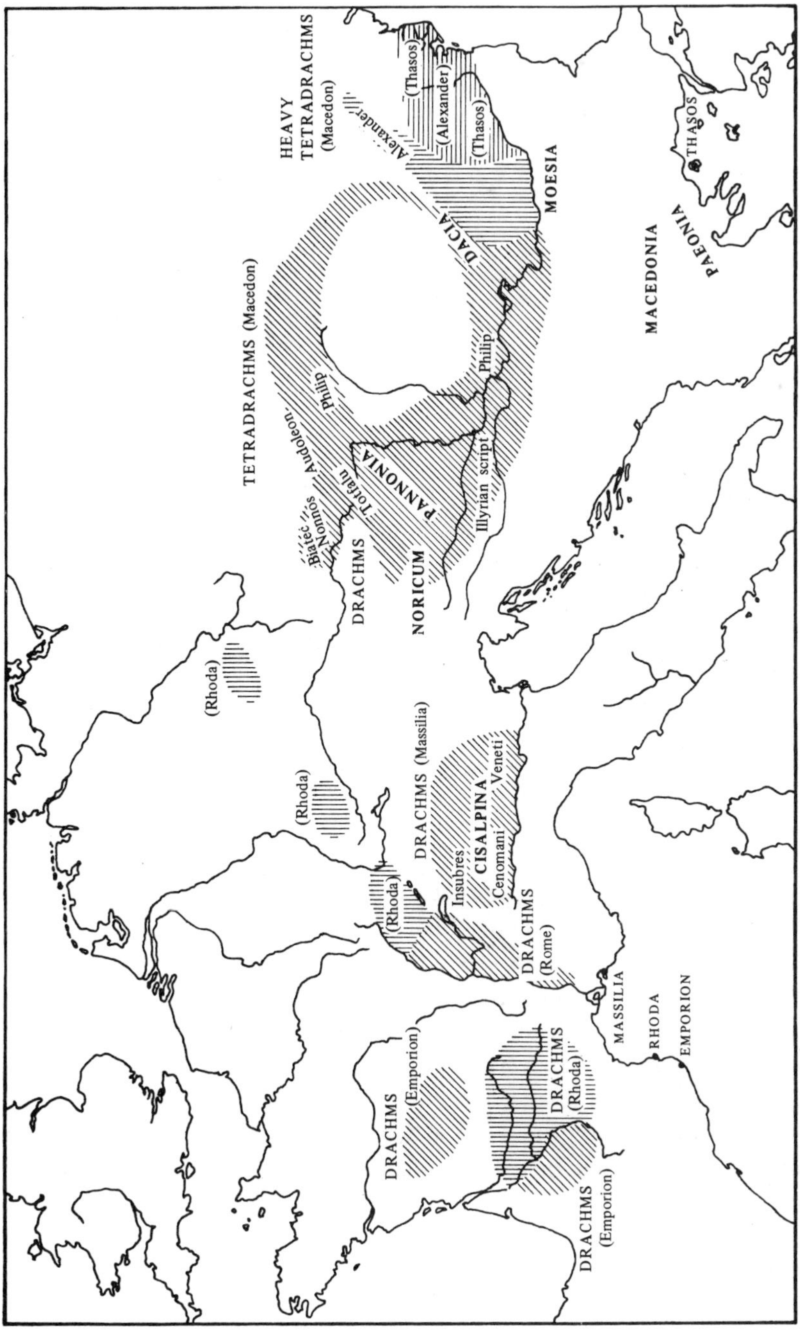

Map 5. Silver coins of southern Europe

Figure 11. Cisalpine Gaul drachms

main streams of imitations, each found in a different locality. They are distinguished by the form of the 'lion' and the pseudo-legends, and they can confidently be ascribed to the three main tribes of the area known to history – the Insubres round Milan (**6**), the Cenomani in the Ticino (**7**) and the Veneti near the mouth of the Po and on the Adige (**8**), the latter not recognised as a Celtic tribe. The different types can be shown from hoard evidence, such as the Paul hoard from Penzance, Cornwall, which consisted of the first two types, to have evolved in parallel.

The beginning of the coins of the Cenomani can be dated by the presence of eight examples in the hoard from the Capitol, Rome, found in 1933, which contained Roman coins ending with the earliest of the quadrigati and halves on which the legend ROMA is in raised letters. The precise date of these remains controversial, but it cannot have been later than 214 B.C. This uncertainty is of minor importance here because the Cenomani coins, unlike the rest of the hoard, were heavily worn; they must have been struck nearer the middle of the third century B.C. They may well have been brought back to Rome by soldiers who had fought at Telamon in 225 B.C.

A century or so after their introduction some of these imitation drachms were given genuine legends in Italiot characters, *Rutirio*, *Pirukoi* and *Rikoi* (**9**, **10**), if they are correctly read; they may be compared with coins reading *Anarekartoi*. We also have uninscribed half pieces (**11**, **12**). The inscribed coins seem to come mainly from the valleys on the Swiss side of the Alps.

There are a number of hoards that can be dated from the presence of Roman coins – more than in any other sector of Celtic coinage. Thus the hoards from Biandrate, Gambolo, Padua and San Zeno nell'Anaunia can be shown to belong to the last quarter of the third century B.C, while that from Gerenzago, which contained coins with the *Rikoi* legend, belonged to the last decade of the second century B.C. or first decade of the first. Examples of degraded type, including one with the same legend, were found with coins of Augustus and Tiberius in a tomb at Como. The likelihood is that the coinage ceased to be struck in or before 81 B.C, but examples will have remained above ground a little longer.

The coins remained faithful throughout to a single tradition with the minimum of change. A certain Celtic feeling may be detected in the so-called 'scorpion type' of the Cenomani (**7**), compare the so-called 'wolf type' of the Insubres above (**6**, cf. **9**). They had no influence on the coins of other Celtic areas and are not found mixed with them: we cannot, as we might expect, trace them in the wake of the migrating Boii, and the Paul hoard from Britain stands isolated.

The importance of this coinage lies in its demonstration that a prolific but almost unchanging coinage could exist in a Celtic area for something approaching two centuries, from the mid third century B.C to the first quarter of the first century B.C, and that the traditions of the Greek model could survive the overwhelming influence exerted by Rome from the beginning of the second century B.C. onwards. This time-scale, which for once is happily not open to doubt, gives the lie to the theories of Celtic coinage recently fashionable, which would seek to compress its enormous complexity into a narrow bracket of time. It also casts doubt on the common presumption that one should posit a long interval between the circulation of the prototypes and the first issue of Celtic copies. These thoughts are relevant to the interpretation of the coins of the Danube Basin, to which I now turn.

The Eastern Sector : The Danube Valley

An enormous silver coinage is found in the valley of the Danube and its tributaries, particularly the Drava and Sava; it is also found in the ring

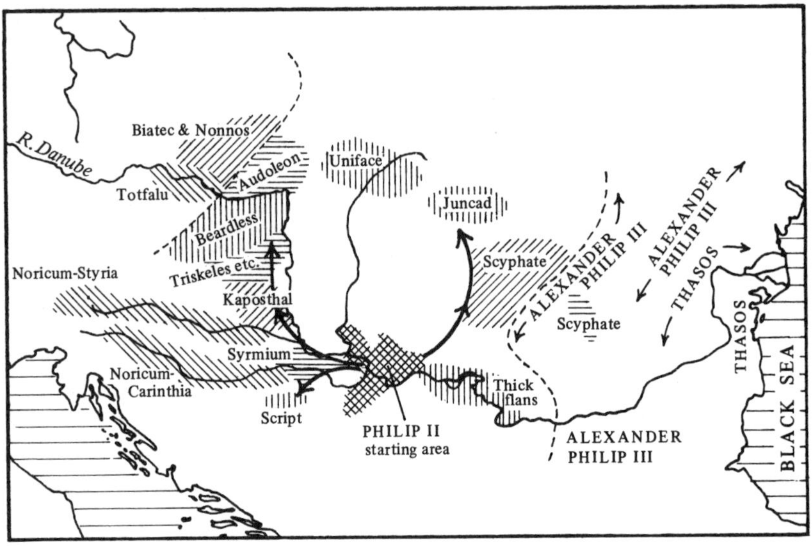

Map 6. Danubian silver : distribution of main types

of the Carpathian mountains.

The regions in which these coins are found were largely, but not entirely, included in Roman times in the provinces of Noricum, Pannonia, Dacia and the northern borders of Moesia. In modern terms the area extends from Austria, through parts of Yugoslavia, Czechoslovakia, Hungary, Romania and Bulgaria to the shores of the Black Sea. For the most part the inhabitants were Celts, at least from the fourth century B.C. onwards, but there were certainly some tribes in it that were not, and on the fringes there was intermingling with Illyrians, Scythians and even Sarmatians. From a variety of sources we know of some of the tribes which lived in this vast area; but as yet it is only in special cases that tribal names and coin distributions can be connected. Great strides are being made in the archaeology of this area and a fuller understanding and better plotting of these coins will be fundamental to it; the work of Constantin Preda on the Geto-Dacian coinages of Romania is an important advance in this direction.

The origin of most of this coinage is to be found in the silver tetradrachms of Philip II and his successors as rulers of Macedon. A subsidiary but important source lies in the coins of the small Thracian kingdom of Paeonia. Finally, a large section is derived from the coins of the Thracian island of Thasos. The principal coin types copied were issued between 359 and 286 B.C, though the Thasos type did not begin until after the cessation of Macedonian coinage in 146 B.C.

Macedonian tetradrachms remained in circulation for a great many years and it is open to argument when the Danubian peoples began to make imitations. Pink's view, that the process did not begin until after the defeat of the Macedonians by the Romans at Pydna in 168 B.C, and did not flourish until after the Roman defeat of the Celtic Scordisci in 101 B.C. near the junction of the Danube and the Sava in north-east Yugoslavia, has now been convincingly refuted, e.g. by Preda, on the basis of hoards containing early Celtic (Geto-Dacian) and Macedonian coins together. In the absence of positive proof, the probability is that no great length of time elapsed between the date of issue of the coins chosen for copying and the initial copies. Certainly the coinage developed slowly at first in a limited area and then suddenly expanded.

The source of the silver for the coinage of Macedon lay in the silver mines of the Balkans, and the likelihood is that, as Macedonian coinage declined, the produce of the mines in Celtic territory came to be turned into local coinage. This could have begun at any time after about the middle of the third century B.C. If we do not assume such a starting date, the wealth of coinage, the long circulation of the earlier, and even some of the later, pieces, and the steady but controlled decline in weight of the Philip tetradrachm to little more than half the original weight defies adequate explanation.

Like all Celtic coinages, Danubian coins are essentially imitative, and the models carefully selected from those available. The basic type throughout the Danube area is the tetradrachm on the Phocaean standard of 14.5 g of Philip II of Macedon (359–336 B.C.), on the obverse of which is a bearded head of Zeus and on the reverse a horse with rider to left or right (**13**); **14–15** are close copies. Much the greater part of the coinage of Pannonia and Dacia consists of variations on this theme. This coinage is associated with less abundant imitations of two Paeonian kings, Patraos and Audoleon, the immediate Thracian neighbours of Macedon. The coins of Patraos, 335–315 B.C, have on the obverse a beardless head of Apollo and on the reverse a horseman with plume on his helmet, spearing a fallen foe (**16**). The influence of this coinage was strong in Pannonia, in some parts of which beardless faces, like **17**, became established. The coins of Audoleon, 315–286 B.C, have a facing head of Athena and on the reverse a standing horse without rider (**18**). The reverse of this coin, but not the obverse, was much imitated, even to the legend and symbols, and it had great influence on the coins north of the knee of the Danube and in Noricum. The obverse of coins of Lysimachos of Macedon, 306–281 B.C, have a beardless head of the deified Alexander the Great with the horn of Ammon in his characteristically loose hair (**19**); the contemporary coins of Tenos have a bearded Zeus Ammon (**20**). A similar horn in the hair becomes a common feature on Danubian tetradrachms, particularly, but not exclusively, in the east.

These are the principal sources of the main coinage, but other influences from time to time occur. Notable amongst these are the fourth-century facing heads of the coins of Amphipolis, Larissa or Pheros, the bearded Janus of third-century Roman origin, the Artemis of second-century Macedon and the cow and calf of Dyrrachium.

The earliest stage of the Philip tetradrachms consists of direct copies. They were not properly a local coinage, but local substitutes for the real thing. The centre of this copying appears to have been on the northern frontiers of Macedonia in Serbia and Bosnia, an area probably occupied by the Celtic (or Celt-Illyrian) tribe of the Scordisci, with whose name some, one cannot yet say precisely which, of the coins should certainly be associated. The key hoards (which may lie outside the true area of circulation) come from the Banat and Arad in south-west Romania. One group of early coins (the Huşi-Vovrieşti group of Preda pls XXI–XXVII) is almost always found cut or countermarked, indicating that their metal had been tested in the course of their long life (**21**); other specimens of the earliest issues are also found tested in this way, though less regularly (**15**).

Soon the coins began to acquire an individuality that distinguishes them from copies, and their areas of distribution may be plotted with more accuracy. The central core now lies either side of the frontier between Hungary and Croatia and also in Transylvania. From this centre there spread what may for the first time properly be called coinages in at least three directions, east-about round the Carpathians, south-east into Serbia and, more densely, west-about up the Danube into lower Austria. The east-about and west-about routes meet in Gallicia, a significant name, which was probably the home of the isolated Celtic tribe of the Cotini. The west-about coins spread across the Burgenland into Styria and Carinthia, which formed the ancient Noricum. No coins are found in the marshland of the Tisza valley, which was inhabited by Sarmatians. Preda has shown that there is a close association, at least in the first two phases of the Danubian coinages, between the presence of Celtic peoples and the issue of tetradrachm coinages of the type under discussion here.

These basic movements did not happen quickly. The opening stages, I believe, should be placed around the middle of the third century B.C. The great period of expansion of the Celts in central Europe dates from their dramatic appearance in Greek history, when they sacked Delphi in 279 B.C. and invaded Asia Minor in the following year. At this time the current coins of Macedon and its neighbourhood were already precisely those adopted by the Celts as the principal models for their own coinage. The collapse of the great Macedonian output of coins after the battle of Pydna in 168 B.C. will have encouraged an independent Danubian coinage, and may be associated with changes in it, but it was certainly not the cause of its origin. The floruit of the coinage undoubtedly lay in the second century B.C. and it had reached its most westerly point, Noricum, well before the end of that century.

About the close of the story we are better informed. Thus in Noricum it seems certain that coinage survived until the region was overrun by Rome in 16 B.C, and, as in Britain, it may have been tolerated as long as a native dynasty was allowed to remain in power, perhaps until near the end of the century. This accords with the known date of the associated Biatec coinage from South Slovakia. But in Pannonia the local coinages had probably disappeared a little earlier, say by the middle of the century. In Hungary and Slovakia there occurs a local coinage based on the Roman Republican denarius, some with the legend *Ravis* or *Ravit*, which possibly refers to the supposedly Illyrian Eravisci (**22**). It may be roughly dated by the Budapest hoard to some time after 76–74 B.C. (the date of a Roman Republican coin in it) and by one of the types which appears to copy a denarius of 63–62 B.C. This implies that the denarius coinage, which is never found mixed with the tetradrachms and was a successor to them, was in existence before the Pannonian campaigns of 12–9 B.C. But here again it looks as if continued use of this native coinage was sanctioned during the early years after the Conquest. In Dacia the Lunca hoard, containing Roman coins down to 49 B.C, also brings the use of the coinage down to the mid first century B.C. It may well have ceased following the unification of the country by the non-Celtic Burebista in *c*.44 B.C, following his defeat of the Celtic Boii and Taurisci.

Thus it looks as if the coinage in the Danube basin began in the third century B.C, reached its full extension before the end of the second century B.C, and for the most part terminated in the middle of the first, though in the west and north it probably survived until near the end of the century, reflecting in consequence a measure of the Roman influence so notably absent from the rest of Danubian coinage.

We may now follow some of the main varieties in rough geographical order. Going east from the Arad and Banat, perhaps the home of the

Scordisci, where we encountered the early and close imitations of the Philip II tetradrachm, the first distinctive local coinages occur in south-west Romania, near the Serbian frontier (**23–6**). One distinctive example is the tetradrachm – there are no quarters in this direction – with a great Celtic curl on a beardless cheek, found in the Criciova hoard (**27**). Such Gallicisms are rare here, but the hair on **28** is another example.

Amongst the Dacii in the south-east Carpathians we soon encounter cup-shaped or scyphate coins, broad, of poor metal and degraded but distinctive style (first **29–31**, later **32–4**); their home lies in the central and east Carpathians. Further north the coins are closer to prototypes from the Banat, but acquire characteristic local symbols.

Finally, in the extreme north of the range, in Gallicia, at the junction with the west-about route, we have coins of east-about derivation that have wholly lost the obverse and almost the reverse pattern (**35**, **36**). These uniface coins, which we may attribute to the Cotini, have been found in the O'Hulta hoard mixed with the coins of their western neighbours. Cotini coins include drachms with a monogram on the obverse, probably reading *Camul.* Moving southeast from the Banat, the coins in Moesia offer many of the same features, but in what is now north Serbia the flans became markedly thick and lumpy (**37**, **38**); many varieties are found with details comparable to those of neighbouring Romania, but they are instantly distinguishable by their fabric. Here too is the home of the remarkable coins with the facing and Janus heads (**40**, **41**). The facing head imitates coins of Larissa (**39**).

Returning to the Banat and moving westwards, the variety of coins found in Pannonia is very large and the distributions relatively firm; for instance **42** with the triskeles, from Lake Balaton, in the district that in Roman times belonged to the Hercuniates. There is a tendency for the rider to wear an elaborate plume on his head (**43**), which in some groups becomes a pair of magical horns. These features seem to have their starting point in the helmet of the Patraos horseman (**16**). Another group (**44–7**) comes from Kaposthal (perhaps corresponding to the tribe of the Andizetes), a little to the south, in the angle between the Danube and Drava. One variety showing markedly Celtic features from the district of Zagreb had a legend in Illyrian characters, *Sasthieni*, perhaps equivalent to the Greek Sosthenes (**48**). It is the only legend of its kind; **49** is a comparable coin with normal head and blundered inscription. Further north the Audoleon influence is added to that of Patraos. In the extreme north, at the junction with the Cotini (perhaps in the area of the Osi) we have coins with a bearded head in the Philip tradition combined with a reverse at first imitating Audoleon (**18**), including a recognisable legend (**50**, then **51**, **52**). In Burgenland (perhaps amongst the Eravisci) we have several striking series of coins with beardless faces, ultimately derived from the obverse of the Audoleon type, with or without rider on the reverse (**53**, **54**, cf. **17**). Another important group is found in the district of Sirmium, later the Roman capital of Lower Pannonia, between the Sava and the Drava, corresponding to the tribe of the Amantini. These have heavily bearded heads and riderless horses, again combining the traditions. In this part of Pannonia drachms and quarter drachms appear and Gallicisms abound. But the coins that show the clearest evidence of contact with the Celts of the west are those from Noricum.

The coins of Noricum (or perhaps more correctly of the Taurisci) descend from a type of beardless-head tetradrachm known from the hoard found at Warasdin, Križovljan, near the junction of the Drava and the Mur. The distribution is not confined within the Roman boundaries of the province of Noricum, but runs much further east. There are two closely related series here, the Styrian and the Carinthian, that is, along the Sava and the Drava respectively. Each starts with a beardless face wearing an elaborate head-dress with wreath (**55–8**); each ends with coins showing a horseman throwing a spear, accompanied by a legend in Latin characters. These legends include the names *Eccaio* (**59**), found also in North Gaul, and *Tinco*, which is reminiscent of Tincommius in Britain. The evolution is closely parallel with that of British coinage; in both cases, for instance, the wreath around Apollo's head plays a major function in the design. In one type, reading *Svicca*, the wreath takes the centre of the coin, and, instead of a face, a horse is superimposed (**60**).

In a series of fractions found in the important hoards of Simmering (**61**) and Tótfalu (**62–4**) in Bohemia, the same prominence is given to the wreath. These coins from the district inhabited in Roman times by the Azati form a bridge between the Norican coins of Carinthia and the Bohemian-Slovakian series of Biatec, which are discussed below; the floruit of the latter can be securely dated to the third quarter of the first century B.C. A rare variety of Norican fraction has a reverse copied from a denarius of 87 B.C. Noricum is also probably the home of very rare coins with Lysimachus head and a legend in Italiot script.

There can be no doubt that the engravers of the Norican coins were familiar with certain coins of the Rhône, Seine and Somme valleys in the late second century B.C. It was in 113 B.C. that Noricum came under pressure from the Cimbri and the kingdom was unsuccessfully supported by the Romans. The new influences revealed in Norican coinage may reflect the wider contacts forced on the people in that turbulent phase.

In addition to the tetradrachms inspired by the coins of Philip II of Macedon, there was to the east a large, but poorly located, group of imitations of Macedonian tetradrachms of Alexander III (336–323 B.C.) and Philip III (323–316 B.C.) (**65**, **66**; imitations **67–70**). Their main home is in Moesia in the modern Bulgaria, though some varieties are found much further north in Romania. On the obverse is the head of Heracles in a lion skin and on the reverse Zeus seated with staff and eagle. There are also similar drachms (**69**, **70**). This coinage went through changes little less drastic than those of the Philip II tetradrachms (though much less invention is involved), but the coinage has not been closely analysed (Preda pls. LXXII–LXXIV). These tetradrachms were struck on the Attic standard of 17.4 g. The drachms by contrast appear to have been on the Phocaean weight standard of 14.5 g and, in fact, sometimes spread to the west, where they have left a trace of influence on Celtic coins as far away as the Rhineland. The weight of the tetradrachms is always relatively high, and they may prove to be earlier than the next series on the Attic standard.

This consists of imitations of coins of Thasos with, on the obverse, a head of the young Dionysus with vine leaves and grapes in his hair and on the reverse a standing Heracles (**71**). These were extensively and crudely copied and the designs eventually reduced to incomprehensible lines and dots (**72**, **73**). An example exists on which the Heracles is replaced by a horseman with spear and the legend ΔHMHT in Greek characters (**74**). The Thasos coins that were copied all date from after 146 B.C. It is therefore likely that the floruit of the imitations is in the first century B.C, while that of the Alexander III/Philip III type may be in the preceding century. Very little, however, seems to be recorded about either group.

Another important group of coins on the Attic standard of 17.4 g comes from Bohemia and south Slovakia, especially the Bratislava area. These coins adjoin the main Philip tetradrachm area to the northwest, but are separated from other Attic tetradrachms. They are usually known as the Biatec series, from the first and commonest of the legends, but there are many others. The coins have a multiple origin; the reverses with rider of some of them are related to the Philip horseman and the inscribed coins of Noricum, while the obverse and reverse of others has a clear derivation from Roman denarii of 60 and *c*.46 B.C. (**75**, **76**).

At the same time the coins have a link with a different past, since there are late gold staters and fractions of the 'mussel' type with the *Biatec* legend, which will be discussed in the next chapter (**142**).

In the Gerlitzen Alps hoard of 1903–4, coins of *Biatec* and *Nonnos* were found, as were also coins of Noricum inscribed *Adnamati*, *Nemet* and *Atta*, with a Roman quinarius of 43 B.C. In several other hoards the coins are associated with fractions of Simmering and Tótfalu types. The start of this series is, thus, exceptionally well dated to the middle of the first century B.C.

There are in all sixteen different legends on the silver tetradrachms, of which some are common, but the majority known only from a single pair of dies. On the earlier coins there is a rider on the reverse (**77–80**), which some have seen, unconvincingly, to be connected with Spanish coins with horseman reverse (*jinete*). The later coins have a great variety of types in a partly Romanised style comparable with those on contemporary British coins of Tasciovanus and Cunobelin – lion (**81**) winged griffin, stag-headed horse (**82**), harpy in helmet (**83**), bear with trainer, winged female centaur (**84**), curled snake, beast eating man, and so forth. There are fractions of *Biatec* and *Nonnos*, the latter of traditional Tótfalu type.

The coins presumably precede the campaign against Pannonia by Tiberius in 12–9 B.C. Indeed, the wave of hoards from Bratislava containing these coins may well date from that event, or possibly from the full reduction of Pannonia in 7–9 A.D. They are amongst the most remarkable of all late Celtic coins and offer a particularly close parallel with Celtic coinage in Britain.

The Western Sector

The Rhône Valley

We have now reviewed the eastern half of the map from the Po to the Danube basin and the Black Sea. I turn next to the west. The first silver coinage encountered is in the Rhône valley. The coins here (**87–9**) had their origin in some of the coins of the Carthaginians in Spain, or conceivably in the earliest silver coinage of Rome, via Northern Italy (**85**, **86**) for the horse's head on the reverse is common to both. The coinage eventually adopted other reverses, with whole horses or goats in place of the horse's head. At the present stage I shall only refer briefly to this coinage, which I believe may not have begun till the second or third quarter of the second century B.C, because I shall revert to it in chapter 5, on the origins and development of small silver and bronze money in Gaul. It will be sufficient here to say that the coinage is inscribed. The first legends on these coins, like those on the first coins of Cisalpine Gaul and on a few of those of Noricum, are in Italiot script. The coins agree in weight with those of Cisalpine Gaul; both are based on the same joint Massiliot-Roman standard. The Rhône is, however, a frontier of importance. Coins of this class are not found to the west of it, but instead coins that owe their origin to the Massiliot colonies in Spain, Rhoda and Emporion, to which I now proceed.

Rhoda Imitations in Gascony and Guienne and Elsewhere (monnaies-à-la-croix)

From the early fourth century B.C. the Greek colony of Rhoda was striking fine silver drachms with the head of a nymph in Syracusan (or Carthaginian) style on one side and an open rose on the other (**90**). These were copied in the region shown on map 7. The copies are readily distinguishable because from a very early stage the punning rose of the reverse, seen from underneath, became misunderstood and converted into a wheel, sun or cross pattern (**91–3**). The nymph's head also underwent the influence of Celtic treatment. The first generation of copies cannot yet be accurately located. It is not long, however, before the dominant feature of the coins becomes the cross suggested by the rose's four calices, in each angle of which there is a crescent suggested by the petals. The four quarters are then filled by a variety of devices, at

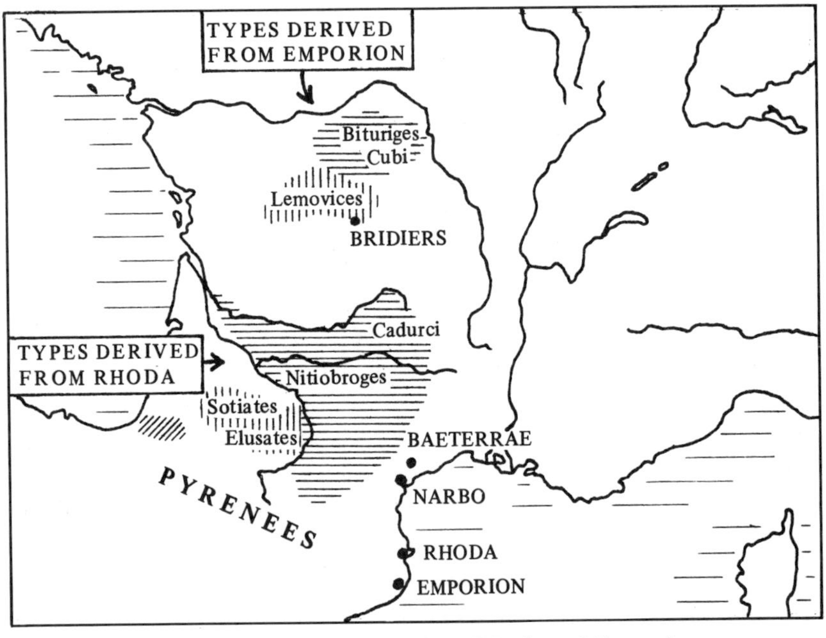

Map 7. Coin types derived from Rhoda and Emporion

first pellets, rings, S's and other emblems; then ears, eyes, flowers, shields and, pre-eminently, axes (**94–9**).

This coinage is not found in significant numbers in Spain, but in adjacent areas on the French side of the Pyrenees, in Guyenne and Gascony or, in Roman terms, Gallia Aquitania. Some forty hoards have been found in the valley of the Garonne and to the south of it in an area from which other Celtic coins are largely lacking. Most of these coins are, as I mentioned in the Introduction, struck on cut, not cast, flans (**99**). We know from Strabo that 'the Gauls of Aquitania were considered more akin to those of Spain than of Gallia Celtica' (Strabo 4.1.1, 4.2.1). With the exception of a single early copy in gold, if it is genuine, all these coins are struck in silver, despite the gold mines of the Tarbelli and the Tolosates in this area, which were well known in antiquity.

The usual difficulties of chronology should be capable of full solution, because in this area, as in the Po valley, there was the kind of contact with Rome and Roman Spain that should establish correlations. Up to now, however, records are defective. For the starting date we have no indisputable evidence; weights seem to show that the earlier copies were more or less continuous with the originals, presumably in the late fourth and early third centuries B.C. The monnaies-à-la-croix proper, however, do not appear to be continuous with these, as they start on a lower weight standard. Blanchet, following Barthélemy, suggested that the coinage began in the last quarter of the third century B.C, in the wake of Hannibal's incursion by land into Italy. This may well be the right chronology, but it did not require Hannibal to establish contact between the Celts of Aquitaine and Spain. When the Roman consul Q. Servilius Caepio reduced the Volcae Tectosages in 106 B.C, he captured (but lost on the way back) an enormous treasure of gold and silver (AV 100000 lb, AR 110000 lb; Strabo 4.1.13), several hundred times larger than the largest hoard of Celtic coins ever found; this would have contained monnaies-à-la-croix. Indeed it is to this campaign that many of the surviving hoards may be attributed. This dating is suggested, for instance, by the hoard from Bompas, near Perpignan, which contained thirteen Roman denarii with some six hundred worn cross coins of fully developed type. The two latest Roman coins, which were in mint condition, were of C. Valerius Flaccus, Imperator in Gaul, where the coins were struck, in 83 B.C. Since the hoard must have been buried within a year or two of 83 B.C, the worn cross coins in it were certainly struck some years earlier. Worn coins were still circulating up to 51 B.C, as shown by the finds at Alesia, but there were also late issues struck around the time of the Caesarian war, for a silver coin of the Cadurcan leader Lucterius, mentioned by Caesar in 52 B.C, and probably struck around that time, is based on this cross pattern (**102**). One was found in the Cuzance hoard in Lot.

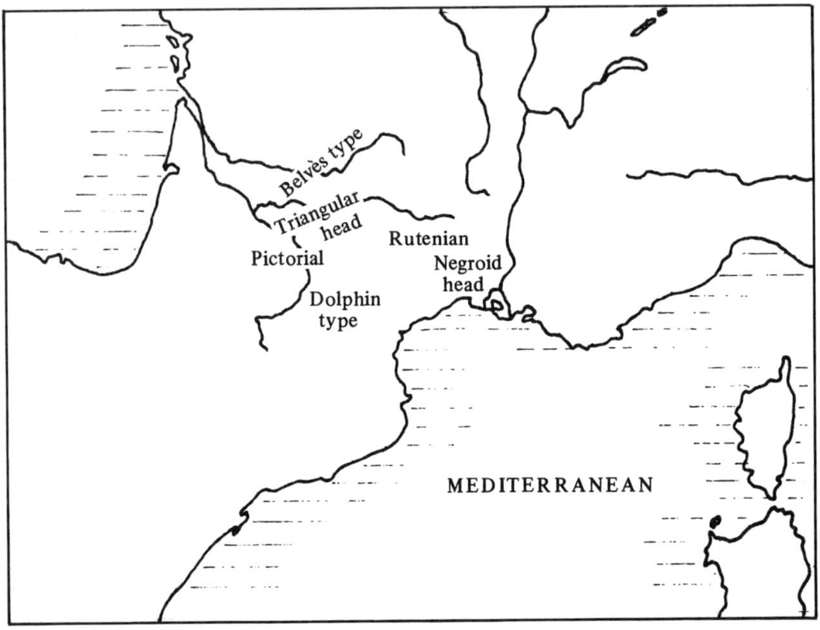

Map 8. Distribution map of monnaies-à-la-croix

There are many varieties of cross money from Aquitaine (**94–102**), some with Roman and others with Celt-Iberian legends; **101** is a fraction. It has now been demonstrated that there are geographical as well as chronological distinctions between many issues. The tribes in the area in Roman times were numerous: they include the Nitiobroges, Petrocorii, Cadurci and, most famous, the Volcae Tectosages. The coins are generally known under the last of these names, but this represents an oversimplification, since very few of the hoards come from their known territory. Nevertheless, the Volcae Tectosages are important, not only because they feature in Roman history, but because we know something of their migrations. They are believed to have reached Tolosa (Toulouse) from the Mainz area about 300 B.C. Later, part of the tribe moved back to the Hercynian Forest, while part moved on to Illyria and Pannonia. The remainder wandered on down the Danube into Asia Minor, where, with other tribes, they were amongst the founders of Galatia after their defeat by Attalus I in 230 B.C. What appear to be traces of these movements can be seen in the cross-type coins of Rhaetia and Bohemia (**103**). Characteristic of the Rhaetian finds is the hoard from Lauterach, Vorarlberg, which also contained a Roman denarius of 110 B.C. Similarly at the great oppidum of Stradonitz in Bohemia (whose floruit was between 110 and 103 B.C.) and on the Magdalensberg in Austria the same cross pattern survives on coins reduced in size and weight to the smallest money of convenience (**105**). The same small coins are found in the hoards of Gurina and Eis, which show them to be contemporary with the later inscribed coins of Noricum. We may even see a trace of the cross pattern in Britain. A British gold quarter stater, only known from the Clacton (Essex) hoard, appears to be connected with the Rhaetian version of the type.

The Aquitanian custom of cut flans is not wholly confined to monnaies-à-la-croix, as is demonstrated by a group of coins found to the east of the principal area of distribution of monnaies-à-la-croix. In the Goutrens hoard from Aveyron, associated with monnaies-à-la-croix, there were silver coins made similarly on cut flans, with a head on the obverse and a well-designed boar on the reverse (**104**). In type, but not in fabric, they have much in common with first-century B.C. silver coins of the Massif Central and the Arverni.

Emporion Imitations in Limousin, Poitou and Berry

The second Greek colony in Spain, Emporion, lay close to Rhoda on the bay of Ampurias. Like Rhoda, silver drachms were issued. At first they showed a nymph's head (Ceres) on the obverse and a standing horse on the reverse with a flying Victory above. In the late third century they changed to a head of Arethusa with dolphins on the obverse, and a pegasus on the reverse (**106–8**). A curious feature of many of the later Pegasus reverses is that the head of the horse is replaced by a crouching boy, who superficially resembles a horse's head – the so-called Chrysaor type, which was occasionally copied in detail (**108**). These coins began not earlier than the last years of the fourth century B.C. Emporitan silver was in circulation down to the end of the second century B.C, as is shown by the Segaro hoard.

As at Rhoda, copies start early (**109**, **110**); indeed there are copies of better weight than the later originals and even than the Chrysaor type. We can confidently put the earliest copies, if not into the third century B.C, at least into very early second century B.C. The process of copying seems more continuous here than at Rhoda. There are Celt-Iberian inscriptions and no cut flans, while the only break in the sequence of weight occurs at a very much later date.

The main tradition in Gaul of types ultimately derived from

Emporitan models is found in and near Limousin and Poitou; this is well to the north of the area under Rhodan influence and may represent a division of spheres of interest between the two Greek neighbours. The main hoard of the type is from Bridiers or Breith in Creuse. The Bridiers hoard contained a variety of silver coins with obverses derived from Emporion and a miscellaneous selection of reverses (111–13), some with the two-horse chariot (and legend) of Philip II gold staters, some with a horseman (and legend) from Philip's silver tetradrachms (114, a type not found in the hoard), some from the lion on the coin of Massilia, and some with a winged Victory over the horse as on early coins of Emporion. Inspired in turn by these, but much later in date, I would put those with a rider having wings in place of arms found in Poitou (122). From the form of the Philip legend and horses in the coins of Bridiers type it looks as if we are in the very early second century B.C. It is to this phase or shortly after that we can attribute other experimental varieties, where the flying Victory becomes a pair of wheels (116), the horseman brandishes a shield and sword (114) and finally Chrysaor's head detaches itself into the place of the Victory and the horse acquires a human head (117). By now we are right into the Celtic tradition. Note the triangular locks of hair (113), which become the most durable characteristic of the tradition.

The next phase is the emergence in Berry, spreading to Poitou, of a coinage of large silver pieces, found in two groups of hoards, the earlier in the department of Indre, the later in Vienne and Deux-Sèvres to the west. These start with issues on which there is a dog (or wolf) over the back of a horse and a triple whorl below (118), or two separate horses, one behind the other (119), or a horseman with shield and spear and hand below (120, 121). The later group found in Poitou shows a winged horseman with flower below (122). All these types, the earlier set of which must belong to the middle second century B.C, have some links with the gold coinages that are to be the subject of the next chapter. The silver coins of Berry might be contemporary with the earliest gold staters found in the same area, but I think they came first. Thus the rider with the brandished shield and sword could well be the starting point for the gold coins of this type found further north in Ille-et-Vilaine; the dog-and-whorl type certainly precedes the gold stater with a crane and whorl from Limousin to the south; while the hand below the horse on the first type seems to be the starting point for the extensive series of Poitou gold staters with a hand. The form of locks on the head on the obverse of these coins had a decisive effect on the obverse of many of the first-century gold staters of Armorica on which there is no trace of the philippus wreath in the hair. The coins of Armorica are, in fact, a fusion of the philippus and Emporitan traditions.

Other coins with the same hair style were struck on a much reduced weight standard, which accords with the general weight of silver coins in the first century B.C. in Central Gaul (**123–5**). On the reverse the horse is sometimes accompanied by a severed human head above or below, sometimes by a sword above or a symbolic tree. On others we have legends. These coins are found in Berry and Limousin, and should probably be assigned to the Lemovices. A small number were found at Alesia – they certainly belong to the first half of the first century B.C.

The same hair style also travelled north of the Loire into the department of Eure-et-Loire, in the area of the Carnutes. It is found on bronze coins having a bird with snake or lizard on the reverse (**369, 370**). It occurs again in Loiret and Yonne, probably amongst the Senones, with a different bird and the legends *Ullucci*, *Koiaca* or *Vlaccos* (**371**). Finally we have coins with the legend *Giamilos Senu* (**372**), which are related to silver and bronze coins copied from Roman denarii of 64 and 45–43 respectively. While the *Ullucci* coins are found at Alesia and are thus pre-51 B.C, *Giamilos* are not, and bring the Emporitan tradition down from its origin in the fourth century B.C. to post-conquest Gaul.

There is another Emporitan tradition. There are common silver coins, attributed to the Elusates (of Eauze) having on one side an incomprehensible series of dots and dashes and on the other a stylised horse, which are known from the hoards of Manciet and Laujuzan in Gers (**127, 128**). There are corresponding obols. The origin of the drachm can be traced back, through a unique coin in Glasgow (**126**) and other copies, to certain standing horses on later third-century drachms of Emporion (**106**). Nearly all the features of **127** and **128** can be found in embryo on the Glasgow coin. Furthermore, we have inscribed bronze coins of a chieftain Adietunnus mentioned by Caesar in 56 B.C. (*B.G.* 3.22.1, 4) which read *Adietuanus*, *Rex Sotiota* (of Sos) (**129**), which reproduce the otherwise unintelligible dots and dashes of the silver obverse. These coins must have been struck immediately after Caesar's campaigns. Thus again the influence of the coins of Emporion can be traced continuously from the third century B.C. to immediately after Caesar.

Summary

We have now passed briefly over the whole of the main body of Celtic silver coinage of southern Europe. We have seen silver coins in the

Danube basin, the Po and Rhône valleys, and in Gascony, Guienne, Poitou and Berry. In every case, except the Rhône valley, there are reasons, possible or presumptive, for a start in the third century B.C, sometimes in the middle of that century. In every case there is evidence that the coinage, so begun, continued in some form down to the middle of the first century B.C. Of course the coins did not immediately spill from their initial centres over the whole of the area, but by the middle or end of the second century B.C. virtually all the habitable parts of the southern half of Celtic Europe has some silver coinage of its own.

In an age of migrations these parallel developments in different places are more than coincidence. Though the interchange of actual coins between one part of the Celtic world and another is the exception, styles and concepts travelled more easily than physical objects. That the coins employ similar horses and riders in widely separated areas is due not only to the historic chance of the models chosen but to a common preoccupation with subjects that led to the choice of these models. In the next chapter I shall move into the comparable belt to the north where the preference instead was for coins in gold. The geographical spread is not quite so wide, but the variety of coins is greater, and they are, perhaps, more strikingly within the Celtic idiom than those I have described in this chapter.

3

The Gold Belt

In the last chapter I described the great belt of Celtic silver coins stretching from the Atlantic to the Black Sea. I turn now to the comparable belt to the north, between Finistère and the Elbe, where the coins were of gold. This falls into two parts, the eastern and the western, which may loosely be described as the Germanic and the Gallic. Coinage goes through parallel developments in each.

The underlying prototype of the eastern group was the gold stater of Alexander III of Macedon while that of the western group was the gold stater of Philip II of Macedon. Other influences are secondary. Both prototypes were of the same weight; they existed in enormous numbers and circulated side by side during the third and second centuries B.C. As models they were equally available, but the Germanic tribes preferred the helmeted head and winged Victory of the Alexander staters, while the Gallic tribes chose the wreathed head and chariot with horses of the Philip staters. We do not know for certain which series began first; they developed independently, and through more or less the same time-scale. If Britain is included with Gaul, then the Gallic sequence lasted about a century longer.

The Eastern Sector : The Germanic Group

I start with the eastern group. What I have to say owes much to the work of Dr Karel Castelin of Prague. We have little of this material in Britain, where no specimens have been found.

The Nike Type

The earliest Celtic coins of this group are plain copies of the gold stater of Alexander III (**130**) reproducing more or less accurately the helmeted head of Athena on one side and the standing figure of Victory with spear and wreath on the other – the so-called Nike series (**131**). They approach the full weight of the originals. Their home lies in western Moravia and the neighbouring part of Bohemia; they are associated with the Celtic oppida of Nechanitz (near Nový Bydžov), and Okluky. No doubt the originals travelled here up the Danube,

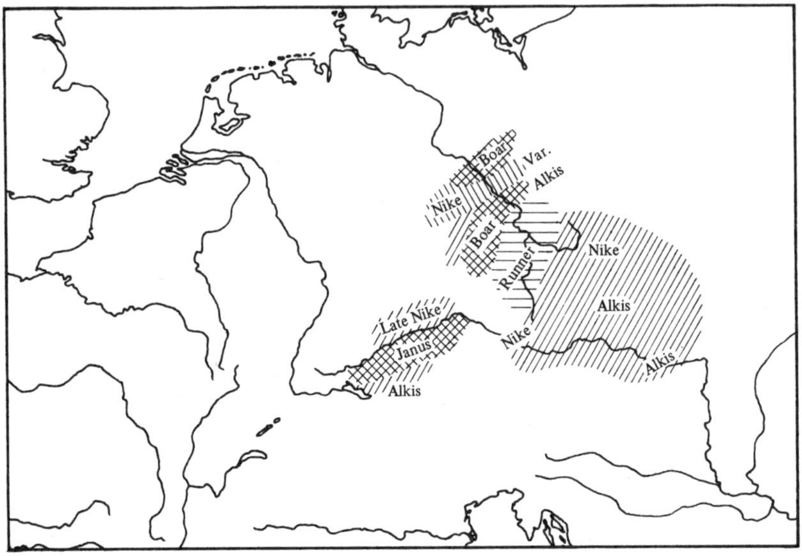

Map 9. Early gold coins of Germany

whence the copies in turn travelled further afield up the Morava and the Elbe.

Weight and type both show these coins to have been the first of the Germanic series. Their date can only be deduced from subsequent coins – the Alkis series – whose origin lies in the second quarter of the second century B.C. We shall probably not be far out if we place the beginning of the Nike coins in Moravia only shortly before, in the closing years of the third century B.C.

The Nike imitations were themselves copied. We find light versions (not more than two-thirds of the original weight) in a Celtic treatment, further west: in **132** you can just see the bill and talons of an enormous bird to the right of the swordsman. The key find-spot for these is Ingoldstadt on the Danube in Bavaria. Weight suggests that these could be as late as the early first century B.C. Finally, there are strongly stylised versions, even lighter, certainly of the first century B.C, from Lake Constance (**133**).

The Alkis Type

The Nike coins were supplemented by a later and deceptively similar series known as the Alkis type from the figure on the reverse. The earliest coins in the series are one-third staters; the full denomination does not occur until later.

The origins of obverse and reverse are different. The obverse has a helmeted head, which is derived not from the Athena of the Nike coins but from the Roma of one of the earliest coins of Rome, in the so-called Romano-Campanian series (**134**). The head reached the Alkis coins by an involved route. It was originally used on Roman didrachms with a standing Victory reverse dated by Crawford to 265–242 B.C. There are barbarous silver coins that combine a close copy of this head with another Romano-Campanian reverse, the horse's head (Castelin, *Goldprägung* pl.3, 33). Unfortunately, we have no find-spot for these, though their home is believed to be North Italy. Only two pairs of dies are known, but one of the obverse dies also occurs as a silver coin, again reduced by one-third in weight, in combination with a typical early Alkis reverse (*ibid*, no.34). An example was found at Stradonitz, the main Celtic oppidum of Bohemia. This early, if tenous, connection with Rome is valuable, not least because the connections of the reverse of the Alkis coins are with Macedon. The reverse is in fact directly copied, even down to the monogram, from a tetradrachm of Philip V of Macedon (220–170 B.C.) with a reverse of Athena Alkis, carrying spear and thunderbolt (**135**). The type belongs to the first ten years of his reign.

It will be seen that the prototypes of both obverse and reverse of the Alkis series lie in the last quarter of the third century B.C. The Alkis coins themselves (**136**, **137**) probably start in the second quarter of the second century B.C. This accords well with the known history of the Celts in Bohemia. During the last quarter of the third century B.C. and at the beginning of the first, the Boii living in Cisalpine Gaul south of the Po were in constant conflict with Rome. In 191 B.C. they were driven out and moved to the district round the Ister, where they lived with the Taurisci and engaged in warfare with the Dacians. While the exact location of the territory of the Taurisci is in dispute, it was certainly south and west of Bohemia; but the assumption that these Boii drifted on to Boiohemium, where another part of the Boii already dwelt, is probably to be accepted.

The Mussel Series

The Nike and Alkis types went through many degradations, and the Alkis type in particular has been closely studied by Castelin in conjunction with the so-called Mussel series of staters, to which I come next.

The Alkis and Mussel series together represent the progressive breakdown and recreation of the original Alkis type. They go through the kind of transformation that constantly recurs in Celtic numismatics, but the coins do not in the process acquire intelligible or representational patterns; they often show no more than lumps or lines on the metal. **141** is Mussel, **138–40** are developed Alkis types. The series continued down to the third quarter of the first century B.C, when, as was shown in the last chapter, we have examples of staters, thirds and ninths, with the legend *Biatec*, whose common large silver coins are found in south Slovakia (**142**). These silver coins are datable with fair precision from 50 to 40 B.C, which gives a clear termination date for the Alkis and Mussel coinage. Between these limits it is possible to subdivide the coinage into four successive main classes and a number of subsidiary groups.

The home of these numerous coins lies in Bohemia, Moravia, Hungary and the north-east of Lower Austria. We need to assume one principal mint, but there are correlated deviations, which probably come from other mints. There is no regularly associated silver series throughout most of the period, but there are some late small silver coins from the oppidum of Stradonitz, some of the cross type described in the last chapter (**105**), others with a horse on the obverse. In rare and relatively late cases there has been an interchange of gold and silver dies. The probability is that from the final years of the second century B.C, Stradonitz was the mint for the main series. A group of third-staters can be located, which deviates but is derived from the main series, at the walled oppidum of Staré Hradisko in Moravia. Among other find-spots of this type is the large hoard from near Cecina, Livorno, in 1912. It is attractive to link that displaced hoard with the incursion of the Cimbri in the last years of the second century B.C. Castelin's dating would, however, place the hoard a few years too late.

The Alkis Variants

Beside the main stream of Mussel and Alkis coins there are a number of rare and lesser known coinages, linked by type and weight. Some of these have types directly derived from the Alkis pattern. Thus, we have a stater, with thirds and ninths, also probably from Bohemia and Moravia, on which there is a head with Celtic locks and a variant of the Alkis reverse (**143**). Recollections of the type occur as far away as Lorraine.

Other series have a less direct link with the Alkis coins. The two principal ones are the Boar-warrior (**144**, **145**) and the Runner (**146–8**). The first of these has a plain Gallic style boar on the obverse, extremely like the boar we find later on Gaulish potin coins of the east. The reverse has a standing warrior remotely connected with the Alkis figure. These coins are found in the middle Elbe and in Saxony. There are thirds, ninths and twenty-sevenths. The running man coins are in a similar crude style. The obverse of the better examples has a bow. The runner on the reverse, holding crossed arrows, again owes a debt to the Alkis figure. There are thirds and ninths. The coins are found in a distinct area, south-west of the Boar-warrior, centred on the Berounka river. Both Boar-warrior and Runner coins are on the Alkis system. Their weight links them with the earlier part of the series; they should, therefore, belong to the middle of the second century B.C. or soon after. So far as coinage is concerned, they represent the fullest extension of the Celts, or more correctly of Celtic culture, towards Denmark and the Baltic.

There is also a later group of staters and fractions, which are poorly located but probably belong to the valley of the Elbe and to Saxony. These have yet more developed Celtic characteristics. One group, the earliest, has a Celtic head on one side and a steer on the other (**149**); another has a horse instead, with apparently a broken-up head for obverse (**150**). There are several later types with horse reverses, one with an Alkis obverse (**151**), one with a thunderbolt pattern (**152**), and another with three revolving wings. Geographically, these coins are far removed from the main stream of Celtic coinage; but in other respects they are, as it were, in full communion. One type (**152**) even has, below the horse, a band based on the wreath of Apollo and a pseudo-legend between parallel lines above. The association here seems to be with coins of Noricum of the early first century B.C, but the revolving pattern can best be paralleled in Britain. It will be recalled that the Cimbri attacked Noricum in 113 B.C. and that at about the same time they and the Teutones were successfully resisted by the Belgae. If these issues were German, there were opportunities in these expeditions to bring back the ideas that we see reflected in the coins; but it is probably nearer the truth to regard them as issues of Celtic or Celto-German tribes or tribesmen settled on the Elbe, in locations that it will be of the utmost importance to establish more exactly.

The Janus Type

There is also a small group of minute twenty-fourth or twenty-seventh staters located between the source of the Danube and Lake Constance, in the area of the oppidum later known as Augusta Vindelicorum. These have a Janus head obverse and on the reverse a horse to left or right, some with a severed head above (**153**). The type clearly belongs by weight to the Alkis series, but the obverse is derived from the Roman quadrigati of the last quarter of the third century B.C. The coins should probably be dated to the middle of the second century B.C, and form another bridge between the gold series of eastern Europe and of Gaul.

The Serpent and Rainbow Types

I return now to the 'mussels' of Bohemia and Moravia, as a starting point for the coins to which map 10 relates. In the third quarter of the second century B.C, to judge by weight, an attempt was made to improve on the formless patterns of the Mussel and Alkis series. Stater dies were produced which have on the obverse an axe of a type known from North Italy, Tyrol and Vorarlberg, and on the reverse a coiled serpent. This beast is beautifully engraved, and has Scythian antecedents from the Black Sea. With this go quarters having on one side the axe and on the other a torque.

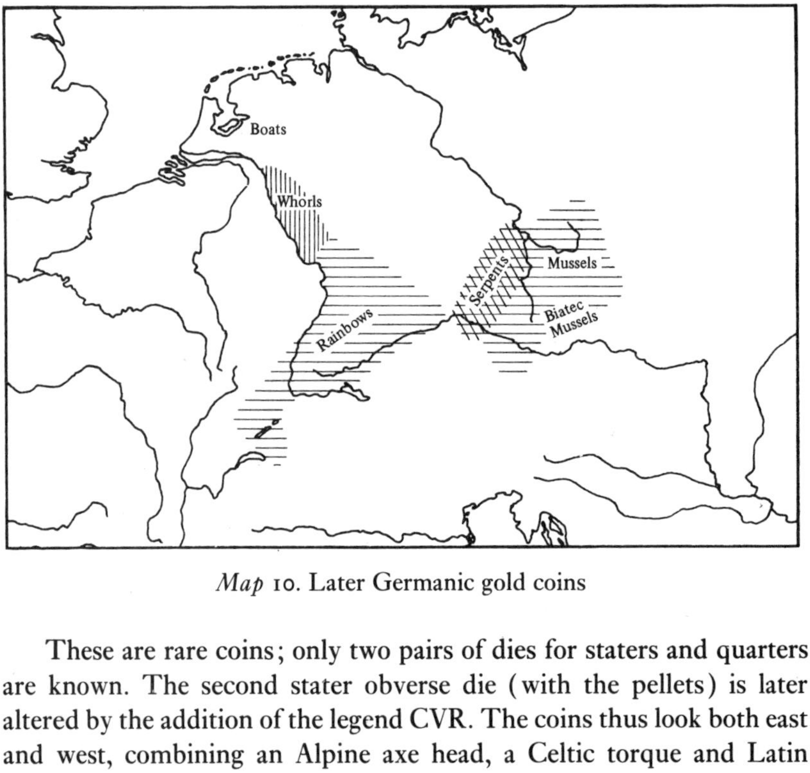

Map 10. Later Germanic gold coins

These are rare coins; only two pairs of dies for staters and quarters are known. The second stater obverse die (with the pellets) is later altered by the addition of the legend CVR. The coins thus look both east and west, combining an Alpine axe head, a Celtic torque and Latin letters with a Scythian serpent. The coins are found in Bohemia in the Stradonitz area, which has given five of the eight recorded find-spots. They mark an altogether new development, which failed, however, to establish itself at its point of origin, where the mussels proceeded on their uninspired course.

Instead the Serpent coins became the prototypes of a common and widespread coinage, known as 'rainbow cups' (*Regenbogenschüsselchen*). The coins begin with copies, in which the Scythian serpent is reproduced on the obverse, while the torque appears on the reverse, enclosing a group of six (or three) pellets (**154**). Next, the snake's head becomes a severed bird's head, while the snake's body is detached to form a chevron border (**155**). Eventually the bird's head gets forgotten and we have a wreath instead (**156**). These coins have not received the same attention as the mussels (the standard work by Streber is more than a hundred years old), and there is much in doubt about them; but the types I have described are essentially the coinage of Bavaria, and predominated in the key hoards of Gagers and Irsching (near the Celtic oppidum of Manching).

There are several varieties. Amongst them, a type with three 'lyres' or paired S's instead of the torque belongs to the south-west and is found in Switzerland and the borders of France (**157**). There are also coins with a Gallic head on one side, borrowed from the Aedui, and this reverse. A type with four-pointed star and S's in place of the six pellets (**158**) is shown by the St Ludwig bei Basel hoard to belong to Switzerland, and the type is also found across the St Bernard pass in North Italy. A hoard from Prague establishes an interesting correlation with a small silver coinage with debased bearded head and horse. There is more than a possibility that the staters are coins that the Cimbri and Teutones took with them on their way to Italy and the west. The type, for instance, occurs at Vercelli; there are rare examples, including one from Vercelli, which have the legend *Atull* added in Roman letters. The staters can also be traced across France and formed the bulk of the Courcoury (Charente-Maritime) hoard.

A certain number of cup-shaped pieces from Bavaria and Württemberg are either completely blank or have only vestigial marks such as a small cross in the centre of the reverse. It has been shown by Castelin that these strange pieces form a well-defined and coherent group, between the Rhine, the Neckar and the Danube, based on the Celto-German oppidum of Finsterlohr; and that the Serpent and Bird-head coins lie to the south, many of them actually south of the Danube. It is also abundantly clear from the weight that these smooth staters are, contrary to opinion hitherto, earlier than the bulk of the Serpent and Bird-head coins. There is clearly some link between these smooth cup-shaped staters and the strange globular gold lumps of Belgic Gaul (**159**); both have small central crosses and no other marks. The lumps have been found as far away as Scotland, where a hoard of them was found at Kirkud in Peeblesshire with the remains of a torque.

Finally a whole generation of Rainbow coins (**160–2**) is found in the Rhine valley, starting with gold and declining to good silver and eventually bronze (compare our Durotriges coins). The bird's head of the Bavarian coins is trebled on those of the Rhineland to form a whorl or triquetra, a common Celtic design. On the reverse, rings replace pellets. The main area for gold coins is the Meuse and Lower Rhine, both banks of which were occupied by Celts; there is a clear frontier with the Sun type and other staters. The principal find is from Mardorf bei Marburg, 1880, where the Rhine type was associated with Bavarian bird-head types; it is thought that the centre lay at or near Bonn. The silver versions occur as far north as the Utrecht district and are the only Celtic type regularly found in the Netherlands. The bronze coins spread into the borders of Belgic Gaul. We find the influence of the coins both on the gold and bronze coins of the Nervii in the Meuse-Trier district. The Rhine types certainly continued until a fairly late date in the first century B.C.

I have mentioned several points of contact between the gold coins of the east and those of Gaul. These and others exist, but they are not extensive and lie mostly on the Rhine frontier. Some Gaulish coins have been found in the east, most notably at Stradonitz, but also at other Celtic sites; they tend to be post-Caesar in date and mainly of silver or potin. Eastern coins do not occur in the west, except in the few gold hoards linked with the incursion of the Cimbri and Teutones. This does not leave an impression of close contact. The coins of the east were poor things compared with those of the west and it is natural, perhaps, that the drift of coinage was generally in the opposite direction to the recognised flow of peoples. There is nothing to suggest that the main central German tribes, the Chauci, Cherusci, Chatti and Hermunduri or Suevi themselves adopted the practice of coinage. If Ariovistus brought any coins with him to Gaul from Germany, they have left no trace.

The Western Sector : The Gallic Group

As the gold coinage of east Europe originates in the staters of Alexander III, so the gold coinage of Gaul derives from the staters of Philip II of Macedon (163). Regrettably we still have nothing approaching solid evidence as to when and how the philippus reached Gaul or why it was chosen for copying in preference to other equally available models. There is no reason to believe that the original philippus ever had wide circulation in Gaul: very few indeed have ever been found in France. Since the early copies are very little lighter than the originals, and plenty of such copies have been found, it is not enough to plead Gresham's law in explanation of the vanished originals; they never came in bulk, and, as the hoards prove, only Celtic coins regularly circulated there until the Roman conquest. The likelihood is that the philippus was chosen simply because the Gauls preferred a gold type with horse and chariot and perhaps also beardless head.

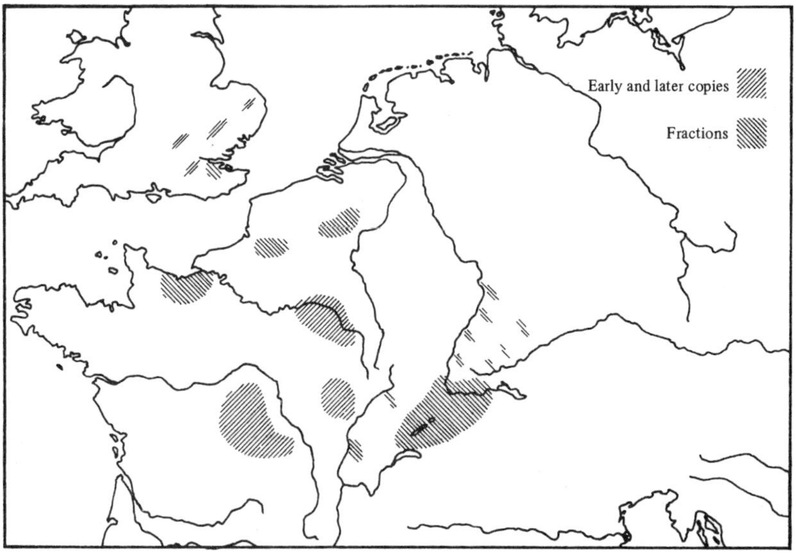

Map 11. Gold Philippus coins

Imitations of the philippus close enough to the originals to rank as direct copies are confined to Switzerland and the Rhineland, and to a lesser extent to Berry and the Bourbonnais, with Bourges, Issoudun and Moulins as the key towns in the latter area. Here, in the heart of France, the originals could have arrived as easily up the Rhône from Massilia as along the Danube through the Jura, but the latter is in fact the more probable route, along the whole of which greater or lesser traces of Macedonian coinage are found, whereas the philippus did not at any time establish itself in the Rhône Valley or the relatively poor parts of Gaul most easily reached from it.

The question of route is less important for itself than for its implications. Supporters of the Rhône route argue that the philippus could only have reached Gaul after the Romans had brought home the enormous spoils of the Macedonian wars in the late second century B.C. This severely restricts the time available for the complex development of Celtic coinage. But the Danube route was available at any time, and coins did not have to travel up it in bulk to provide a starting point for what was initially a limited gold coinage in the Rhineland and the bend of the Loire. Unfortunately there are no early hoards (or no descriptions of any) that can be used to fix the starting point, but, in the absence of demonstrable evidence, the strong presumption must remain that the date was not radically different from that of the Celtic gold coinage of Bohemia or the first Celtic silver coinages of the Po valley and the Atlantic coast, that is to say, at latest, near the beginning of the second century B.C. and more probably before the end of the third.

At its maximum extension, the philippus coinage spread from Switzerland to the Atlantic coast north of the Charente. Its most southern point is the Auvergne; in the north it extends across Britain from Kent to the Humber–Severn line. In the east the Rhine forms the frontier south of Mainz or Koblenz. The coinage peters out in Belgium north-west of the Ardennes. Its true home lies in the great plateau of northern France, over which we can to some extent trace the manner and order of its spreading.

First-Generation Copies

The first generation of copies can be recognised by eye and this can be confirmed by weight (8.10 g or more). The determining features are a more or less recognisable ΦΙΛΙΠΠΟΥ legend and two horses drawing a chariot on the reverse. The coins often reproduce the small mint and magistrate's symbols from the originals, such as the trident, thunderbolt, cup or sun. The monogram AP (alpha-rho) associated with the thunderbolt, is also copied (**164**, **165**). Initially the choice of individual models is fortuitous; later the symbols themselves grow more prominent and are confined to particular localities. But in this whole phase any attempt to attribute the coins to tribes is misguided. Thus the traditional attribution of many of these coins, on the strength of the copied AP monogram, to the Arverni is nonsense, especially as the coins are not found in the Auvergne. Strabo's mention of the gold and silver treasure of Luernius, father of Bituitus in the mid second century B.C. (Strabo 4.2.3), may well refer to Celtic or other coins, but, if so, it is certainly not to these as a local currency.

As always, an imitative coinage deviated with time from the originals. The records are not good enough for satisfactory allocation of all the varieties to regions, but certain trends, most easily described in terms of symbols, can be detected. The most durable symbol is the thunderbolt, combined with the AP monogram, which has its centre in the rich plateau north of the Massif Central extending to Burgundy, in direct continuity with the earliest copies (**166**). The monogram itself evolves into a triskeles. To the east in Franche-Comté we have the cup symbol (**167**) and elsewhere there is an inverted lyre, which becomes confused with Helios, the sun (168–70). Tridents are also found (171).

In this early phase we find the first half and quarter staters, particularly in the Swiss area, though their greatest development comes later. We meet now for the first time an isolated example of a genuine inscription in small Roman letters, EIQITIVICO (the Q and T upside down). It is on a coin with the triskeles symbol from Gracey, Cher (172).

Even though we do not know for sure when this early phase started, there are so many varieties that we can be confident it lasted for an appreciable time. If any of the Gaulish gold coins belong to the third century, it is these.

Second-Generation Copies

The second generation of copies grew out of the first. The traditional formula of Apollo head and two-horse chariot is maintained, but the coins no longer aim to look like forgotten originals. Deliberate variations often appear, in the form of intrusive animals and ornaments, and the symbols grow in size and importance (173–88). Pseudo-legends in pattern forms take the place of Philip's name (175, 182) and the second horse tends to disappear, especially on the fractions (177, 180). This is pre-eminently the period of halves and quarters; there are even very rare thirds. The stater itself is in some areas, notably Belgic Gaul, the exception or absent, and it is only in this early phase that the half flourishes. The coinage is generally anonymous, but an unlocated stater has the legend KABAΛΛ in Greek letters (178).

One of the most prolific centres of production of second generation staters is in Berry and the Bourbonnais, where the thunderbolt and AP monogram remain, the latter now firmly in triskeles form. The triskeles ornament is also found east to Cote d'Or and in the Vosges, Jura and Switzerland (174). Here the coins acquire a broad cup-shaped character. The sun ornament starts from Berry and Limousin and apparently moves north. The inverted lyre (to which the KABAΛΛ coin belongs) is certainly located in the north since it influenced the coins of Armorica and Belgica. Another distictive coinage of this period is that of the Treveri, which is related in type to an early Armorican coinage (183, 187).

Some halves and quarters are better located. Distinctive types are found in Manche and Calvados (189–91), in Picardy especially near Amiens, and in the valley of the Meuse up to Namur (193–4). Others are found in and on the way to north Switzerland and in the valley of the Rhine down to Strasbourg (184–6). By now the coins have intentional distinctions; thus in Manche and Calvados, the charioteer holds a symbol such as a sword or miniature ship, while in Switzerland a cockatrice appears beneath the horse. A bearded face with hair in ƲƲ formation is characteristic of Amiens and Pas de Calais and has even been found in Britain. The staters tend to come from the centre, the halves and quarters from the Channel coast, the Meuse, the Rhine and Switzerland.

The period was certainly protracted and it lay entirely within the second century B.C. A full study of the surviving coins should permit us to map north, central and east Gaul into a dozen or more distinctive districts, not necessarily to be equated with any known tribes, but, given the poverty of published records, this is seldom a practical proposition.

Parallel Experiments

The mid second century was a phase of experiment. Although the dominant tradition throughout remained the philippus, with its wreathed head and horse with chariot, other influences were freely absorbed. Of these the most important is the stater of Tarentum of the late fourth century B.C, with a veiled head of Demeter and a youthful rider on horseback (**192**). Copies of these are found in the coastal area of Belgic Gaul (as if it had reached there by sea) and may have affected the coins of Manche and Calvados. From Picardy there starts a rider tradition, while Demeter's veil seems to have influenced the head and wreath pattern on the obverse of later Belgic coins. A strange half-stater in the Tarentine tradition (**194**) has on the obverse a human head dividing a horse, as if the forequarters were coming out of one ear and the hindquarters going into the other.

An important early group have large wreathed heads of philippus type, while on the reverse there is a naked, probably female, rider, brandishing shield and spear or sword (**195**). Their home lies in Manche and Ille-et-Vilaine, to the east of Armorican Gaul. Here is a blend of Macedonian Apollo head with either the Tarentine rider or the Emporitan rider described in the last chapter, both being subjected to the usual transformatory fashions of Celtic coins. Other types, less well located, but lying between the Seine and the Loire, have comparable obverses, while on the reverse the charioteer of the normal philippus type is replaced by an eagle and the horse is accompanied by a foal or a cockatrice. Countermarks, in one case a dóuble countermark, appear, showing that the coins had a long life and recognised values.

As interesting group consists of staters and quarter staters on which the obverse die has either been deliberately defaced with lines or cuts (**196**, **197**) or the defacement is simulated (**198**). On the reverse the horse at first is accompanied by a regular charioteer. This type is found both in Gaul and in Britain, more particularly in the London district where it is currently described as Gallo-Belgic B. Of all types found in Britain, the reverse of **196** is the closest to the original philippus.

Figure 12. Gold Gallo-Belgic B stater, reverse type

These and other deviations from the main tradition were taking place in parallel with what I have described as the second generation of the coinage, but it is not yet practicable to present a wholly coherent picture of them either in terms of time or place. All one can say is that they must have occupied the greater part of the second century B.C, mostly in the north-centre.

The Tayac Hoard

One of the first fixed points in the philippus coinage is provided by the important hoard found at Tayac, near Libourne, in the Gironde in 1893. Of these coins seventy-eight were 'rainbow cups', and the remainder of philippus types. Some sixty-five were early examples of the main early coinage of Belgic Gaul (**199**), another sixty-five pale gold staters with a triskeles below the horse, which belong probably to Cote-d'Or or Yonne (**174**), and the remaining 195 were red gold staters with the trident mark, which are probably local to the Gironde area (**201**). The trident symbol is found elsewhere to the west – compare the silver coins with this mark which came from the Bridiers hoard. Five coins similar to the Tayac trident variety were in the hoard from Rouquette, near Eymet, in the Dordogne, with a large number of silver monnaies-à-la-croix in the Rhodan tradition.

The Tayac hoard thus brings together coins belonging to the west, north and east of Gaul. This establishes a vital correlation. The hoard has frequently been associated with the incursion of the Cimbri and Teutones, and although it is impossible to establish this with any certainty, its date may be fixed independently in the decade from 120 to

110 B.C. on the basis of the probable chronology of the Belgic and Burgundian coins in it. It should be seen beside the hoard of a hundred rainbow staters of south Bavarian type from Courcoury, which may tentatively be connected with the Cimbri and Teutones. The date marries well with the Rouquette hoard, because the most likely historical occasion for the burial of the wave of similar hoards was around 106 B.C.

If this general date for the Tayac hoard is correct, it provides an essential fulcrum for the dating of the philippus coinage. Broadly, coins weighing 7.50 g and over, up to 8.10 g, that is to say the block of coinage I have described as the second generation, will belong to the first three-quarters of the second century B.C. Those that weigh less come after.

The Tribal Coinages

It is from this stage on that the gold coinages of Gaul may legitimately be ascribed to tribes. The coins become more common, more individual, more precisely located, and at the same time our knowledge of tribal names and affinities becomes vastly greater. Even so, there are many doubtful cases and it may well often be better to speak of areas rather than tribes.

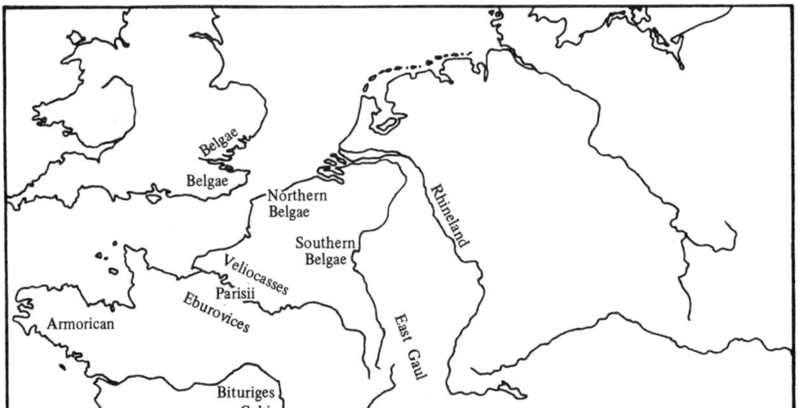

Map 12. Later Philippus gold coins

The period runs from some time in the last quarter of the second century B.C, that is after the Tayac hoard, to the middle of the first century B.C, some sixty or seventy years in all. The latter date is provided by the finds at the burial ground in Alesia and confirmed by several slightly later dated hoards. Between these limits there is no detectable wave of hoards that can be associated with any known historical event. We can be confident that gold staters were still in circulation at the time of Caesar's campaigns in the Auvergne, Berry and Poitou, but also that by then gold coinage was very much on the decline. It is certain, too, that in central Gaul gold coinage disappeared from circulation almost immediately after the conquest, no doubt as a result of the booty extracted by the conquerors. In Armorican Gaul, gold had undoubtedly been disappearing from general use for some time previously. In Belgic Gaul however, indications are that it continued to be used and issued appreciably after the conquest.

Of necessity I must be selective. We can best start with the coinage of the Arverni in the south-centre (**202–5**). Arvernian coins are at first uninscribed – there are many varieties – but later have a series of names: *Ater*, *Camulo*, *Seno-Omodon*, *Cas*, and finally *Vercingetorix*. Towards the end these are accompanied by bronze coins with different legends. On the head side the original wreath is soon lost amongst the locks, which become loose; the horse stands free and the earlier ornaments, the triskeles or the inverted lyre, are replaced by an amphora, crescent, bird or other device. Coins of Vercingetorix (**203**, **204**), Caesar's last and greatest opponent in Gaul, were found at Alesia in the mass grave deposits of 52 B.C.

Moving west and north from the Arverni, we meet the fine coins of the Bituriges Cubi in Berry. They are generally inscribed, for instance *Abudos* or *Solima* (**206**, **207**). They too are accompanied by bronze coins (**208**, **209**). Next we may look at the coins of the Pictones in Poitou, where the head is certainly derived from the Emporitan tradition (**210**, **211**). It is here that we first encounter the human-headed horse, which we will meet again and again in the north and north-west; it was found on Emporitan silver as was shown in the last chapter. The coins had a very long life, and all have a hand below the horse. Many also bear the inscription SA (**211**). The coins of both Bituriges Cubi and Pictones were found at Alesia.

Moving north of the Loire into Armorican Gaul, the coins of the Namnetes in the Nantes district (**212**, **213**) are closely connected with the hand coins of the Pictones, but what started as dolphins in front of the face on these coins have become elongated straps, to the ends of which small detached human heads are added. There is often a cross in the hair. Beneath the human-headed horse there is a half figure with outstretched arms. The type occurs in silver too.

Next we have the coins of the Veneti in Morbihan and Southern Finistère (**214, 215**), where the locks of the head have acquired a pattern of S-shaped curls, two or three backwards and one forwards; there is often a boar, a lyre or a cockatrice in the hair. On the reverse a prostrate winged figure with helmet replaces the half figure.

The type settles down in the north-west corner of France amongst the Osismii, where the fallen winged figure was replaced sometimes by a lyre, wheel or other ornament (**216–18**). There are many varieties, some of which can be located – that of the Guingamp hoard for instance being confined to the north coast of Finistère and Côtes-du-Nord, clearly a sub-area of the Osismii. The same general type then travels round the north coast of France to the Unelli and Baiocasses in Manche and Calvados (**219**) where it comes into contact with other traditions stemming from the Seine.

All these Armorican types start as gold coins, but well before Caesar's day had been replaced by versions of the same types in base silver or billon. These base silver coins are found in large numbers in hoards buried at the time of the wars, probably in 57–56 B.C. It is these types, especially those attributable to the Coriosolites (**220–1**), that form the bulk of the great hoards found in the Channel Islands.

Parallel in date with these Armorican coins, but further east and inland, there is another group, the heads of which clearly stem from the Philippus tradition, since they have a pronounced wreath, but their mixed origin is betrayed by the presence of a feminine ear ring. What seem to be the earliest are found near Angers, in the district of the Andecavi. They have first a winged figure (**187**) and later a fallen warrior holding shield and spear (**222**). To the north-west, in the district of Rennes, amongst the Redones, we have connected coins with a wheel below the horse instead (**223**); the head on these is sometimes bearded.

Having followed the course of the stater west and northwards from the Arverni, we may now turn to the east. The staters of Franche Comté, including the coins of the Sequani and the Leuci, not yet distinguished, are more direct derivatives of the philippus than those of the Arverni. Their immediate models may have been the second-generation quarter staters of Switzerland, but they are broad, thin, cupshaped and generally base (**224**). Many of the earliest retain the triskeles mark, which later becomes a wheel. We find similar coins in Switzerland with rose or sun instead; an obverse die of one of them has survived at Avenches. Further north in Lorraine are found other coins of the same family, to be attributed to the Mediomatrici of Metz and the

Viroduni of Verdun (**225**, **226**).

Also traditionally attributed to the Mediomatrici, though of entirely different character, is a group of coins with a beardless Janus head of Roman derivation (**227**, **228**), which is die-linked with coins having a philippus head (**229**). Other coins, occasionally found in silver, with a Roman-looking Pegasus on the reverse (**230**), occur on both banks of the Rhine, with Frankfurt-am-Main or Wurms as the centre, and may be related to one of the groups of silver coins from this area.

We have now followed tribal staters of Gaul eastwards and westwards from the Arverni. Before I come to Belgic Gaul, contained within the Seine, the Marne and the Meuse, I will mention three tribal coinages that lay to the south and west of it, each of which provides a bridge with the coins of the Belgae.

The magnificent coins of the Parisii, in the Seine district (**231**) are broad and flat like the earliest Belgic coins we met in the Tayac hoard; but the hair style has links with the Armorican coins from Manche. They are lighter, hence later, than the Tayac coins. A useful correlation is the hoard from the Schwartzwald, where they were found with uninscribed coins of the Treveri, little, if at all, earlier than the conquest. **232** is an accompanying potin coin.

The coins of the Aulerci Eburovices from Evreux (**233**, **234**), and the Veliocasses (or perhaps Caletes) across the Seine (**235**) are interconnected. Note the boar upside down on the neck of **233** and the tattoo across the face of **234**. The gold staters of the Veliocasses are associated with bronze coins (**236**). The horse on both is similar; but in place of the face on the obverse we have on the bronze a runner who turns out to be an enlargement of the charioteer from the coins of the Aulerci Eburovices (**234**). One might have expected any of these coins, like those of Armorica and Belgica, to be found in Britain, but in fact they are totally lacking.

Belgic Gaul

The gold coinages of Belgic Gaul in the first century B.C. almost without exception are descended from the broad gold staters of Tayac hoard type belonging to the last quarter of the second century B.C, of which figure 5 shows the full patterns. Even in its own day the type was certainly striking. There is very little on the obverse with any debt to the philippus, but on the reverse the chariot wheel, the triskeles, and even a pseudo-legend survive. Afterwards they had a long life and went through many varieties. They are the first type imported on any scale into Britain where we call them Gallo-Belgic A (**199**, **200**), and their successor (**237**) Gallo-Belgic C. Gallo-Belgic A is basically a coinage of

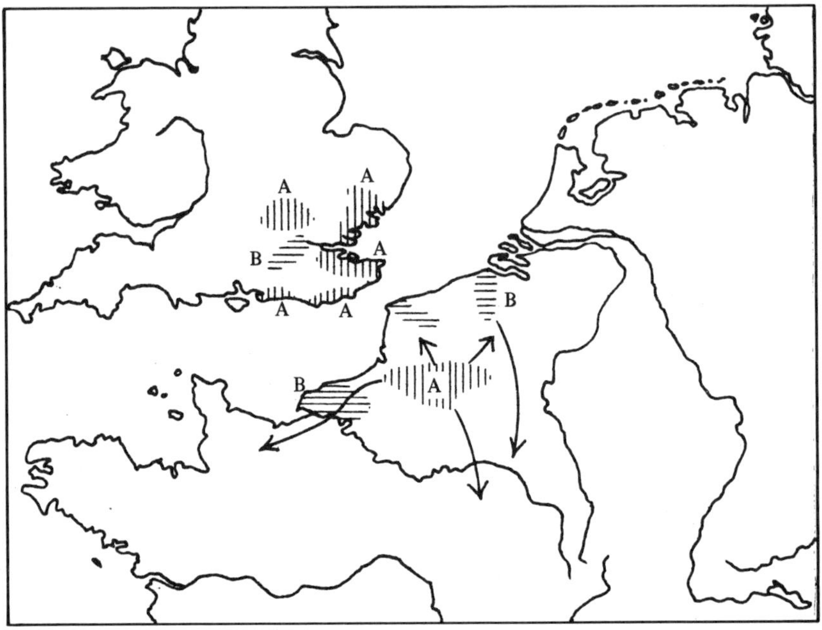

Map 13. Early Belgic coins found in Britain

the Somme Valley, but no tribal name is warranted. The successor coins in Belgic Gaul, which start as degradations and turn to variations on the same themes, are, however, essentially tribal. They are found in well-defined areas, and were probably struck by the Ambiani.

The gold coins of Belgic Gaul may for some purposes be divided into two groups, those which are also found in Britain and those which are not. The types found in Britain mainly lie in the north and centre of the area, especially on the Somme; those not so found, lie to the south and east.

I shall pass quickly over the first group because the coins are well known in this country and I have given an account of them elsewhere. It consists of the coins that have come to be called in British contexts Gallo-Belgic c, d and e (**237–40**). The three types formed the basis of the development of the gold stater in Britain; sometimes more specimens of each are recorded in Britain than in their true home in Gaul.

The prevailing choice of tribal names attached to these, as to many Celtic coins, needs critical review in relation to the other coins of Belgic Gaul. Thus, I have come to realise that the real reason why such an obvious Celtic tribe as the Ambiani (Amiens) were not until recently

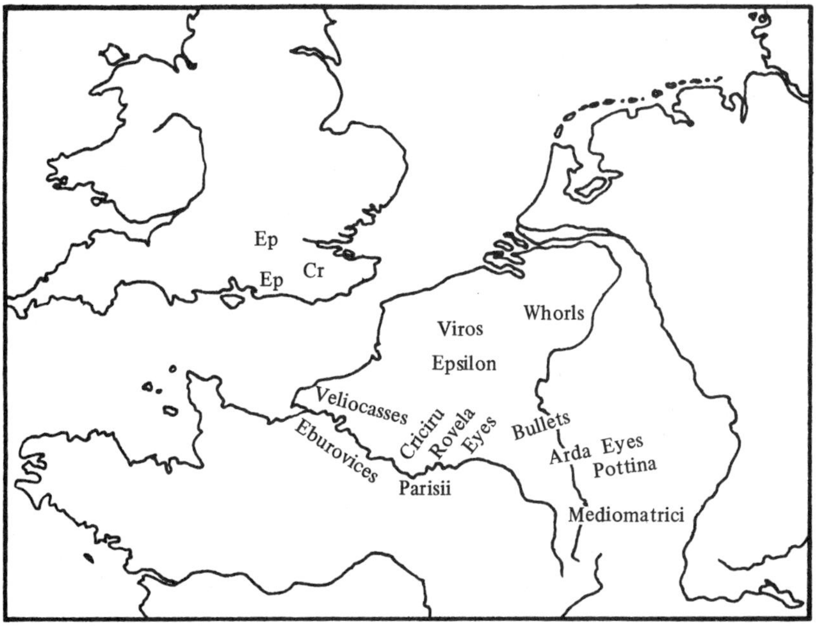

Map 14. Belgic gold coins not found in Britain

considered responsible for some of them is simply that this name had been pre-empted for other, and much earlier, coins. On the basis of find-spots we are as entitled to attribute Gallo-Belgic C coins to the Ambiani as to the Atrebates (Arras), and there are other grounds to make the Ambiani attribution most appropriate. The uniface coins of Gallo-Belgic E, also usually called Atrebates, actually occur widely over northern France, in Pas-de-Calais, Seine-Maritime, Somme and Nord as well as in Belgium (**238**). The Gaulish prototypes of our triple-tailed horse coins, Gallo-Belgic F, which are not themselves found in Britain, could well prove to be those of the Bellovaci (Beauvais) who, with the removal from them of the wrongly assigned prototypes, are left improbably without any gold coinage at all (**241**). Much greater confusion reigns over the application of tribal names to Belgic gold coins than to any others.

We can now turn to the Gallo-Belgic types not found in Britain. The first group (**242**), a large one, is derived from the type that should be ascribed to the Ambiani rather than Atrebates (**237**). Here the face pattern on the obverse is built round two joined locks, which have combined to form an epsilon. These overlap with the uniface coins and are probably correctly ascribed to the Nervii. The latest coins have the inscription VIROS (**243**). The Kwaremont hoard, which contained both inscribed and uninscribed examples, was buried in the reign of Tiberius. There is also a bronze type reading VIROS, with head and horseman, which would almost pass as a coin of Tasciovanus (**244**). After his original destruction of the tribe, Caesar treated the Nervii with special clemency in 57 B.C, sending survivors back unharmed to their towns and villages. It seems likely that some of these coins were still being issued by the Nervii after their return.

Another type, not found in Britain (**245**), in base metal, has a generally similar reverse, but the obverse is occupied by a whorl of three locks, or crescents. This device is certainly borrowed from the Rhineland 'rainbow' staters, since these coins lie precisely at the point of the contact with the Belgae, and they may probably be ascribed to the Eburones. Since the Eburones were practically wiped out by Caesar in 53 B.C, the coins are likely to precede that date.

Of the remaining Belgic gold coins not found in Britain the majority are derived from the triple-tailed horse coins, Gallo-Belgic F, which I have tentatively suggested may be found to belong to the Bellovaci (**241**). Perhaps the most important type is that which may be ascribed with certainty to the Treveri, whose oppidum lay near Trèves. The forest of the Ardennes divides these from the Epsilon coins, with which they are never mixed. The centre of the obverse design is a large triangular device containing what looks like an eye (**246–9**); it is actually a version of what is left of Apollo's face on the Gallo-Belgic F coins. Initially uninscribed, they later acquire legends *Lucotio*, *Pottina*, *Vocarant* and finally *Arda*, to the last of which some inscribed romanising bronze coins correspond. The appearance and development of these coins, with their neat legends, invites comparison with the post-Julius Caesar inscribed coins of Britain. There is evidence in the Hussigny-Godbrange hoard to suggest, but not to prove, that *Arda* bronzes are post-Caesar. Scheers dates *Arda* to the 40s B.C. One suspects that here again we have a gold Belgic coinage that did not cease suddenly on Caesar's victory.

Moving south-west, in the direction of Paris, we have gold coins that can be assigned to the Suessiones (around Soissons) and the Meldi (around Meaux). They bear the legends *Criciru* and *Roveca* respectively (**250–3**, **254–8**), and are also derived from the triple-tailed horse type. Both have this in common with British coins, that they are accompanied by full sets of silver and bronze pieces, the bronze reflecting Roman types, in much the same stage of independence as the coins of Tasciovanus in Britain. One may wonder whether the name *Criciru* is not a Celticised rendering of the name Cicero, with which it is certainly cognate. Q. Tullius Cicero, M. Tullius' younger brother, served in the Belgic area in 54–52 B.C. under Caesar and his name would have been a good compromise choice for a collaborating Celt. However, there is evidence that the oppidum of Pommiers, Noviodunum Suessionum, in which his coins are chiefly found, did not long survive the Roman conquest.

I can perhaps best show the relationships in a diagram of the obverses (figure 13). Downwards on the left we have Gallo-Belgic C, leading to *Viros* of the Nervii and *Criciru* of the Suessiones; on the right Gallo-Belgic F, leading to the Treveri and finally the form of the Gallo-Belgic C adopted in Britain.

There are now no gold coins that can be reliably attributed to the most faithful supporters of Rome, the Remi of Reims. For all but small change they will perhaps have preferred to use Roman coins.

Just as in Britain we have increasing evidence of some coinage taking place in all four main outlying tribes (Durotriges, Dobunni, Coritani and Iceni) after the Roman conquest of Britain, so there is at least some reason to think that in the remote Belgic north-east, some gold coinage probably was allowed to continue after Caesar's wars. If so, development of the inscribed coins here may have proceeded in parallel with the inscribed coins of *Commius*, *Tincommius* and *Tasciovanus* in Britain. This is consistent with Hirtius' statement (*B.G.* 8.49.1–3), in relation to the winter of 51 B.C, which Caesar spent amongst the Belgae, that to avoid provoking fresh unrest, Caesar treated the local governments honourably and the chieftains generously and refrained from the imposition of fresh burdens.

I shall not attempt to pursue this story into Britain, where the course of gold coinage is already well known. Suffice it to say that the traditions in Britain grew out of the coinages described above and that they continued to flourish for nearly another century up to the reign of Claudius or beyond.

This brings to an end what has necessarily been a greatly abbreviated and simplified survey of gold coinage of the Celts in Europe, from its origins in Macedon and elsewhere, through more than two-and-a-half centuries of intricate development. It may be seen that this phasing is exactly parallel with that of the main silver coinages discussed above. Together they represent the basic currencies of Celtic Europe. The purpose of my next chapter will be to describe the bronze coinages of the Mediterranean belt, and then the vast quantities of small silver coins and bronze coins, cast and struck, which, as time went on, overlaid or

Figure 13. Belgic gold staters
1 Gallo-Belgic C (Ambiani); 2 Viros (Nervii)
3 Criciru (Suessiones); 4 Gallo-Belgic F (Remi)
5 Treveri; 6 Gallo-Belgic C (Ambiani)

replaced the basic currencies of Gaul and came to be used as small change in an increasingly urbanised economy.

4

Spain and Narbonensis

We have now covered the whole silver and gold belts of Celtic coinage from the Atlantic to the Black Sea. I pass to what I call for convenience the bronze belt, though silver was used as well, that is, the Celt-Iberian coinage of Spain and Narbonensis. I shall not attempt to go into detail because the coinage of Spain must be treated as a whole and by no means the whole was Celtic. Nevertheless, parts of this area were inhabited by Celts and it would be wrong to omit them altogether. For coin legends see chapter 6.

The Celtic and Celt-Iberian areas of Spain are not distinguished from the Iberian and Tartessian by any clearly defined frontier. The general location of the division is known from ancient geographers, but for the details the Spanish antiquaries are largely dependent on the linguistic analysis of the numerous silver and bronze coins which bear city and tribal names in Celt-Iberian script. The transliteration of the script is mainly due to the coins themselves, a number of which are bilingual. In general, the Celt-Iberian coin inscriptions are confined to the Mediterranean coast as far south as Malaga, together with the valleys of the Ebro and the Douro. The coins in these areas are, however, not to be distinguished by outward appearance or by other numismatic details from the remaining comparable coins of Spain. I have therefore shown on map 15 the known mints in the Celtic-speaking area.

The coinage consists of comparatively scarce and mostly early silver denarii (or drachms) of approximately the same weight as the Roman Victoriate or the Massilia drachm (**259–63**), accompanied by a few half-pieces, and a much more extensive coinage of bronze asses or divisions (**264–7**). Silver coins come mostly from the mints of Saguntum, Emporion, Tarraco, Ilerda, Pompaelo and preeminently Osca, which provided almost ninety per cent of the total.

Bronze coins come from some eighty other mints as well, not by any means all securely located. Some silver coins are drawn from non-local prototypes but the majority resemble the bronze coinage. The characteristic obverse type is a male head, with or without beard, often under Punic as much as Roman influence; on the reverse there is a rider armed with palm branch, spear, sword, dart or, in one fascinating instance, a Celtic boar-standard, such as is encountered many times in Gaul. These are the so-called 'jinete' coins. At Emporion itself, the bronze series is in six descending sizes, each with a different animal reverse, comparable with the menagerie we shall meet in Gaul (**268**, **269**).

Map 15. Spanish and Celt-Iberian mints
(after Forrer II, p.24)

The range of dates for this very extensive coinage is well established by hoards and excavations. Saguntum was coining silver with Celt-Iberian legends by the end of the third century B.C, as is shown by the Cheste hoard. Coins of jinete type were flourishing at the time of the siege and fall of Numantia in 133 B.C, as proved by the excavations on the site. They were still flourishing at the time of Metellus' campaign in 79 B.C, as shown by the excavations at Carceres. This chronology is confirmed by the Cordova and Palenzuela hoards of 124–92 and 78–49

B.C. respectively. The main coinage seems to have given out around the time of Julius Caesar's campaigns in Gaul; some bilingual coins fall immediately before that time. Although the circumstances of this coinage are very different from those of coinage in Gaul – it is a matter of controversy how far Celt-Iberian coinages were actually controlled by Roman authority – it will be seen that the time scale was not altogether different. Just as Spain became a Roman province earlier than any other Gallic area, so the system of tolerance or at most loose control over autonomous local coinages is first encountered there. The true comparison of Spain in the late second century B.C. is with Gaul in the late first century B.C.

Celt-Iberian coinage was not widely distributed and left no marked influence outside Spain and the nearby Mediterranean coast of France west of the Rhône, that is, in Narbonesis. It is often said that the Biatec coins of South Slovakia owed their origin to the bronze coinage of Spain but I do not believe it. So many Celtic coins of all areas show riders with boughs or branches in their hands (let alone weapons and standards) that we must take the carrying of such objects to be a feature of Celtic life.

The bronze coinage of Narbonensis is much more closely linked to Spain than to the rest of Gaul. We can rely on an admirable study by Hill. The most important series is that of Narbo, under its Celtic name of Nero – the legend gives the ethnic *Neronenses* in Celt-Iberian characters. The coins have a draped female head on the obverse with charging bull (**270**, **271**) or, on the half denomination, a capped head right with a hippocamp reverse (**272**). More obscure legends also exist, some with a bull type, others with the Spanish rider (**273**). To these we may add bronzes having on one side a Carthaginian Hercacles head, club and hand, and on the other a lion, with a reading in Greek letters of the town name *Betarratis* – Béziers (**274**).

Next we have another series of asses with similar types, Carthaginian Heracles head and lion, but with Greek legends giving Celtic chieftains' names followed by the title Basileus: *Kaiantolos*, *Amytos*, *Bitoukos*, *Bitovios* and *Rigantikos* (**275–80**). There is also a half coin of Kaiantolos with female head and boar. These could have been rulers at Béziers. Finally we have a series of bronzes of particularly varied weight, having on the obverse a Mercury head and on the reverse a tripod taken from some bronzes of Massalia (**279**, **280**). Beside the tripod is given in Greek letters the name of an otherwise unknown tribe, the Longostaletes – and occasionally a further inscription in Celt-Iberian characters. On the obverse we have in Greek letters the personal names *Bokios*, *Loukotinos* or *Loukotiknos*, clearly Celts.

So far only the coins of Narbo and of Béziers can be attributed to known mints, but the remainder must have been struck in the immediate neighbourhood. Examples of Narbo, *Betarratis* and *Bitovios* coins have been found as far away as Vesontio in the Jura.

We have some evidence for the date of the Neronenses coins. They were found in large numbers at Montlaurès, the pre-Roman site of Narbo. They were probably struck there before Roman Narbo was founded in 118 B.C. (conceivably between that date and 71 B.C, when the Sertorian war ended); at this time the comparable bronze coinage of Emporion was flourishing. We have less evidence for the date of the remainder, but they came later rather than earlier. A considerable number of the coins of the Longostaletes were found at Montlaurès. Thus we can be fairly sure that the several bronze series of Narbonesis all existed in the second century B.C, if not earlier, and that, if some of them may have run on into the first century B.C, they did not continue far into it.

5

Subsidiary Coinages of Silver and Bronze

In the last two chapters I have outlined the development of the basic silver and gold coinages of Celtic Europe. I shall devote this chapter to the subsidiary coins of silver, bronze, and potin, which provided the small change of Gaul and Britain (and, to a much smaller extent, of Germany) during the latter part of the same period. They are symptomatic of the transition of the oppidum from a village community to the beginnings of urban life, a process that, in the periods with which we are concerned, had in general advanced further in Central Gaul than in the other parts of the Celtic world.

Silver Coins of Gaul

Rhône Valley Group

The silver coinage of Central Gaul is primarily a reflection of the coinage of Rome, with some influence from the coinage of Massilia. The main route of entry was up the Rhône valley, the great highway from the Mediterranean South to the fertile plains of the centre. From here small silver coins spread throughout the centre, north and east of Gaul and into Britain, for the most part independently of the more valuable gold and silver coinages we have hitherto examined.

The silver coins start on the east bank of the Rhône. The most probable derivation for the first Rhône valley coins is, as I have mentioned before, from a Carthaginian model, via Spain, although an origin from two types of Romano-Campanian didrachm is also conceivable, a head of Apollo being drawn from one and a horse's head on the reverse from the other. The weight of the coins (2.6 g, falling to 2.2) is, however, based on that of the third- to second-century light drachms of Massilia, a weight shared by the Roman victoriate. The coins thus combine Roman motifs of the mid-to-late third century B.C. with a weight that was itself borrowed from Roman coinage in the first quarter of the next century. In the Tourdan (Isère) hoard the coins were found with a worn tetrobol of Histiaea of the third century B.C. Though initially uninscribed, most of the coins have legends in an Italiot script, similar to that used on the coins of the Po valley and the gold coins of the Salasses in Haute Savoie; the first legends are *Kasios* and *Ialikovesi* (**281**). These are followed by generally similar coins, which have a horse instead of a horse's head; some have an Italiot legend, but most often the legend is in Roman letters, e.g. *Vol* (**282**). Next comes a group with chamois instead of horse (**283**).

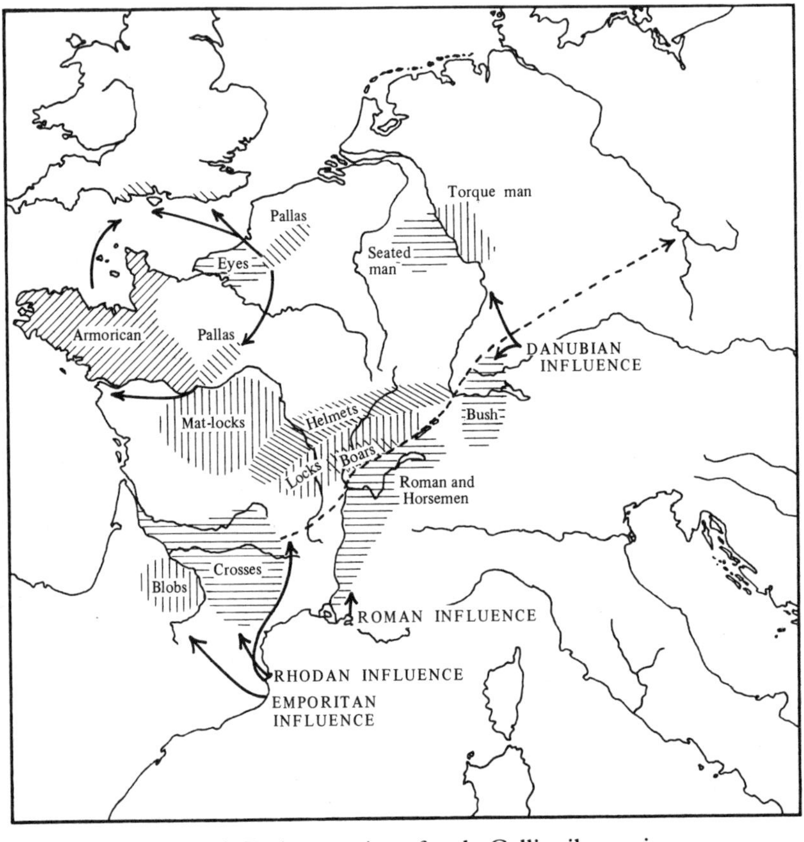

Map 16. Basic grouping of early Gallic silver coins

This group lasted a long while on the east bank of the Rhône and in the valley of the Isère, an area corresponding to the tribes of the Allobroges, the Vocontii and the Cavares. The first is best known to history, since it was the first truly Gaulish tribe with which the Romans became embroiled. They were defeated by Cn. Domitius Ahenobarbus in 121 B.C, immediately before the campaign against Bituitus and the Arvernians. There can be little doubt that the beginning of the coins preceded these events. A coinage started under the impetus of a Roman invasion at this date could hardly have avoided copying the then current Roman denarius, with the helmeted head of Roma and the Dioscuri on the reverse. We may, therefore, place these coins about the middle of the second century B.C, or even a little earlier, when they would be about contemporary with the similarly inscribed coins of the Po valley and early silver monnaies-à-la-croix of Aquitaine. They remained in circulation, however, long after they were issued: a *Vol* coin was still in use at the time of the battle of Alesia in 52 B.C.

This is the starting point for the very numerous silver coinages of Central Gaul. From now on, although head and horse types predominate, silver coins did not generally adopt traditional patterns as did the gold, nor are they copied without modification from Roman coins. The types range widely – most have some element, even if remote, of Roman influence; at the same time few are without Celtic features. The coins are, in fact a fusion of the Roman and the Celtic, in which the Roman gradually takes precedence.

The early developments are characterised by a helmeted head on the obverse. We have, from immediately to the east of the Allobroges, a series of coins occasionally in gold, but usually in silver, which combine a helmeted head on one side, clearly derived from a Roman source, though not directly from the denarius, with a definitely Celtic winged hippocamp on the other (284). Hoards show these to have circulated side by side with the *Vol* coins, presumably at the end of the second century B.C.

Shortly afterwards we have a very large group of silver coins on which the heads are drawn from the helmeted head of Roma on the Roman denarius of the types current throughout the second century B.C. Coins in this class are found not only on the east bank of the Rhône but also in west Switzerland, the Jura and the northern slopes of the Massif Central. They were current amongst the Sequani, Lingones, Aedui and Ambarri in addition to the Allobroges and Vocontii. The initial weight was certainly intended to be exactly half the Roman denarius. This is the kind of coin a Celtic tribe in direct relations with Rome would produce. The starting date is unlikely to be before serious contact began in 124 B.C, but cannot be much later. The final coins are certainly immediately subsequent to the Roman conquest.

There are several subdivisions of the group with helmeted head. The first and earliest series is found on the Rhône and Isère. The reverse is a simplified copy of one of the Dioscuri as depicted on the reverse of the Roman denarii from which the obverse also is drawn. The coins nearly always have two legends in Roman letters, one on either side; more than twenty combinations are known (**285–9**). There is an earlier and a later group. The weights start at 2.2 g but fall in the second group to the standard weights of late silver coins in Gaul – 1.9 to 1.8 g. Amongst the early legends we have *Cn. Volunt* (**285**); the final pair is *Durnacus Donnus*, with the –VS termination which is only used towards the middle of the first century B.C. (**289**); earlier coins have the ending –OS, as in *Durnacos Auscroco* (**288**). The coinage, therefore, seems to have lasted more than, say, sixty years. Rare obols, with a wheel type drawn from small coins of Massilia, accompany the normal denomination (**290**).

Another subdivision of silver coins with helmeted head has on the reverse a legend in Greek characters, *Kaletedou* (**291–4**); on very early examples (**290**) this is accompanied by a Latin monogram of Sulla, which appears on a Roman denarius of 151 B.C. On late coins the legend becomes corrupt and some of the letters are reduced to ornaments, e.g. **293**, where there are remains of Є and Δ. Some have lost legends altogether (**294**). Again this is clearly a coinage with a very long life, existing no doubt alongside the horseman coins, mainly in the area of the Aedui and Lingones. It is of the standard weight.

A closely comparable group is found with its centre slightly to the east, mainly amongst the Aedui and Sequani. All have helmeted head and horse. One series has the Roman legend *Q. Doci Sam F.* (**295**, **296**); this is fairly close to the *Kaletedou* coins. Rather rougher coins have the legends *Togirix* and finally *Q. Julius Togirix* (**297–9**). Both *Q. Doci* and *Togirix* coins are accompanied by potin coins with the same legends, the *Togirix* also by very small bronze coins. The Alesia finds and the adoption of the name Julius bring the end of the *Togirix* series down to, and probably after, Julius Caesar, but *Q. Doci* must be nearer the beginning of the century. Other coins using an improved version of the same head, with legends *Santonos* and *Arivos* and *Orgetirix*, are certainly post-conquest (**300**, **301**).

The early Rhône valley and subsequent helmeted head coins, with their strong Roman affiliation, form the central core of Gaulish coinage in the first century B.C. The later examples were spread extremely widely throughout Gaul, as a result, no doubt, of the dispersion of coins and their users caused by Caesar's campaigns and the events that led up to them. The usual rule that Celtic coins, and especially smaller coins, rarely travelled from their homes, ceased to apply for at least a decade.

Alesia Finds

The key factor for the dating of all these coins lies in the finds in the earthworks at Alesia, which I have several times mentioned. The excavations by Napoleon III between 1860 and 1865 at Alise-Sainte-Reine, the oppidum of the Mandubii, one of the constituents of the Aedui, established beyond doubt the site of Caesar's culminating victory in 52 B.C. over the Gauls allied under Vercingetorix. The 134 Roman coins found in the earthworks cease abruptly at 54 B.C; 449 Celtic coins found likewise in the excavations represent a cross-section of the loose money carried by the tribes present at the siege, less the Belgae and the Armoricans. Ten of the coins were of gold, and I have already relied much on them; 246 were of silver, 140 of bronze and 53 of potin. For the moment I will concern myself only with the silver, which formed the bulk of the finds. Up to the conquest of Gaul bronze and potin played a minor role.

122 of the coins, or more than a quarter of the total, were of the helmeted head types I have already described, *Togirix*, with 72 being clearly the latest. A single Allobroges coin of the *Vol* type was perhaps the earliest. Of the remaining silver coins, a group of twelve with legends *Pictilos* and *Epomeduos*, together with *Epad* (**302–4**), stand apart from the rest, partly by their lively Romano-Celtic types, but also because they are on the weight standard of the earliest Rhône valley types (2.4 to 2.2 g). They are all probably coins of the Arverni, *Epad* being no doubt Caesar's Epasnactus (*B.G.* 8.44.6), a pro-Roman Arvernian chieftain, of whom no less than 59 bronze coins were found (**305**). It looks as if we have a survival in the Arvernian area and on the Rhône of a Massiliot weight standard, which had been abandoned elsewhere in favour of a Roman one.

The remainder of the silver finds conform to the common weight standard (1.9 to 1.8 g), which was universal except in the outlying districts of Armorica, Belgic Gaul, across the Rhine and Britain. A few came from far-away parts of Gaul. From the south-west there were four worn specimens of the monnaies-à-la-croix of Aquitaine derived from the Rhoda tradition, by now reduced to the standard weight. From the east came a worn example of a silver coin of a Rhineland type from the Pfalz district on the west bank (**306**). The seated figure on the obverse is an example of eastern influence, since it must be ultimately derived from a seated Zeus in the Danubian tradition. From the west came twelve examples of the Limousin-Berry (Lemovices) type with large simple locks, derived from the Emporian tradition (**123–5, 337, 338**), and four rather similar coins where the usual horse is replaced by a beast with a boar's head and a hippocamp's tail, from Périgord (Petrocorii) (**307**). All these coins come from south of the Loire. The presence of the

Lemovicans at Alesia is attested by Caesar (*B.G.* 7.75.3, 7.88.4).

The majority of the coins, however, come from nearer to Alesia. It is customary to attribute most of them to the Aedui, but the Lingones and Leuci should also be considered. The largest and simplest group have a head on one side and a plain horse on the other, but there are several other types and several inscriptions, *Solima*, *Anorbo-Dubnorix* (**308**, **309**), *Diasulos* and *Dubno* (**310–12**). It is clear that they are contemporary with some of the helmeted head coins; they borrow their weight and are found immediately to the north. They are the first – or at least first identified – representatives of a group of coins that became extremely numerous after the Roman conquest.

An interesting group from Alesia is of coins reading *Sequanoiotuos*, which have a head on one side and a boar on the other (**313**, **314**). They may belong to the Sequani, as the name may imply, but from find-spots could as well be Aeduan. They are sometimes overstruck (**314**) but I have been unable to identify the undertype. Notice the underlying head at right angles to the first. Unlike in Britain, the boar as a main type on silver coins is rare in Gaul; the use of the animal on the *Sequanoiotuos* coins (as on those of the Goutrens, Aveyron, hoard; **104**) may have been suggested by the silver drachms of the Massaliot colony of Avenio (**315**), which used a fine boar reverse and are dated by H. Rolland to the late second century B.C.

The next group from Alesia consists of coins, beautifully engraved, which pre-eminently represent the combination of the Roman and Celtic. On the obverse is an essentially Roman head and on the reverse a standing, or in one case riding, figure, bearing Celtic weapons. Two read *Dubnocou-Dubnorex*, one with a man carrying a boar standard, the other with a man holding carnyx, boar standard and severed head and wearing a sword (**316**, **317**). One reading *Vepotal* again has a warrior with spear and boar standard, while a fourth, reading *Litavicus*, has a rider carrying boar standard (**318–21**). This highly Romanised group can be attributed to the pro-Roman Aedui. The *Dubnorex* is surely the Aeduan chief Dumnorix in Caesar's narrative (even though he usually appears as anti-Roman), as is also Litavicus. The obverses of the group are derived from Roman denarii of the decade 70 to 60 B.C, which makes it likely that the coins are actually contemporary with Caesar's war.

It will be seen from these coins found at Alesia that by 52 B.C. there had developed in central Gaul a most extensive series of silver coins, mostly with chieftains' or magistrates' names. The types were nearly always distinct from the gold coins, being more or less closely bound up with Roman coinage. On present knowledge it is simply not possible to arrange them in neat chronological or geographical patterns; but the general area from which the coins found at Alesia were drawn is certain. Putting aside the helmeted heads and some of the strays, which were earlier, there is at present no reason to assign any of the rest to a date before about 60 B.C. The decade embracing Caesar's wars in Gaul saw an enormous flowering of the silver coinages, partly, no doubt, to pay the troops.

The Great Silver Hoards

A disproportionate amount of Gaulish silver surviving today comes from a series of large hoards (thirteen thousand in one case), which spread across Gaul from Poitou to Picardy and even Brittany. They mark the next phase of the coinage (**300**, **301**, **322–8**). Several of these are dated by the presence of Roman coins, which now appear in central and northern Gaul in quantity for the first time. The hoards fall into two groups, the first of which may be dated to *c.*50 B.C. or very shortly after; for instance the La Jante (Haute-Vienne) and the Pommiers (Aisne) hoards. These are more or less contemporary with Alesia and confined to Alesia types. They belong to the obscure period of mopping up after Caesar had handed over command. The second group contains additional types not found at Alesia; these hoards represent a cross-section of the currency during the ten to twenty years after the conquest of Gaul. Typical of these are the Vernon (Vienne) hoard buried after 45 B.C, the Rozel (Jersey) hoard, buried after 38 B.C, and the Chantenay (Nièvre) hoard, buried after 36 B.C. There is a strong presumption, and sometimes proof, that the additional coins date from after 51 B.C. We know of no single historical event that could readily explain this wave of similar hoards, but incipient revolts of the Bellovaci are recorded in 46 B.C. and of other Belgae in 30 to 29 B.C; no doubt there were many unrecorded. Almost all the coins in these hoards are inscribed with the name of one or more Celtic chieftains. It is clear that the contents of all the hoards were drawn from a wide area; only in cases when individual coin types (or legends) can be located from the find-spots of isolated coins, can we know their true home.

The majority of the new post-51 B.C. coins have head and horse types of much the same character as some of these found at Alesia, but there is much variety in the treatment of the head; it is usually beardless and with Roman echoes. None of the new names are of people known to history. *Nercod*, *Orgetirix*, *Caledu* and *Biovos* arc examples (**322–4**). Some betray their post-conquest date by the adoption of Roman cognomens, for instance *Durat-Iulios* and *Gaius-Julius-Agedomapatis* (**325**).

The new types are not confined to horse reverses. An important variety, located in Champagne, with the legend *Ateula Vlatos* has a winged bust on the obverse and a bull on the reverse; had it existed at the time, so common a coin could not have failed to be found at Alesia (**326**, **327**). A similar obverse reads *Senodon* (**328**). Another whose absence from Alesia is important has the legend *Epad* (**329**); the obverse is adapted from a Roman coin of 67–66 B.C. (**331**), while the reverse has a standing warrior with a panoply of arms, distinctly more Roman than the Aeduan types from Alesia. Here is probably a post-conquest coin of the same Arvernian Epasnactus whose coins we met before, but reduced by now to the standard silver weight; the type also occurs in bronze (**330**).

The coins of Orgetirix, which I have mentioned, belong to this phase. Different inscriptions on different varieties tell us that Orgetirix was an Aeduan and the son of Atpillos. He must be distinguished from Caesar's Orgetorix, who was Helvetian. The coins form a sequence; the first obverse (**333**) is drawn from an uninscribed silver type (**332**), closely associated with Aeduan gold staters (**179**); it is odd that none of these was found at Alesia. The later ones are indistinguishable in style from the common run of post-51 B.C. silver.

Another striking type has a helmeted head with spear and on the reverse a figure walking beside a wooden idol (**335**, **336**). The legend is *Segusiaus Arus* and it is certainly a coin of the Segusiavi, north-east of Lyons. The reverse motif is derived, by the familiar process of *interpretatio Celtica*, from the Heracles carrying club and trophy of Roman denarii of 47 B.C. (**334**).

The list could be prolonged; the number of new and sometimes ephemeral types was large. It is clear that the new Roman masters, having at once abolished the autochthonous gold coinage, tolerated or encouraged a direct continuance, even expansion, of the pre-conquest silver coinage in Central Gaul from the Channel coast to the Massif Central. This went on down to about 30 B.C. Hoards of later dates are all of bronze coins. The likelihood is that the silver coinage was terminated by Augustus when, freed from other cares by the battle of Actium, he visited Gaul in 27 B.C. The regular organisation of the province within the framework of the Augustan Empire dates from then.

Remaining Silver Types

The Rhône valley, the Alesia and the great silver hoard types provide the central core of Gaulish silver coinage. Scarcely one of these coins has any direct connection with the basic gold coinage of Gaul. None of the many names on silver coins occur also on gold coins and very few even on bronze or potin. They represent an intrusion of silver coins of Roman inspiration into an area where the staple coinage was of gold.

To complete the picture of silver coinage in Gaul, we need to look either side of this central core. We have already met the silver coins of the west. In Aquitaine we have seen the monnaies-à-la-croix, terminating in the silver and bronze coins of the Cadurcan chief Lucterius, mentioned by Caesar. I know of no evidence that any silver in this area is post-conquest. Further north, in Berry and Limousin, we have the silver coins of the Lemovices with Emporitan type locks; several types are distinguishable, and some bear legends such as *Cam* and *Iurcau* (**337, 338**). The most developed type, with the legend *Cambotre* (**339**) occurred in the Vernon hoard and is probably post-conquest.

Further north still, in Armorica, the Rozel (Jersey) hoard has given a number of minute, usually base silver, coins of different type from those generally found in Armorican hoards, which again are probably post-conquest (**340–3**). One, with the legend *Esvios*, has a Massiliot lion on the reverse (**340**).

To the east we may start in Switzerland. The main silver type here, found also in South Germany, was struck, no doubt, in one of the pagi of the Helvetii. It has a normal horse reverse, but the obverse consists of a broken-up bearded head barely recognisable as such, and more often resembling a sort of bush (**344–6**). The head is apparently a final degradation in the west of the bearded Zeus of the Danube coinages. One may compare the borrowing of the Allobroges head in North Noricum on the Tótfalu and Simmering types. The 'bush' coins, though not found at Alesia, certainly covered the first half of the first century B.C. There are many varieties, some inscribed MV (**346**). The post-conquest phase is probably represented by the lively and highly Romanised coins with a Mercury head and a boar reading *Ninno* or *Mau*, alone or in combination (cf. the type of a British Cunobelin; **444**, cf. **484**); they were found in the La Jante and Rozel hoards (**347, 348**).

In the Alesia find there was a Rhineland silver coin with a seated Alexander-type figure, probably of the Vangiones. There are four associated types of the same weight as the Bush coins, from both banks of the river. The seated figure (**306**) is from the west bank; there is a similar type with a head on the obverse (**349**). From the east between Mainz and Coblenz, we have coins with a head and a man carrying a torque (**350**). The earliest of them have a pure Roman helmeted head and on the reverse traces of the legend *Serveilius*, both drawn from a second-century denarius. Later coins have become completely

Celticised; the surround of V's is borrowed from Rhineland gold (or silver) staters. The type with the horse's head turned back is the most northerly, perhaps from the area of the Ubii (**351**). For the raised arms of the running man on the reverse, compare the attitude of the gods on the Gundestrup cauldron (plate 41); he represents either a perversion of the charioteer or perhaps more probably a relic of the Alkis tradition. It will be seen therefore that from Switzerland to the middle of the Rhine there is a series of Celtic silver coins, whose inspiration comes as much from the Danube as from Rome. These form a modest bridge between the two main branches of the Celtic world.

The Pallas Head

We are left with Belgic Gaul. Silver coins here are comparatively scarce and for the most part late; silver played a markedly small part in the currency of this area and this no doubt accounts for the virtual absence of silver in south-east Britain before Julius Caesar.

The first stage, which is often overlooked, consists of coins having on the obverse a head derived from the helmeted head of Pallas Athena on the gold staters of Alexander III of Macedon, the type that gave rise to the Nike staters in Germania. There are in fact gold quarter staters with an obverse of this kind and a typical later second-century B.C. Belgic horse on the reverse, one of which was found at the confluence of the Marne and the Seine. This type was soon adopted for silver coins; the starting point seems to have been in the neighbourhood of Chartres, in the territory of the Carnutes, but from here the type spread both east and west (**352**). To the west we find it established for small silver amongst the Veneti, where it is best known from the Brech hoard. To the east we find it first in the Rouen district and then at Amiens (**353**). By this stage the face has been lost and we have no more than a traditional pattern; ultimately the engraver starts to turn the relics of a human face into a horse's head. The silver types, which certainly belong to an early period in the first century B.C, are of particular interest to Britain, because it can now be positively asserted that Pallas-head coins, probably of the Rouen variety, are the origin of the curious thin silver coins of the Durotriges in Britain (**354**), which are shown by the Le Catillon hoard to precede Caesar's conquest of Armorica.

Two Animal Coins

The Le Catillon hoard also demonstrates that a group of rare silver coins from Belgic Gaul with two facing animals, heraldically arranged, are pre-Caesar in date (**355**; cf. **356**, **357**). They go with a very small number of silver coins with heads that do not look British, some of which have been found at Selsey and elsewhere on the south coast

(**358**). With the Pallas type, these probably represent the first phase of a tentative silver coinage in Belgic Gaul, but silver never became a regular part of the currency there.

Figure 14. Silver coin type from Selsey

Inscribed Belgic Silver

Similarly we have very little from Belgic Gaul to correspond with the great mass of inscribed silver coins from Gallia Celtica. Of such as there are, no examples have been found in Britain. There is a group of badly located coins with, amongst others, the legends *Nide-Arbodios* or *Abrodios* (**359**) and *Pennoovindos*, the former from Aisne. The peculiarity of these base coins is that they do not conform with the weight standard for silver coins, which we have seen from well before Alesia to be pretty well universal; they revert to the old standard of 2.4 to 2.3 g against the usual 1.9 to 1.8 g. These coins have mixed Greek and Roman letters.

A second group consists of silver coins of normal weight, which form part of a gold-silver-bronze sequence of denominations such as are found in Britain. We have already met the legends *Criciru* (**250–3**) and *Roveca* on gold staters amongst the Suessiones or Meldi (**254–8**). The silver and bronze of *Criciru* betray an obvious Roman origin. The *Roveca* silver (**256**) have a Juno Moneta head of a type found on many Roman denarii. We have already suggested that these staters are post-conquest; the other metals support this.

Finally we have in north Belgica a sequence of silver and bronze coins with the names *Carsicios-Commios*, *Garmanos-Commios* and *Carmanos-Andobru* (**360–2**), the former two being in silver, the latter in bronze. The coins are controversial; the silver coins belong to the normal weight group of the great silver hoards, but no examples occurred in the hoards, nor were any found at Alesia, from which Belgic coins were almost entirely lacking. The bronze type occurred in the Hussigny-

Godbrange hoard of *c.*30 B.C. Flines, Nord, is the key site for single finds of *Andobru*. The French view, sustained, for instance, by Dr Colbert de Beaulieu, is that these are coins of Caesar's Commius. My own view has been that such intensely Romanised coins, never found in this country, are unlikely to belong to the historical Commius; it is better to treat them as one of the many series of magistral silver and bronze coins of the early years of the Roman occupation, which were mainly issued after our Commius had made his escape. The head type has close affinities with the coins of *Criciru* and *Roveca*, so that if I am wrong in thinking these to be post-conquest, I shall similarly be wrong over Commius.

Britain

There is no time in a general survey such as this to deal more than cursorily with Britain. It will be seen that in the area of Gaul from which Britain derived the concept of coinage, silver played a minor role, and at the appropriate time there were very few models near at hand to copy. Consequently, when the invasions of Caesar introduced Britain to the concept of a silver coinage beside the gold, there tends to be a marked originality in the types. So far as they borrow, they owe more to contemporary gold coins circulating beside them (even to Gaulish gold) than they do to the contemporary silver coins of Gallia Celtica. Although we have a certain number of isolated silver coins, not forming part of sequences, especially in the Hertfordshire, Bedford and Suffolk districts, but also in Kent, the great majority of British silver coins are attached by legend, type, or both to gold denominations. Almost from the start, but at a reduced weight, they form part of a coherent monetary system; it is only in the west, amongst the Durotriges that our silver (and later bronze) coins are base substitutes for gold coins.

It is only in Britain and Armorican Gaul that we find silver minims. In the advanced central tribes, the silver coins display distinctive Romano-Celtic features not found on the Continent, which are readily recognisable in handling the coins. Thus, amongst the Coritani and Iceni we have boar-horse types that are not borrowed from the Continent but have their own evolution. Amongst the Iceni we also have pattern-horse types of purely British origin, connected with the stater pattern. Amongst the Dobunni we have head-horse types, on which the head, so far as it is influenced at all, is drawn from the gold staters of the Parisii. While the continuity of British gold coinage with the continental coinages is obvious, in the case of silver the connection is tenuous and indirect. The most obvious debt of the late coins is direct to Augustan Rome. Although in weight and monetary purpose our silver is clearly a reduced version of the standard continental denomination, the true analogues for the types and their artistic content are to be sought more in the late coins of Noricum and Slovakia than in those of nearby Gaul.

Bronze Coins

Alesia

Before the Roman conquest, bronze coinage struck with dies in the normal way was slow to develop. The coins were of small intrinsic value and the exact weight of little significance. The scene is again set by Alesia, where 140 bronze coins were found in the grave deposits. Most of them were certainly local coins, current at the time, but some more distant types were represented too. As a whole they represent the first stage of Gaulish struck bronze coinage and none give any evidence of being old when buried. In other words, it looks as if struck bronze coins in Central and Northern Gaul did not begin before the decade 70–60 B.C.

There is no single point of origin for bronze coins in Gaul. Perhaps the first were subsidiary small change to accompany the major gold tribal currencies; but not far different in date there are in the same areas bronze coins that we can associate with independent silver coinages. Thus the gold coins of the Arverni and the Bituriges Cubi, both found at Alesia, were accompanied each by a series of bronze coins with legends. Amongst the Bituriges Cubi at least one name, ABVDOS, is also found on the gold (**206**, **208**) but most names are not (**363**, **364**: *Vandelos*, *Caliageis*; these were common at Bibracte). Amongst the Arverni all the names are different from the gold (*Bucios*, *D canaunos*, **365**). There were forty-two such bronzes of the Bituriges Cubi and nine of the Arverni at Alesia. Also probably Arvernian, but entirely distinct from the preceding, are bronze coins corresponding to the heavy silver coins of *Pictilos*, *Epasnactus* and *Epomeduos*, reading *Caledu*, *Cicedu-Bri-Epad* and *Cambil* (**366**, **367**), of which there were seven, fifty-nine and five respectively. These together comprise more than three-quarters of the bronze found.

Of the remaining bronze coins from Alesia, the most interesting is that reading *Tasgetios-Elkesouis* (**368**); the first name must be that of the chief of the Carnutes murdered in 54 B.C, as the coins come from the Chartres area. The obverse is copied from denarii of L. or C. Calpurnius Piso Frugi (90 or 67 B.C, **331**) which is used on other bronzes also (for instance, the Arvernian *Cambil* coins). They can thus be dated with conviction to 60–55 B.C.

Next we have a series of coins with locks of the kind used on the silver coins of the Lemovices, which I have previously spoken of as in the Emporitan tradition. The normal coins are essentially Celtic with no trace of Rome in their make-up. One group is found amongst the Carnutes (**369, 370**). It has a bird with snake or lizard on the reverse and is uninscribed or bears a monogram KA. One was found at Alesia together with four improved and Romanised variants of the theme. A second group, found a little further east amongst the Senones, has a different bird with a legend *Ulucci* (**371**); six of these were found. There are other legends, including *Senu* or *Giamilos Senu* (**372**). The latter are certainly post-Caesar, for we have silver coins of *Giamilos* that adopt Augustan silver types.

The remaining bronze coins at Alesia come from further afield. There were two specimens of common coins of the Belgic Remi, with the legend *Remo* (**373, 374**); it has three profile heads on the obverse and a Celtic chariot on the reverse. There was also one specimen of another southern Belgic bronze with the legend in mixed Greek and Roman characters, *Deiviciac*, clearly the same name as the very much earlier Diviciacus, king of the Suessiones (Caesar *B.G.* 2.4.7). Finally there was an example of a curious coin with on one side a head wearing a Celtic helmet, accompanied by a spear, and on the other side a grazing horse with tree and cup (**375**). Other find-spots suggest that this coin is Aeduan. Bronze coins tend not to travel far compared with silver and gold. The bronze coins from Alesia will not, therefore, give us anything like a comprehensive coverage of the earlier bronze coinages of Gaul but they are the best criterion we have for the initial phase.

Later Bronze

At the other end of the scale we have two important hoards of bronze coins alone, which give us a picture of the bronze coins circulating in Lorraine about 30 B.C, and in Vendée about 10 B.C. The Hussigny-Godbrange (Meurthe-et-Moselle) hoard contained more than thirty types of bronze coins, worn and fresh, mostly from Belgic Gaul, together with a few silver and potin coins. The hoard gives a cross-section of the bronze coinage of the whole north-east quarter of Gaul around 30 B.C, from which it is possible to draw deductions for the many other comparable bronze types from elsewhere. Most of these were independent bronze coinages of essentially local circulation, bearing the name of their issuers. The hoard, however, contained bronzes of *Arda* and *Roveca*, a name we have seen in the silver and bronze *Commios* sequence. One may compare the Meilleraie-Tillay, Vendée, hoard, which makes it certain that the inscribed orichalcum coins of Poitou, (*Luccios*, *Annicoios*, *Contoutos*, *Atectori*; **376–8**) were circulating and indeed fresh down to the last ten years of the century. In the hoard there were also bronze coins of the Vendée (*Viretios* and *Sactnos*; **379, 380**) and a small number of strays, including examples of the Arverni and Bituriges Cubi types as found at Alesia. No dated hoards of this kind from the first century A.D. have been found; by then all but a few Gaulish coins of particularly wide distribution (for instance the bronze *Germanus Indutilli L.*, **381**) had disappeared.

Intervening Bronze

It is within the range of dates provided by Alesia and those hoards that we must place the main bulk of the enormous quantities of miscellaneous Gaulish bronze coins that have survived to today. There are at least two hundred recognisable types. It is absolutely certain that the great majority of them were struck after the conquest, with Roman sanction; but there is generally no means of accurate dating within the last half of the first century B.C. Although it is sometimes reasonable and convenient to fix them geographically by reference to tribal areas, it is only rarely that they bear the names of issuing tribes; they were issued in the names of individuals, no doubt Celtic chiefs approved by Rome, and it appears that they were intended in most cases for circulation in a single oppidum or civitas. This is from time to time demonstrable when such sites are excavated and local coins provide a majority of coin finds.

There are some coins whose legends or types themselves betray their date. The most notable of these are the coins from the area of Trier that bear the name of Aulus Hirtius, Caesar's friend and legate in Gaul and the continuer of his commentaries. On one type with an elephant obverse, the name stands alone; on the three others he is described as *Imperator* and the name is accompanied by that of Gaulish chieftains (**383, 384**). In 46 B.C, while *praefectus Urbi* in Rome, Hirtius was responsible for the largest issue of gold aurei in the name of Caesar. In 43 B.C, he was killed. It is not possible to pin any of these coins down to a particular year in the bracket 51–46 B.C, but that bracket must contain the starting point; many look like subsequent copies. Another elephant type, however, reads *Carinas*, and is presumably connected with the C. Carrinas who in 31 B.C. became *propraetor* of Belgic Gaul. Both coins occurred in the Hussigny-Godbrange hoard. Another example in the same class is the bronze that gives the name of Gaius Claudius Casticus of the tribe of the Samnagetes, which clearly takes us a great deal later still. There is hoard evidence that the widespread coins of *Germanus Indutilli L.* (L for *libertus*; **381**) with a focus probably on the Treveri, belong to the last years of the first century B.C. The same too probably applies to the comparable southern *T. Pom. Sex. F.* bronzes (**385**) not yet well located.

In other cases, as in some of the preceding, the date is indicated by the models copied or reflected. Thus the three types found in the oppidum at Amboise reading *Artos*, *Acussros* and *Drucca*, all have elements taken from Roman denarii of dates between 88 and 54 B.C. Since the assembled merchants of nearby Cenabum (Orleans) were all massacred in 52 B.C, the three types were with little doubt at all struck after that date. Several other bronzes are derived from post-conquest denarii, for instance those of *Giamilos*, which must be post-49 B.C, and those of *Connos-Epillos-Sedullos*, similarly post-47 B.C. The list can be multiplied. What this amounts to is that in all parts of Gaul, excluding Armorica (though very patchily in the south), isolated small bronze coins continued to be issued, with Roman acquiescence, sometimes by tribes, sometimes by individuals, generally for purely local use, but occasionally on an almost national scale, right into the early years of the first century A.D. Occasionally the coins form part of sequences of magistrates' names, occasionally they are linked with corresponding silver coins; but the majority are local and isolated.

Such Gaulish bronze coins as are found in Britain are, as one would expect, from the northern parts of Belgic Gaul, especially Ambianian territory, but we are singularly ill-informed about them or their history (**386–91**). The principal hoards are the St-André-sur-Cailly (Seine-Inférieure) and St-Jacques (Amiens) finds. Neither is dated. The coins are mostly uninscribed, intensely Celtic, usually with birds or beasts, sometimes paired, sometimes revolving. We have no means of locating many of the individual varieties. There are virtually no typological links with the gold coins of the area. This is the class of coin that is sometimes found in Kent or on the Bedfordshire/Hertfordshire/Suffolk borders and provides the starting point of British bronze coinage. One can be sure that such coins were known to the engravers of Tasciovanus' coins; one cannot be sure when they started but it could well have been pre-conquest. The running-man bronzes found near the mouth of the Seine to the east (**236**), which have an origin in the charioteer on the coins of the Aulerci Eburovices, are certainly pre-conquest, since one, said to be of silver, was found at Alesia, and they are associated in the St-André hoard with the Belgic Bronze types.

Most of the bronze coins of Britain differ from those of the Continent because they form part of a gold-silver-bronze set of denominations. On the continent the full set occurs only in Belgic Gaul with the *Roveca* and *Criciru* legends. A long range of types with a single name, such as we have with Tasciovanus and Cunobelin (**392–7**), is very rare in Gaul; almost the only examples are the bronzes of *Roveca* and of *Pixtilos*, the latter from the Carnutes, the central point of Central Gaul. Except in Kent and the Herts/Suffolk borders, the two areas of Britain where the Gaulish originals are found, there is no reproduction in Britain of the sporadic and miscellaneous character that is the essence of the bronze coinage of Gaul.

Although bronze coins were of small intrinsic values, and there is no means yet of relating their value to silver and gold, there must have been some relationship between the value of coins and the metal it contained. Otherwise we could not explain the reduction by a third in the weight of the bronze coins of Britain as compared with Gaul, nor the appearance of a minim coinage no more than eight millimetres wide in Kent and Colchester. I think the weight of Cunobelin's bronze coins was intended to be twice that of his silver coins, that is to say 120 to the Celtic pound.

Potin coins

The essential small denomination of much of Gaul is not the struck bronze, but the cast potin coin, made of an alloy of copper and tin. The exact composition varied, but in principle it was a token coinage, so that exact weight, size or composition was of little moment. Hoards, and especially mixed ones, are rare, which makes correlation difficult.

At their full extent potin coins are spread over the whole of the central, northern and eastern parts of Gaul but fall short of the coast; they even spread into western Germany, though they were not made there so far as I know. There is also a small pocket near Toulouse, marked with a T. In Britain we have coins of this class in Kent and East Anglia (**398–400**). Nothing comparable was adopted in other parts of the Celtic world. In Gaul, however, potin coins are very common.

The coins of *Q. Doci Sam F.* and *Togirix* (**401–3**) in Burgundy and Franche-Comté are the main instances where potin coins belong to a set with coins in other metals. In the extreme north-east of Belgic Gaul there are related bronze and potin types; a mass of them was found, prepared for melting, as scrap at Mandeure, Jura. *Turonos Cantorix* is known both struck and cast (**404**). But in general the potin stands wholly distinct from coinage in other metals and to some extent cuts across regions marked by the gold and silver distributions. We find, for instance, no frontier between Belgica and Celtica as we do with gold and silver. Some types are very widespread, and one would be hard put on published information (which is often imprecise) to identify their centre; they were probably made in many places. Others, however, are

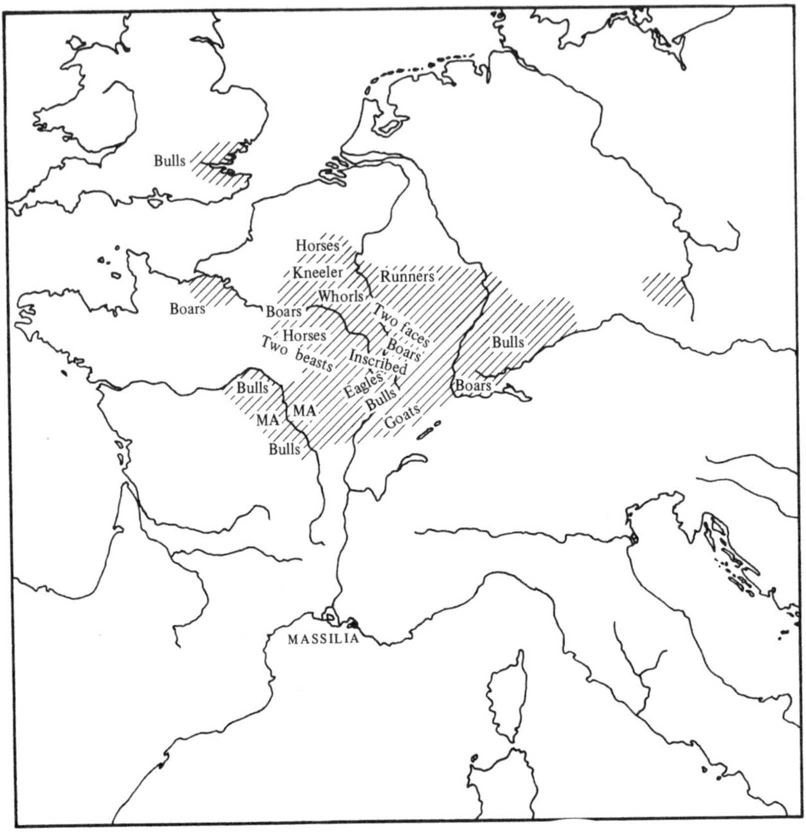

Map 17. Cast potin coins

as strictly local as any Celtic coins. If gold coinage shows the affinities of the rich classes in the community, potin coinage similarly shows the groupings of the poor.

There is no classical model for the concept of a cast coinage of this kind, but the first potin coins are almost certainly those that copy the butting-bull bronzes of Massilia (**405**). The originals are usually dated to the second century B.C, and it is common to assert that the potin coins began in that century. This still seems to me possible in the case of the rare coins that closely imitate the Massilian originals and those close to them (**406**). They appear to come from the upper Loire valley. But it is not possible to rely on the so-called second-century tomb at Ornavasso, in which two coins of advanced types were found, because the argument is circular; the tombs have been dated from the coins.

As with the silver and bronze coins of Gaul, the best fixed point for the potin coins is provided by the finds at Alesia. Of fifty-three potin coins found, eighteen were of the type into which the Massilia butting bulls had early turned; there are a great many varieties with degraded head on one side and deformed quadruped on the other, spreading from Lyons to the bend of the Loire in the west, to Switzerland and Württemberg and Baden in the east. The commonest type at Alesia, however, of which there were thirty-two examples, substitutes a horse for the bull (**407**); it is presumably at home amongst the Aedui and Mandubii, though horses also occur further to the north-west. The remaining three Alesia coins help fix correlations of time; one has replaced the quadruped on the reverse with a boar or boar standard, the characteristic type of Franche-Comté and the upper waters of the Seine, and is found in great numbers at Châté de Boviolles (**408**, **409**); the remaining two have lost the head. One of these has a three-armed whorl on one side and three revolving beasts on the other (**410**). Its home lies in the Aube district between Troyes and Reims, with Langres as the centre. The other has two confronted beasts on each side, as do many bronze and some silver Belgic coins; but they come from the Seine valley in the neighbourhood of Paris (**411**).

It will be seen therefore that, by 51 B.C, what had started as a sub-Massalian coinage had deviated into a strange collection of essentially Celtic types. There are many others, some of great originality, for instance a monster consuming a man. It is probable that the majority of potin types were in existence before the conquest, since the Alesia finds are typical of the whole, but it is certain from the excavation finds both in France and Germany, for instance the find from Châteaumeillant, Cher, which brings them down to the Augustan Age, that the coinage continued in use into the first century A.D. The Hussigny-Godbrange hoard contained six types, all different from those found at Alesia, including the well-known type with standing figure and thunderbolt (**412**); this has been found straggling across Germany and as far east as Stradonitz, which has also given examples of other Gaulish potin coins. The parallel kneeling-druid type was not found in the hoard and is conceivably later; it too was found at Stradonitz (**413**, **414**). An 'improved' Roman version exists of the standing-figure type (**415**). A number of types are inscribed in Roman or occasionally Greek letters.

The so-called tin coins in Britain are a direct continuation of the Gaulish potin with butting bull or deformed quadruped (**416**, **398–400**). They are not derived from the many models available in the non-coastal parts of Belgic Gaul, but from central Gaul. The earliest are, in fact thicker than the normal British type, and their Continental connection more obvious. It seems to me likely that they were introduced relatively early into Britain, to Kent, which is certainly their main home, before the full spread of potin coins had taken place in Gaul. It is difficult otherwise to imagine why the butting-bull type was chosen. The type, an 'immobilised' one, in numismatic parlance, had a very long life in Britain, being still in circulation in 43 A.D, and a special technique of casting was developed. As in Gaul, however, the potin coins in Britain stand apart from the main stream of coinage and we do not have the evidence of correlations. We do, however, have the happy confirmation from the Snettisham finds that the potin coins in Britain go back at least to the third quarter of the first century B.C, and in my belief appreciably further.

The period of time and the geographical area I have attempted to cover in this outline of the silver, bronze and potin coinages of Gaul have been less than in the previous chapters, but the volume of surviving material is such that the treatment has necessarily been cursory. I have tried to show a few fixed points to which the rest can be related. I have avoided dealing with the problems of interpretation of the legends and types. My next chapter, therefore, will be devoted to an account of the legends found on Celtic coins, their script, language and interpretation. In the course of it I shall mention incidentally many of the varieties of silver and bronze coins that have not been included above.

6

Coin Legends

The Purpose of Coin Legends

I shall try now to give some account of the legends on Celtic coins. They present many problems of reading and interpretation, but they are often the first known use of writing in their areas.

The use of an inscription on a coin implies some familiarity with the arts of reading and writing, but it does not mean that many of those who used the coin could read the legends. What it shows is that the issuer wished to put on public record whatever it is that the legend says. It implies an awareness of the value of writing, either as a means of communication or record, or conceivably for the prophylactic purposes of magic.

My first aim will be to record, my second to interpret. My knowledge of the Celtic language is superficial, but any study must start from reading the legends themselves, which are written in ordinary classical scripts, mainly Latin and Greek. This is a task for the numismatist. It often takes several coins to complete a legend and you will sometimes have to take my word for the full readings on the specimens illustrated.

The earliest of Celtic coin legends probably belong to the second century B.C, and the floruit of the legends is during the first century B.C. In Britain they do not begin until after the middle of that century and continue to the middle of the first century A.D. We are dealing, therefore, with a total period in the order of two to two-and-a-half centuries.

Professor Jackson has said that these partly Latinised legends do not imply a written Celtic literature at that date; anyone who was sufficiently educated to read or write would have been sufficiently educated to know some Latin – to which I would add – or Greek. What I have to say here amply bears out that judgement, but I hope that the fusion of Celtic, Latin and Greek in these legends is not without some significance for the study of Celtic language and institutions.

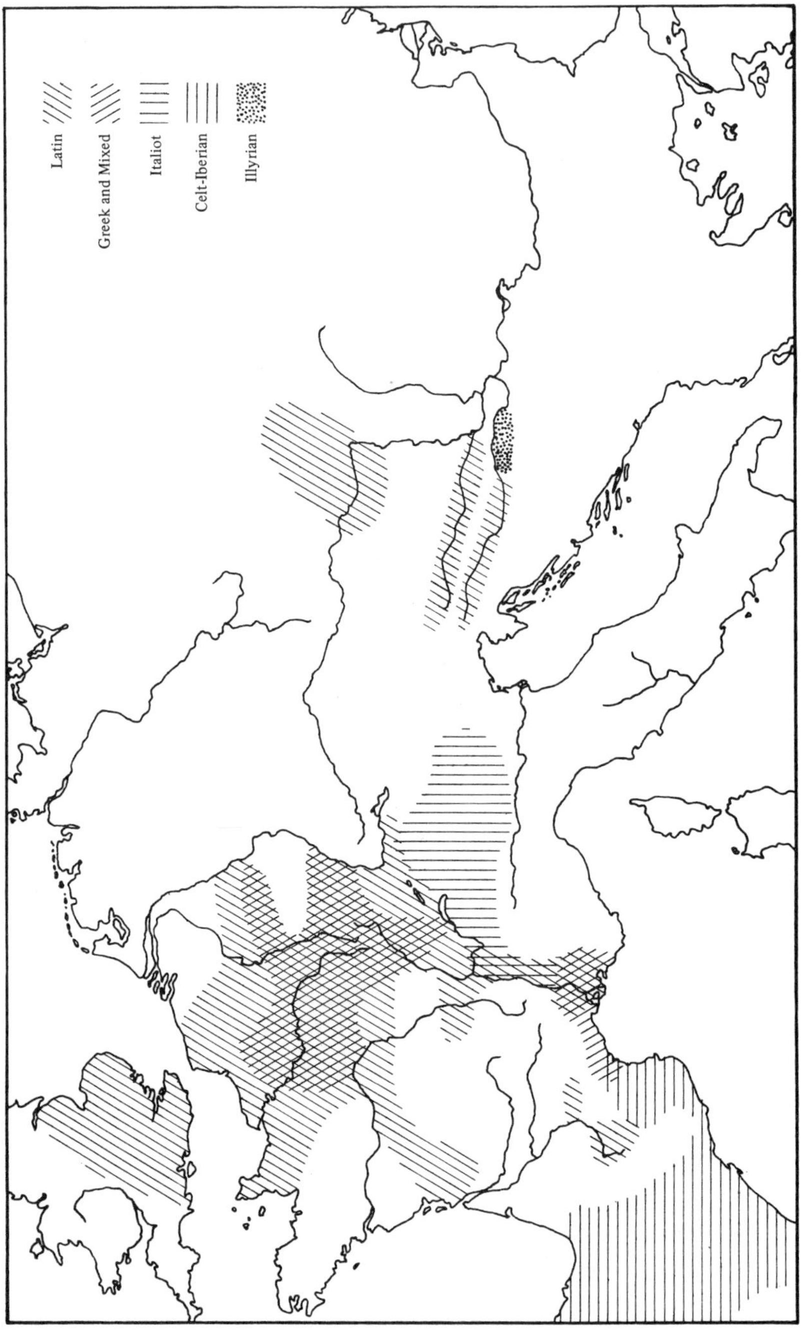

Map 18. Scripts on Celtic coins

Copied Legends and pseudo-Legends

We start with a complication. Nearly all the earliest Celtic coins are copies of Greek or Roman models, which themselves bore legends, monograms or symbols. The first generation of Celtic coins tends to reproduce these legends, often correctly or at least legibly. Later generations display blunders and modifications and before long these legends are reduced, without losing their identity, to patterns (**417**). A monogram may readily grow into a decorative element. One must suppose that to their engravers and users such legends, Greek and Roman, conveyed no meaning, but that without them their coins would not have conformed to the proper standards of coin design.

Thus letter and monogram shapes formed, from the earliest days, part of the die sinker's repertoire, and one must beware of assuming too readily that apparently new combinations of these shapes were intended to convey a phonetic value. They may be no more than decoration. When true legends were first introduced, this was done in an unmistakable and deliberate manner, even if the results were sometimes crude.

We can thus dismiss from a study of Celtic coin legends all but a few of the silver tetradrachms from the Danube basin and gold staters from Gaul that bear the name of Philip of Macedon, or some corrupt version of it. The same applies to the silver tetradrachms and gold staters from south Germany and the eastern Balkans with the name of Alexander III or Philip III of Macedon, and to the Danubian silver coins with the name of Audoleon of Paeonia, as also to the Cisalpine silver coinage bearing the legend ΜΑΣΣΑ, the opening syllables of Massilia. There are examples, too, of legends copied from Roman Republican denarii (**291**, **418**, **419**).

Excluding all such false legends, together with those where decorations have been wrongly interpreted as writing, there survive something in the order of five to six hundred distinct coin legends on a larger number of coin types. A complete tally is not possible because many legends are still only partly read or suspected. True legends extend from mid-Spain to south Slovakia and from the Po Valley to the Humber.

Scripts

Celt-Iberian Script in Spain

Celtic coin legends are written in a variety of borrowed scripts, occasionally with local adaptations. I start in the south-west. The silver and bronze coinage of Spain during the second and first centuries B.C.

has legends in Celt-Iberian characters. This script, which has been much studied, is derived from the Tartessian script. It owes little to Greek, more to Semitic, and nothing to Roman. It was apparently first used in the third century B.C. Its correct transliteration, on which there is now broad agreement, depends largely on the existence of late bilingual coins of such towns as Celsa and Saetabi. Out of twenty-eight or -nine regular signs, fifteen or sixteen are syllabic. With modification, the script was used consistently throughout most of Spain, except in Andalusia; it was, therefore, as much the script of the Iberian and other peoples of the Peninsula as of the western Celts. The coins issued by the Celts and Celt-Iberians of north-west Spain cannot be distinguished numismatically or by reason of their script from the similar coins issued by the other ethnic elements. What alone distinguishes them is that the inscriptions on the coins use Celtic forms.

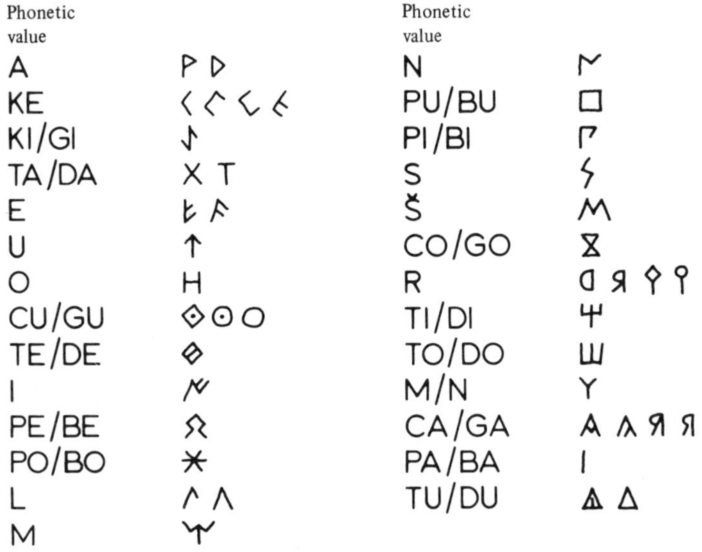

Figure 15. Celt-Iberian script on coins

Thus the typical inscription on coins from the Iberian areas of Spain gives a tribal name terminating in the genitive plural *-scen* (for instance, *Untikescen* (**420**), *Sedeiscen* or *Icalcuscen*). The distribution is distinct from that of legends terminating in *-cos* and *-com* (for instance *Arsacos* (**261**), *Lovitisacos* or *Tuitiscos* or *Contabacom*, *Carbicom* or *Beligiom*), which belong to the Celt-Iberian area. There are, in addition, Celtic language legends with other terminations, for instance the vowels *-a*, *-e* or *-o*. In many cases the legends can with certainty be read as giving town names of Celtic origin, some of which survive in use to this day. For instance, the name *Iaca* on coins is undoubtedly the Roman Iacca and the modern Jaca. *Saetabi* of the coins is the Roman Saetabis, which is now Játiva. Celtic names terminating in *-om* are thought to be in the genitive plural and thus to be tribal names, but the large number of inscriptions ending in *-os* look like personal names, as analogy with other Celtic coins would suggest. Nevertheless in Spain the form may well be ethnic and adjectival; thus at the Roman Calagurris, modern Calahorra, the bronze coins read *Calqoriqos*. In other cases we have tribal names in the nominative plural – *Ilterces* is presumably Ptolemy's Ilergetes, who lived in the region of Ilerda. Another form is represented by the Celtic-sounding legend *Corucoruatin*.

There are instances of secondary inscriptions in Celt-Iberian characters. These may sometimes be the opening letters or syllables of magistrates' names, usually singly, occasionally in pairs. The principal examples of single names in Celt-Iberian script are on the later coins of the first century B.C. at Indica, the native part of the Greek town of Emporion. At other towns, such as Turiaso and Calagurris, there are, in Augustan and Tiberian times, coins with magistrates' names in pairs, which actually describe them as *duumviri* or sometimes, at Turiaso, as *aediles* (**421**). Then we have cases, as at Osca, the modern Huelva, where two symbols on the obverse reproduce the first and last letters of the town name as given on the coins, Hiloscan (**422**). The same two symbols occur in the same place on the coins of nearby Iaca and Sesaes and it looks as if these symbols indicate that the coins were not minted locally but at Osca. Another case of a probable mint name is *Konquida*, which occurs on the obverse of coins of *Kontan* and of the Vascones. Secondary inscriptions, thus, follow no single pattern, but have been thought to give, in addition to the names of magistrates and mints, the values or denominations of the coins, or in other cases to be merely imitative.

I do not propose to enlarge on this complicated subject, on which there is no general agreement, since the coins of the Celtic tribes in Spain stand apart from the rest of Celtic coinage. But I have said enough to show that the great majority of them bear legends giving Celtic town or tribal names, occasionally in adjectival or ethnic form. More rarely the coins may bear the names of authorising magistrates. Although this is the basic pattern, there are many variants and unexplained details. We shall find both contrasts and analogies elsewhere.

Celt-Iberian Script in Aquitania

Celt-Iberian script was used to a small extent outside the frontiers of

Spain. We find it in Aquitania and in Narbonensis, both of which areas had closer affinities with Iberia than with the rest of Gaul.

There are examples of the silver 'cross' money of Aquitania derived from coins of Rhoda, with pure Celt-Iberian legends, for instance *Acoequntin* and *Untga* (**100**). The former may be compared in form perhaps with *Corucoruatin* in Spain. It seems likely, from the Spanish analogy, although this is rare elsewhere in Gaul, that the legends give us place names. We do not know the origin of Caesar's name Aquitania; could it be cognate with *Acoequntin*?

Celt-Iberian and Greek Script in Narbonensis

A series of bronze coins generally similar to the bronze asses of Spain is found in Narbonensis. One group within the series has legends in Celt-Iberian script. The most frequent reverse legend is *Neroncen, Neronc* or *Neronen* (**270–2**); here again we have secondary obverse legends. Other reverse legends are *Selonencen* and *Pricantio. Neroncen* undoubtedly refers to Narbo, the present Narbonne, and seems to be in the form of the tribal name – Neronenses is the Latin equivalent. In the third we presumably have a town name, Brigantio: but the root is the same as in the Brigantia from which the Lake of Breganz, the Brigantia on the Danube, and our own Brigantes in Yorkshire take their names.

Parallel with the Celt-Iberian legends there are other groups of inscribed bronze coins from Narbonensis, which have legends in Greek characters reflecting the influence of nearby Massilia. One small group with Greek legends are those of Béziers, the name of which occurs in the form (BHTAPPATIC) *Betarratis* (**274**). Again this seems to be the name of the people rather than the town. Another group consist of the coins of the Longostaletes (**279, 280**). The name is given on the reverse in good Greek characters in the genitive plural (usually with a C for Σ) while on the obverse there is generally a personal name, also in Greek characters and in the nominative – *Bokios, Loukorinos* or *Loukotiknos.* On the reverse – an inscription in Celt-Iberian letters – PURP. The explanation can only be conjectural. The same word occurs on one of the secondary obverse legends on coins of the Neronenses. The choice again lies between the names of mint, magistrate, the coin denomination or the ruler's title. Finally, we have five Celtic kings whose names occur on coins accompanied by the Greek title *Basileus* in the nominative – *Kaiantolos, Amytos, Bitoukos, Bitovis* and *Rigantikos* (**275–8**).

Thus Narbonensis furnishes a wide range of inscriptions – tribal names, sometimes at any rate in the genitive, town names, certain or possible, rulers' names with and without title, and a variety of unexplained legends. The variety of the legends in Greek, which we can read with certainty, may warn us against looking for too great consistency or logic in the Celt-Iberian legends of Spain. The series as a whole belongs to the end of the second century and the first quarter of the first century B.C, during the floruit of the Iberian coinage in Spain.

Greek Script in the Marseilles Area

As would be expected, the nearer we get to Massilia the stronger the influence of Greek script; but the actual area of this influence was remarkably small. Apart from Narbonensis, it occurs only in the immediate hinterland of Massilia; here we have what are, in effect, Greek coinages, all with regular Greek legends, of the Caenicenses, the Glanici and of Avenio (**423**, **424**, **315**). We have also a series of first-century B.C. bronze coins from the vicinity imitating regular bronzes of Massilia, with what are presumably Celtic rulers' names in Greek characters beginning *Krisso, Elkiot, Lom, Aoss, Aora*. Altogether later we have a bronze of Massilia type with the name of Gaius Claudius Castico of the otherwise unknown tribe of the Samnagetes (**425**). But that is about all.

In view of all that is said about the commercial pre-eminence of Massilia and its multifarious influence on Gaul, it is striking how little effect the Greek script of Massilia exercised over the spread of writing as revealed by Celtic coinage. We shall meet the Greek script again in Gaul, but in situations where it by no means follows that the only source was Massilia.

North Italian Script in Savoy and the Alps

In the area to the north and east of Massilia, where on historical grounds Greek legends might have been expected, there in fact occur legends in the scripts of North Italy, generally akin to Etruscan. They are found on the gold coins of Haute-Savoie and the Swiss borders, the first silver imitations of Roman coins in the Rhône Valley, and the imitations of Massilia drachmae from the foothills of the Alps and the Swiss valleys. The scripts in each have features in common, but they are not necessarily identical in all respects. The coins only give some of the alphabet in each case (figure 16).

On the gold coins of Haute-Savoie (**426**), traditionally and correctly ascribed to the gold-producing tribe of the Salassi, six legends are known: *Ases* (or *Asem*), *Prikou* (the Brigantes root again), *Ulkos, Anatikou, Kasiloi* and *Kat*. The legends read either from right to left or left to right. They were placed prominently between parallels in the middle of the coins. They were certainly meant to be read. They form no doubt a series of personal names, probably in succession, and in a single organised State distinct in coinage and in customs from its neighbours. Typologically, the coins stand apart from all others. The obverse represents a totally broken down and formalised face, not necessarily in the philippus tradition; weight implies an early mid-first century B.C. date. The Salassi were not conquered by Rome until the campaign of Valerius Messala in 34 B.C. One suspects that the end of the series did not long precede this date despite the out-of-date script.

Figure 16. North Italian scripts

On the silver coins of the Rhône valley, which are to be dated about the middle of the second century B.C. or soon after, we have four legends in Italiot characters, generally similar to those used by the Salassi – *Iazus, Ialkovesi, Kasios* and *Ailos*, clearly personal names (**281**). Very soon these legends were overtaken by others in unmistakably Roman characters, starting with VOL (**282**), to which I shall come later.

Again in Cisalpine Gaul we have four silver coins with legends in a similar Italiot script, to be read as *Anarekartoi, Rutirio, Pirukoi*, and

Rikoi (**9**, **10**). The legend *Anarekartoi* occurs on an imitation of a heavy drachm of Massilia and may well belong to the third century B.C. The other three legends are on copies of the light drachm; the coins reading *Rikoi* are in base metal and poor style and undoubtedly come at the end of the series, say in the first quarter of the first century B.C, the other two no doubt before.

Thus between the Rhône, the Po and the Alps, at a variety of dates between the third century and the mid first century B.C, we find a true Italiot script in use, sometimes to the exclusion of Greek and Roman, to give what are probably all names of Celtic chieftains. In most cases the names appear to run as a sequence, one ruler more or less carrying on from the previous one.

Celt-Illyrian Script in Croatia

We have another example of a distantly related script, this time from the vicinity of Zagreb in Croatia. A hoard of silver tetradrachms in the philippus tradition, but influenced by the coins of Patraos of Paeonia, contained examples with a Celt-Illyrian legend read as *Sasthieni*, thought to be equivalent to the Greek name Sosthenes. The legend on the reverse reads from right to left (48); other coins have a blundered version, showing how unfamiliar writing was to the engravers. The type stands alone. There are no other coin legends in this script, and not more than a handful of Danubian tetradrachms on which it is conceivable that such Greek or Roman letter forms as were used were intended to be read; in no case is this likely. We shall come later to the legends in Roman letters regularly used in Noricum, but two legends in a true Italiot, not Celt-Illyrian, script are in fact probably also Norican. Weight suggests that the Sasthieni coin is of the second century B.C, while the analogies of the Noricum coins are with the first century B.C.

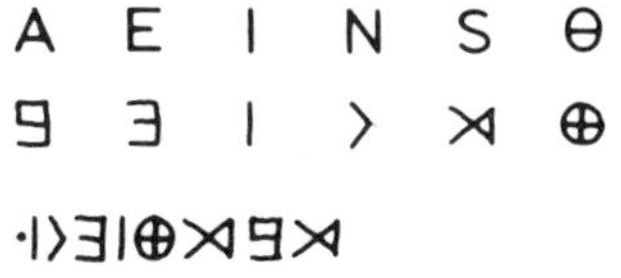

Sasthieni (= Sosthenes?)

Figure 17. Celt-Illyrian script

Writing in the Celtic Homelands

I now turn to the legends of the centre and north. Here the universal scripts are Greek and Roman, often mixed, with Roman strongly predominating. Writing in one or other of these forms was throughout most of the area clearly a growing usage, from the latter part of the second century B.C. onwards. There are sporadic traces of it before that.

Nevertheless, at no time was uninscribed coinage wholely superseded; there are mute coins and areas to the end.

Much confusion has been caused by the mention in Caesar's commentaries and in Strabo (Caesar *B.G.* 6.14.3; Strabo 4.1.5) of the use of Greek letters (not the Greek language) in Gaul. Caesar states that the Druids employed Greek characters. He also describes a nominal roll of the Helvetii which was in Greek letters. Nevertheless, a letter sent from the territory of the Nervii to Q. Cicero was written in Greek characters (not necessarily in the Greek language) to make sure that, if it fell into enemy hands, it would not be understood. These remarks seem to imply both that the Gauls did, and did not, understand Greek characters. Celtic coins show beyond any doubt that the writing used was mainly Roman, sometimes Greek, occasionally both seperately, and more often both mixed. There are few distinct indegenous traits. It could be that the Druids, who, so far as we know, had no particular connection with coinage, did use Greek letters, but that on the whole those to whom coin legends were addressed did not.

Early Stater Legends

The use of legends on gold coins in Gaul before the middle of the first century B.C. is essentially occasional and unsystematic. The earliest legends, which are generally not at present located, are very rare and in Roman, not Greek, characters. The most notable is EIQITIVICO (**172**) on an early gold philippus stater. The letters are Roman, occasionally upside down, and the early date is marked by the use of EI for E and Q not followed by V. Similarly, the first gold legends in the east, CVR on the coiled serpents, ATVLL on the rainbows and BIATEC on the mussels are in Roman letters. We have in fact only two pure Greek legends on gold coins; the legend KABAΛΛ on middle period gold staters is not located but perhaps comes from East France, while the legend ΘΙΟΛΕ is found on late pieces from the area of Metz and the Marne (**428**). There is no connection between the two.

The Legends of the Rhône Valley

We have much fuller information about the silver coinage, where we can trace the development of legends. The process starts in the Rhône valley, where we have already met legends in Italiot script in the middle of the second century B.C. It can be proved from hoards that these were immediately followed first by coins reading in Roman letters VOL, backwards or forwards, and then by the horseman series on which there are pairs of names, again in Roman letters (**286–8**). From this point on there are two separate lines of development; one common group of coins, derived from the same Roman helmeted head as the horseman,

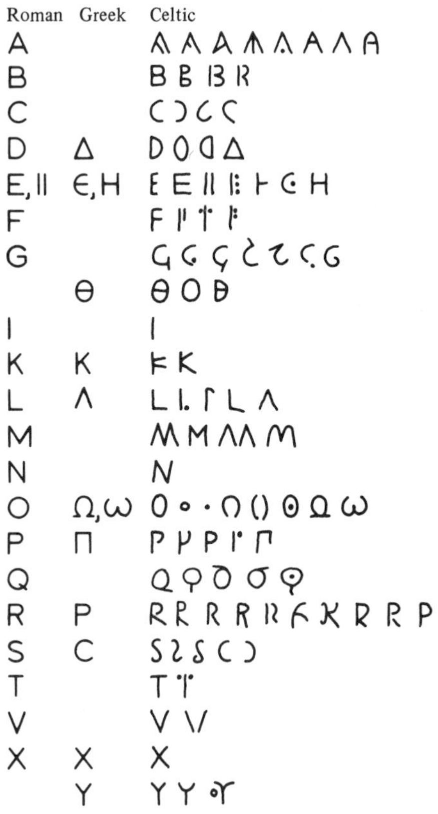

Figure 18. Celtic scripts on coins

have a legend in Greek characters, *Kaletedou* (**291–3**), while another, in parallel, has the legend *Q. Doci Sam F.* and other legends, both in form and content positively Roman (**295–8**; compare *Arivos Santonos*, **300**).

Greek Script in Central and North Gaul

I take the Greek legends first. The home of the *Kaletedou* coins is in Côte-d'Or and Haute-Marne, well away from any contact with Greek colonies. The earliest coins have a purely Greek legend (**291**). The significant fact is that very soon the type becomes an established or immobilised one, and is copied, like so many Celtic coins. **293** shows the latter part of the legend decaying into a pattern, in which the true letter forms are lost; the process is nearly complete in **294**. It looks as if the engravers were not at home in Greek. Much the same occurs with another common silver coin from the same general area, probably from Bibracte, which initially read *Doubno* in Greek characters (**311**). This very soon became corrupted to a number of largely incomprehensible variants (**427**). Corrupt Latin legends occur too but they are relatively few.

On bronze coins Greek legends are even more scarce. The legend *Smer* is not well located, but may belong to the Marne (**429**). On potin coins we have two apparently plain Greek legends, *Aged* and *Ouindia* which belong to Oise and Côte-d'Or respectively (**430**, **431**). In their case, however, appearances would suggest that they are very late and probably post-Caesar. In general the rarity of bronze coins with plain Greek legends seems to suggest that this script was on the way out before the great floruit of bronze coins in the latter part of the first century B.C.

Mixed Scripts in Central and Northern Gaul

Mixed legends and scripts are much more common. The first class consists of coins, on one side of which has a legend in Greek characters and the other the same legend in Roman. There are three instances of this. Firstly there is a silver coin from the Vosges and Lorraine (just to the north of the *Kaletedou* and *Doubno* coins) reading *Solima* in Roman letters on the obverse and Greek on the reverse (**308**). Secondly, in the Seine district east of Paris on the southern borders of Belgic Gaul, are found gold, silver and bronze coins with the legend *Roveca*, occasionally *Rovecu* (**254–8**). Among the bronze coins there are several examples of dual legends of this kind and there is a very similar bilingual bronze coin reading *Epenos* from the same area. The legends are equally prominent, which seems to suggest that in this part of Gaul it was expected that those who could read should be familiar with one or the other of the two civilised scripts of the time, or perhaps that a civilised ruler should display acquaintance with both. The *Solima* coins certainly precede the conquest, the bronze coins may well be after it, but not long after.

There are other examples of the same linguistic duality. We have bronze coins from north of Paris which have the legend *Deiviciac* (clearly the name we know as Diviciacus) either in mainly Greek letters or in plain Roman (**432**). The Greek version was amongst the coins found at Alesia and shortly precedes the Roman conquest of Gaul. A ruler of the Treveri, *Arda*, gives his name in Greek on his gold coins but in Roman letters on his bronze ones (**433**, **434**).

By far the largest class, however, is composed of coins with legends that themselves contain a mixture of Greek and Roman characters. A good example is the bronze coin from the Paris district, with the legend *Venexetos*, but I fear not clearly shown on the specimen shown as **435**. It is boldly engraved and forms a prominent part of the pattern. It starts with a Roman V, uses an X probably for a sibilant, and ends with a round Greek C for S, the usual form on these coins. The letter K is somewhat of an interloper in Latin, but it is commonly used on coins with otherwise Roman letters; on one bronze type from Belgic Gaul it is interchangeable with C, *Conat* or *Konat*. The legend KPACCUS might be a rendering of the name Crassus in partly Greek letters, but to confuse the issue it ends in a Roman S. The finest example, which can be dated to a few years before 54 B.C, is the bronze coin with on the obverse the Roman legend *Tasgetios* and on the reverse the mixed legend *Elkesoouviz* (**368**). Here again we seem to have two forms of S. Probably the first inscribed Belgic coin, with the legend *Nide* / *Arbodios* (there are variant spellings) is also in mixed characters; it uses ⊦ for E.

In all, about one in fifteen Gaulish coin legends contains some Greek element. In mixed legends, if we assume the Roman script to be the basis, the letters commonly borrowed are Γ Δ Є Η Θ Κ Λ Ρ C Υ and perhaps X. There does not seem to be borrowing of Φ Ψ or Ω. One can fairly say that mixed legends, which are most common on bronze coins, are centred on the Seine at Paris, but spread some distance either side. If we exclude Θ, which is a special case, and the problematical X, it can be said that mixed legends are rare in Belgic Gaul and absent in Britain, Armorican Gaul and south of the Loire.

We can now sum up the use of Greek on coin legends in Gaul. Excluding the rulers of Narbonensis and the immediate vicinity of Marseilles, where Greek was the natural script, Greek legends proper first occur on silver coins in a belt running from the Vosges and the Jura to the approaches to the Massif Central; they belong to the first half of the first century B.C. Another pocket where Greek was in regular use, but alongside Roman script, was on the north-east bank of the Seine in the vicinity of Paris, spreading towards the Marne; these are mainly bronze coins and are probably later than the silver. Spreading from here, there is a rather scattered area of mixed scripts combining some Greek and some Roman elements. The letter Θ, however, and possibly X also, established itself in Celtic usage and turns up as far afield as Britain. One may conclude that it is wrong to deduce from Caesar's famous remarks an implied generalisation that Greek was, in his time, the script of Gaul. There may well have been pockets where Greek letters were positively unfamiliar. Apart from the Mediterranean belt, wherever in Gaul, Germany or Austria there is writing on the coins, some of it is always in Roman characters and most of it is consistently Roman (figure 18).

The Dominance of the Roman Alphabet

The great majority of legends on Celtic coins are in clear and unmixed Roman letters. This applies not only to the coins of Central Gaul and Britain, but also to those of the Danube Basin. It is also true of all periods during which the legends are found. The lettering is sometimes, especially on earlier coins, scratched on to the dies in a linear fashion that can make it very difficult to read. At times the legends recall the cursive script of popular writing, and some of the letter forms, for instance I I for E, come from it. Often, however, the tops and bottoms of the letters are marked with large or prominent pellets, punched or drilled into the dies, in the place of normal serifs. Legends are sometimes placed between ruled parallels or in rectangular panels, where they form a prominent part of the coin design. Yet other legends are cut in bold Roman letters of inscriptional type. The gradation from one extreme to the other is infinite and, though localities sometimes have preferences for one letter form or style rather than another, it is only in a very broad way that one can indicate different Roman scripts in different areas.

Style of Script

The Roman alphabet on Celtic coins consisted of nineteen letters: A B C D E F G I L M N O P Q R S T V X. To this must be added the Greek Θ, making twenty in all, since it is regularly used in such legends as KARIΘA or VELIOCAΘ. In Britain it generally takes the form of Đ (D with a cross bar) and so anticipates the Anglo-Saxon Đ (thaugh). The forms of the letters are generally those normal in the late Republic or early Empire, but there are occasional variants. Traces of archaic forms are few. Thus the cross bar to A, if present, may slope either way or be horizontal or even, in one instance (*Diasulos*, **310**), vertical, as in Roman cursive writing. Points are occasionally used in this and other letters in place of cross bars (E F G T). E as often as not takes the form I I (double I), lapsing occasionally into a single I. This occurs on Roman coins and inscriptions, but is particularly characteristic of Gaul. O may be large or small, oval or round. Of the consonants, C and G are not always clearly differentiated, but there are several forms of G, one, as far as I know, confined to Britain. F is extremely rare. R and P are particularly subject to local variation. S is reversed as often as not. One usually presumes X to be the Latin X (as in *Rex*) but in some otherwise Roman letter contexts it is probably a sibilant related to the Greek X (chi).

The great majority of legends read from left to right, but retrograde

Figure 19. Coritanian gold stater: *Volisios–Dumnocoveros*

legends occur at all times and letters (Greek and Roman) are occasionally inverted, especially on early or slightly barbarous coins. Circular legends generally, like Roman coins, read from the centre, i.e. clockwise, exergual legends from outside, i.e. anti-clockwise, but this is not universal. Outward-looking legends tend to be the earlier. Where a legend is split into two lines, it does not follow that the upper line must be read first; both arrangements occur. Letters are sometimes arranged in the quarters of a cross; they then read clockwise or anti-clockwise.

Monograms

To save space it is a common practice to compound consecutive letters into monograms. Some are very common and the interpretations obvious. The most familiar example in Britain is the version of *Camul* for Camulodunum (figure 20; **436**); the same form occurs on the Danube on coins of the Cotini in the Danubian area. Others are much more complex and difficult. There is, for instance, a very late bronze coin found in the west of France, perhaps *c.*20 B.C, with only four characters, which are now read, rightly I believe, as VRIDO·RVF (**437**). These were as difficult to read correctly when the coins were made as they are today (figure 20).

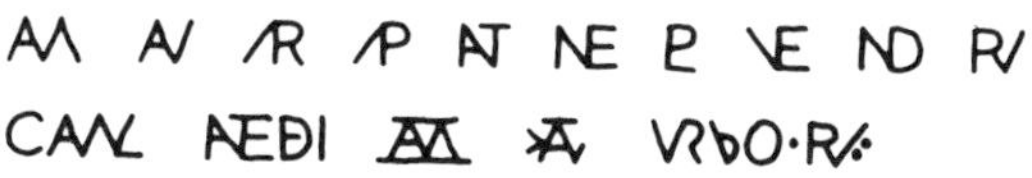

Figure 20. Monograms on coins

Animal forms

An intriguing practice, confined to Britain, so far as yet observed, is to combine letter forms with parts of the coin type (figure 21). The first instance noted is on coins of Tincommius, where the letters TIN are followed by the two ears of the horse, which take the form CO. On coins of the Iceni and Coritani, the legs of the horse on the reverse regularly form the shaft or down stroke of A,E,D or L; the legend is *Antedi* (**438**, **439**). In the legend *Dumnovellaunos* both forelegs are used to make a double L. On coins of the Dobuni the G of RIG in the legend ANTED-RIG, takes the place of a traditional fetlock on the preceding uninscribed coins, no doubt serving, in the engraver's eye, a double purpose.

Figure 21. Animal forms : coins with legend *Antedi*

A promising field of study lies in the different spellings of individual names on the coins, which may sometimes be compared with the versions of the same names in classical writers and in inscriptions. It would take too long to describe all the variants but they should give clues to the pronunciation at this date of Celtic names. The spellings must have been phonetic, not conventional. I can best illustrate what I mean by taking two British examples. Adopting only the longer versions, the ruler we call Tasciovanus has his name spelt on the coins in eight different ways. The ruler we call Dubnovellaunus in Kent spelt his in four; the same name occurs in Lincolnshire as Dumnovellaunos and on different texts of Augustus' *Res Gestae* as Dumnobellau and Domnoellaunos (figure 22). In Gaul the opening syllable is sometimes Doubno, sometimes Dubno, but is never spelt with an M.

TAXCIOVI	DVBNOVALLAVNOS
TASCIAVA	DVBNOVELLANVS
TASGIVA	DVBNOVELLAVN
TASGIO	DVBINOV
TASCIOVANI TASCEOVAN	DVMNOVELLAVNOS
TASCEOVANTI	DVMNOBELLAV
TASCEOVANTIS	ΔΟΜΝΟЄΛΛΑΥΝΟϹ

Figure 22. Variant spellings of *Tasciovanus* and *Dumnovellaunus* (II shown as E)

Of the vowels, A and E often interchange, also A and O; the commonest interchange of all is long I with E (usually written in the form II), or EI. Of the consonants, no clear distinction was drawn between C and G; the name Diviciacus of history appears as *Deiviciac* or *Deivigeag*. CT and XT are used (in *Pictilos*) as equivalents, the X perhaps having an aspirated sound as in the Greek chi, but in other contexts X before a consonant (e.g. *Tasciovanus*) is equated to S. D and S are closely associated (e.g. *Abudos* or *Abudod*, *Caliageis* or *Caliageid*, *Vodenios* or *Vosenos*). And plain D in some, but not all, contexts is distinguished from Θ or Đ. BR and RB can interchange (*Abrodios* or *Arbodios*). Doubled letters are frequent and used consistently; it is rare, even in different areas, for a doubled letter in one not to recur in the other. Thus *Eccaio* in Noricum and *Eccaios* in Gaul are both spelt with two C's. In Britain *Epaticcus* has one P and two C's as consistently as *Eppillus* has two P's and two L's. But so that an exception may prove the rule, *Epillos* on the the Continent has only one P. In addition to I, the letters found doubled are C L M N P S T Θ; in Roman inscriptions doubled consonants were not introduced before the middle of the second century B.C, but become common before the end of the century.

The Language of the Legends

The great majority of legends consist simply of personal names, sometimes in full, more often truncated so that we do not know the terminal letters. They are not Latinised; thus the universal termination of the ordinary form of name is -OS down to the Roman conquest of Gaul. The termination -VS was only introduced in Gaul after that, and it never wholly ousted -OS. In Bohemia it is equally late in names like *Busumarus*, *Cobrovomarus*, *Iantumarus* and *Maccius* (83, 84); compare the earlier *Nonnos* (78). In Britain, -VS only occcurs in Kent in the names *Dubnovellaunus*, *Eppillus* and *Ammius* and as a rare spelling of *Cunobelinus*; it is never found in the outlying areas of Britain, where -OS is universal.

These personal names are nearly always in the nominative, when they are given in full. There are numerous terminations; in addition to -OS and -VS, many end in A or V, some in -IX, -EX or -EIX, yet others in -IS, -ES or -AS. Legends ending in -O or -IO or sometimes in -I, -E or -IA may leave us in doubt as to the true ending of the name; unquestionably the final -S or many legends ending in -OS is omitted as in archaic Roman inscriptions, while in other cases -O is certainly the correct nominative ending. There are a few examples of the principal name in the genitive. Thus in Britain the name of Cunobelinus is occasionally given as *Cunobelini*, and there are coins of Tincommius and Tasciovanus that end in ambiguous monograms, which may contain a genitive. On the Continent the best example is a coin of Vercingetorix that ends with the letters -RIXIS (204) presumably the genitive form. As a rule, however, the genitive is ordinarily used only where there are two names on the coin and it then indicates the issuer's father.

The normal full form of the Celtic personal name has always been so-and-so the son of so-and-so. This does occur, but outside Britain it is not common. However, many double legends where one or both names are truncated may conceal such pairs of father and son. The best example from Gaul is on the Aeduan coin which reads *Orgetirix Atpili F. Q. Doci Sam F.* is another (295, 301). In Britain we have coins of the three sons of Commius who give their father's name in the genitive with or without some abbreviation of *filius* (440–2); similarly two sons of Tasciovanus (443–5). It is interesting that the word used to indicate 'the son of' is the Latin *filius*, never the Celtic *Mac*. Where on these coins – and it alone arises over late ones – some word is wanted in addition to the name or names, it is normally a borrowed Latin one.

In Gaul, but not elsewhere, we meet both before and after the conquest traces of Roman influence in the customs of naming. Thus on silver coins that are certainly not later than the early part of the first century B.C. we have a legend *Cn. Vol.* or *Volunt* (285), and again pre-conquest is *Q.Doci Sam F.*, while on a later bronze we have *T.Pom.Sex.F.* (385). It became fashionable in the forties and thirties to attach the name Julius (never Caesar) to a Celtic name; thus we have a *Q.Julius Togirix, Julius Duratius* or *Gaius Julius Agedomapas* (this one in the genitive) (**299, 325**). On a rather different level the legend *Germanus Indutilli L.* (for *libertus* or freedman) is notable as a Roman usage. It is right at the end of the series (**381**).

Another feature of post-conquest coins in Gaul is the widespread use of tribal names in conjunction with the normal personal name. These tribal names have caused some confusion because they are not descriptive of the tribe of the coin, but of the issuer; the fact that he uses a tribal name at all can mean that he was a stranger in the area where the coin was issued, but not always. Caesar describes many chieftains in this way, Commius Atrebas, or Lucterius Cadurcus for instance; the coins give us, to mention a few only, *Orgetorix Eduis, Arivos Santonos, Arus Segusiaus,* and *Atesios Remos* (**300, 335, 336, 446–8**). This usage is to be distinguished from the use of a tribal name for the coin itself, like the legend *Remo* (**373, 374**).

The persons whose names are on the coins only sometimes tell us their function. In Spain we have already met *duumviri* and *aediles*; in Narbonne we have met the title *Basileus*, King. In Gaul, despite the frequent use of *Rex* by Caesar to describe tribal chieftains, we only have one coin that uses this title; this is the coin of Adietunnus of the Sotiates or Sontiates, who is noticed by Caesar in the year 54 B.C. as exercising the *summa imperii* at the tribal oppidum (*B.G.* 3.22.1). The coin reads on the obverse *Rex Adietuanus Ff*, and on the reverse *Sotiota* (**129**). The final letters of the obverse legend F F have been thought to carry a Latin interpretation such as Felix, Faustus or Fortunatus, but perhaps more probably represent *flavit feriit*, 'cast and struck' (compare AAAFF on Latin coin inscriptions). In Britain, by contrast, we have three kings who describe themselves regularly as *Rex*: Eppillus, Verica and Cunobelinus (**449–51**), and one who described himself as *Rigoni*, Tasciovanus (**452**) – if this is not part of a double-barrelled name. The concentration of regal inscriptions in Britain is a mark of its continuing independence after the conquest of Gaul.

Only slightly more common in Gaul are coins that give a magistral title, and they all appear to be post-conquest. Bronze coins of the tribe of the Lexovii, who lived around Lisieux, introduce two titles, *Vergobreto* and *Arcantoda* (**453–5**). Caesar mentions elected magistrates amongst the Aedui who were called *vergobreti*. There were one or perhaps two at a time; both interpretations are possible. On the coins of the Lexovii with the *Vergobreto* legend there are also two personal names in the nominative – *Cisiambos* and *Cattos*. The first of these names occurs too in other combinations, or alone, without the title. In one of these combinations the second name, *Maupennos*, is accompanied by the word *Argantoda*, without doubt another title, although it is unknown from literary sources. We find it again on the Belgic bronzes of *Roveca* in the form *Arcantodan* (**456**) and as *Arc* or *Arg* on bronzes from further east reading *Ambact(us)* (**457**, **458**). We can be certain that this word, which incorporates the root argent- (cf. Latin *argentum*) is the word – or at least a word – for the moneyer magistrates of the Celts in the Roman era.

One may suspect that the title had also a wider currency. Several of the silver tetradrachms of Noricum have a subsidiary legend AR in monogram, high up behind the rider on the reverse (**60**); but other explanations are equally possible. Other comparable unexplained secondary legends could also convey magistral titles in pretty well all areas, for instance the monogram *Mat* (or it could be *Tam*) on silver tetradrachms of Bohemia; but this particular legend may have a magical significance – compare the *Mat* that marks the long or strong months of the Coligny Calendar.

Oddly enough we do not find the Latin title *Duumvir* on Gaulish coins at all, although there is much reason to suppose that many of the silver and bronze coins of Gaul were issued by or in the name of magistrates operating in pairs, that is to say *duumviri*. We have many instances of two names in the nominative, usually on opposite sides of the coin, sometimes on the same side. In even more cases we have abbreviated names, which look as if they may stand in the same relationship. In the horseman coins of the Rhône valley we have a sequence of some twenty different pairs of names (e.g. **285–8**). At a later date we have several series of bronze and silver coins that show the same feature on a smaller scale; for example in Belgic Gaul we have seen the sequence *Carsicios / Commios*, *Garmanos / Commios* and *Andobru / Garmanos*. An interesting coin reads *Orgetirix Coios*; since from other coins, already mentioned, we know that Orgetirix was an Aeduan and that his father was Atpilos, Coios can hardly fail to be a colleague. There seem to be only two gold coins in Gaul with a double name of this character, read as *Anteribid/Solim* and *Seno/Omodon*; but we have a sequence of seven such legends abbreviated in Britain in the gold and silver coins of the Coritani (**459–61**).

There can be little doubt that underlying this series of double names is a magistral system that the Romans would have described as *duumviri*; there are even cases of possible *triumviri* in the legends *Epad / Cicedu / Bri* and *Connos / Epillos / Sedullus* in Gaul or *Dumno / Tigir / Seno* in Britain. The earlier double (and treble) names occur amongst the silver and bronze coins found at Alesia. The system certainly preceded the conquest, but the majority of them are probably post-conquest. One must not, however, jump from this to the conclusion that all Celtic moneyers operated in pairs; indeed one can point to long series of names in different areas of Gaul, Britain, Austria and Bohemia, where quite clearly one single ruler or chieftain succeeded another as the issuer of the coinage. The double name *Ateula Vlatos*, for instance, must go closely with coins showing the single name *Senodon*.

Both in Belgic Gaul and Britain (the Dobunni) we have staters with a sequence of single names (**462**, **463**).

A special case of double names lies in the group of coins associated with the name of Aulus Hirtius, Caesar's collaborator. In addition to the coins of Belgic Gaul in Hirtius' own name (**383**, **384**, **464**) there are similar coins in the name of Carrinas – we have a series of three types of bronze coin which have Hirtius' name with the title *Imperator* on the obverse and the names of three different Gallic chieftains on the reverse. Similarly from Languedoc we have coins with the name of L. Munatius Plancus, *propraetor* of Celtica in 44–43 B.C, with three obviously Celtic names on the reverse.

The emphasis throughout is on personal names, but some other legends occur. Only a few Celtic coins bear the name either of the mint town where they were struck or of any issuing tribe as such. Outside the area of Greek and Celt-Iberian legends, where there are plenty of examples of town names, and the more or less Romanised coins of Nîmes and Lyons, there is no sure example on the Continent of the use of a town name. Only in Britain do we have the three definite mint names *Calleva* (**465**), *Verlamio* (**466**) and *Camuloduno* (**436**, **467**), in full or shortened, to indicate these major oppida. In each case the name is in the Latinised ablative or locative form. This may imply that in Britain of the late first century B.C. and the early first century A.D. towns mattered more than tribes; on the Continent it has been the Celtic tribal, not the town names, that have survived into the contemporary language.

Outside Britain, although even these instances are rare, the name of the mint town is taken by that of the issuing tribe. In some cases, mostly bronze, the legend consists solely of the tribal name. From before the conquest we have seen the coins of the Remi with the legend *Remo* on both sides; from a later date no doubt, we have three types of the Aulerci Eburovices, which give the name as *Aulirco* or *Aulirco Eburovico*, or simply as *Aulircus*, interesting as the use of the ethnic adjective in the singular. Other examples are the Volcae Arecomici (**468**) and the Mediomatrici (**469**). We have already met the coins of the Lexovii, where the tribal name is given either as *Lixoviatis, Lixovio* or

Lexovio (453–5). On a silver coin from the Vernon hoard of *c.*45 B.C. we have the legend *Lemiso Ex S.C.*, referring no doubt to the authorising decree of the senate of the local civitas.

In Britain we have only one possible use of a tribal name on the coins, *Ece* or *Ecen*, which is found in the region of the Iceni (470). It is one of a series of names, the others of which are with little or no doubt personal; but it is the commonest, and within the coins of this legend there are three distinct blocks of dies, as if there were three distinct issuers. It is, therefore, likely to reflect the tribal name, but it is salutory to compare a silver coin of Gaul, found at Alesia and hence pre-conquest, with the legend *Sequanoiotuos* (313, 314). The type comes from the general area of the Sequani and the name appears to be a personal one employing the tribal name as the first element. One may suspect other such cases.

Another recognisable form of legend is the description of the denomination. This occurs in full only on the bronze coins of the Lexovii, as *Publicos Simissos* or *Semissos* (chapter 1, above), a typical combination of Latin loan word with Celtic termination. An independent S or Z on some other bronzes has been noted, which may also refer to the denomination, but in no instance is this certain.

The Significance of Legends

I will now, at the expense of generalisation, try to draw the threads together. Whose names are on the coins? Why were they there? What were the legends intended to convey?

The persons who put their names on the coins were not all of the same capacity. We have met those who call themselves Kings, Duumviri, Aediles, Vergobreto, Arcantodan and in one case a Freedman, but most offer no description. They are, in each case, no doubt, the person who took honourable and public responsibility for the value of the coins. Some issuers may have been no more than the smith, turned moneyer, who made the coin. Others were great men, the recognised head of the tribe or confederation of tribes, such as Vercingetorix or Cunobelin. Far more, however, were probably magistrates chosen, amongst other duties, to supply the coinage; this was the practice in the late Roman Republic and it was certainly borrowed both before and after the Roman conquest. The commonest inscriptions are of persons unknown to history. Of the plethora of chieftains who appear in the pages of Caesar, we can plausibly identify less than a dozen as the issuers of coins, yet coins of the war years abound. After the conquest, we can be sure that the issuers, like the freedman Germanus, were favoured citizens in their respective areas, acting with the tacit approval of Rome.

The general absence of coherent patterns on the Continent contrasts with the relative order of coinage in Britain. This is because inscribed British coinage is post-Caesar and influenced by the Imperial Roman coinage available across the Channel. It is no coincidence that in Britain we can identify Commius, Tincommius, Verica, Dubnovellaunus, Cunobelin and Caratacus of the coins with kings or chieftains known to us from other sources. Yet even in Britain, there are gaps; if Cogidubnus issued coins at all, they were no more than copies of the bronzes of Claudius.

Consistent throughout is the stress on the personal name; only in Spain and Narbonne and on a few post-conquest coins from Gaul do the legends mention tribes. The tendency of commentators has been greatly to over-emphasize the tribal character of Celtic coinage. The gold coins of Gaul, on which legends are rare, are generally found in isolated places, perhaps near the homes and farmsteads of their owners; in contrast the silver, and more especially the bronze, are concentrated in the oppida. While we are no doubt right to group many of the late pre-conquest coinages under the main known tribes, everything points to the issue of much silver and bronze on a more local basis. One may state as a general rule that it is the chieftain, not his tribe or city, who issued the coins from the oppidum where he held sway. Eventually we should be able to prove many of the oppida of issue, as *Criciru* has been fixed at Pommiers.

The presence of legends implies some one to read them; but it was not the public at large. The educated few will have contained the merchants and the bankers and perhaps the priests and other leaders. They would have known that, as on Roman Republican coins, an honorific superscription was proper to the maker or magistrate. The language of the coins carries no implication of a written Celtic literature; on the contrary the legends in Gaul, when not giving simple personal names, go out of their way to emphasize the admixture of Latin or occasionally Greek. The mixed Greek and Latin scripts, as well as the bilingual legends, suggest that the spread of classical cultures before the Conquest, and even afterwards, was confused and superficial. Writing, whatever the script, was always recognised as a borrowed practice, for public and business purposes. There is nothing on the coins to suggest that writing was in any way the prerogative of priests or druids.

The coins show heads, beasts, scenes and objects, many no doubt with ritual or symbolic meaning, but in no single instance does an accompanying legend give us an interpretation. There is much in common between the legends, spelling and writing of the coins in Britain, Bohemia, and Gaul. This is partly due to common origins in the coins and cursive writing of Rome, partly also to the existence of a common language and the repetition of Celtic names in different areas. But one doubts if it ends there; the coins did not pass to and fro in any quantity, except in the confused period of Caesar's wars and immediately after, when Celtic coinage became thoroughly mixed. The inference surely is that, even if the money did not travel, ideas or fashions did.

The legends fail to give us any picture of the true value of the coins to their owners or of the use to which they were put. This can only be deduced from the circumstances of their finding, for instance from waves of hoarding, from association with temple deposits or from juxtaposition with contemporary Roman and Greek coins, on which we are better informed.

Although, compared with the number of legends, the sum total of conclusions is not great, I hope that it adds up to an intelligible picture. There are still many readings in doubt, and what I have been able to assemble here has depended to a large extent on new and reliable readings on Continental coins provided by Dr Colbert de Beaulieu.

In my final chapter I shall turn to the theme of Celtic coin types. If the coin legends leave many questions unanswered, the subjects depicted leave many more; but they do, I believe, provide, in a limited way, a picture of how the chieftains, whose names we have met, sought to present themselves to their contemporaries, and of the world in which they passed their lives.

7

Coin Types

I shall devote the last chapter of this book to an analysis of Celtic coin types. In the previous chapters, incidentally to the story, a great variety of designs, subjects, and treatments have been described. Now I shall try to arrange these and other coin types so as to give, if possible, some insight into the minds of their engravers and users.

As we have seen, there was an element of imitation in the types of most Celtic coins. It was the first intention of their makers to produce what would at any given time look like familiar and acceptable coins. No doubt the Greek and Roman models were themselves subject to some kind of 'interpretatio Celtica', and certainly each deviation carries us further away from the original towards something specifically Celtic.

We must not attribute to the engravers artistic intentions outside their age and place. Their job was to produce in a traditional manner something for ordinary use; innovations were permissible only within a general convention and sometimes a more local one as well. This basis in a tradition is common to all primitive art but Celtic coinage has the distinction that, instead of growing from seeds within itself, it never entirely forgets its link with the sophisticated culture of the Greek and Roman world to the south.

May I remind you of the four stages in the development of Celtic coinage. In the first place there is plain imitation of Greek or later Roman models, with which I couple recollections at several removes. Secondly there is disintegration, the break-up of the original design into fragments. Thirdly, there is re-integration, when the engravers tried to create their own kind of sense from the pieces; this is generally the phase of greatest inventiveness. Fourthly and finally, there is the reassertion of the Roman influence, often producing a hybrid phase of much interest, which is neither Celtic nor Roman, but both at once. The finest craftsmanship in engraving may be met with in any of these steps, which did not derive from the skill of the engraver, but from his objective.

I shall be particularly concerned with the third and fourth of these stages, since it is then that the full range of the subject matter of the coins is reached. One is never far away from Roman inspiration, but the actual copying of Roman coins without deliberate variation or adaptation is surprisingly rare. In the process of adoption the original assumes a new form, which one cannot doubt had a clear meaning to the Celts by, and for whom, it was made. We can be sure that it is insufficient merely to call a coin type a Janus, a Medusa or a Pegasus, but if we try to go beyond the simple Greek or Roman interpretation, we are instantly in difficulties.

At the time of the coins in question, our knowledge of the religion of the Celts is mainly drawn from classical writers, who automatically subjected what they saw and heard (sometimes inconsistently) to the concepts of the Roman pantheon. A little later this source is supplemented by the inscriptions and monuments of the Roman Empire, which are somewhat coloured by the same class of equations. Finally we have the magnificent literatures of Ireland and Wales, with their rich stories of deities and heroes.

From these sources it is clear that we have not one Celtic religion but many. Even if the gods and heroes of different times and places have powers, attributes and interests in common, even if the approach to worship and propitiation were often similar, there is nothing that can properly be called a system. The gods of the Celts dwelt on earth; they belonged to the local soil and woods and rivers. There was no biblical canon of myth; the tales of the seers and poets grew longer and wilder in the telling.

It needs no argument to show that the heads, figures and beasts of Celtic coins, once released from the thraldom of plain imitation, were basically religious, mythological or heroic. In some cases their supernatural character is self-evident; in others, where the outward appearance is of ordinary men or animals, it may be inferred; no clear distinction was drawn between the earthly and what lay beyond. It should occasion no surprise that in scarcely more than half a dozen cases can we even guess at the name of the deity or hero depicted; in no single instance do we have a legend that identifies the subject. It follows from the nature of Celtic religion that, while we can to some extent group and classify the subjects, which have a cousinly relationship with some of the figures of Celtic religion as known from other sources, we cannot construct a pantheon from the coins. Yet collectively they remain one of the most extensive and suggestive sources for the religion of the Celts in the second and first centuries B.C. There is nothing on the Gundestrup cauldron that does not have its parallel somewhere or other on the coins.

Representation as such was never at any time a main purpose of the

Celtic coin engraver; but sometimes it was incidental to the effect at which he aimed. Given the mythological and heroic character of the coins, we should expect what is depicted on them to be twice the size of life. The coins do not present any simple picture of life as it was lived in Celtic times; nevertheless, engravers drew something from their day-to-day experience, which comes through.

Though we can sometimes legitimately treat coins of this, as of other ages, as works of art, it must not be overlooked that they were objects of mass production, even in those times (say ten thousand coins struck per die), and to some extent also of mass consumption; standards were not maintained continuously against the pressure of demand. The best is representationally and ideally very good; but by any proper standard of art there is much that was rubbish.

Heads

Most Celtic coins have a head on one side. The tradition began on the coins copied, which bore on one side a Zeus, an Apollo, an Artemis, a Persephone, a Janus or a Bellona, to mention only the best known. At first it was simply these heads that were reproduced, but most subsequent coins, long after the models had been forgotten, have a head side too. These later heads must have held some meaning for those who used the coins, probably apotropaic. I suspect that in most cases this was the deity, male or female, under whatever local name, who in each locality was regarded as tutelary of the coinage or of wealth.

A large group are positively male. The predominant type is the bearded head of Zeus of Macedonian origin, an awesome father figure (e.g. **13–15**). Bearded heads are not confined to the Danube; occasionally staters from Gaul are bearded, mainly from the Armorican and Belgic areas (**471**, **472**). On Spanish silver and bronze there is frequently a bearded head drawn from the Heracles of Carthaginian coins (**259**, **262**). Beards of all varieties are found on post-Conquest silver and bronze coins, especially in Britain (**473–5**). Most, perhaps, have neat beards and moustaches to match, but there is a large class with flowing, unkempt hair, like classical River gods, which they may well be. The most remarkable, certainly, is the spiral goatee beard on the coins reading *Andecombo*, which belong to the period of, or immediately after, the conquest (**476**).

Two bearded gods deserve special mention. We have heads on the Danube, in south-western Gaul, and again in Britain with a horn in the hair (**25**, **477**, **478**), the Zeus Ammon of classical antiquity commonly shown on coins. We may link him with the antler god Cernunnus of the

Reims statue or the Nodens of the Lydney and Verulamium mosaics, or even the seated figure on the Gundestrup cauldron. His most interesting form perhaps is riding on horseback on tetradrachms from central Hungary (**479**, **480**). There is also a horned female head on the silver coins of Litaviccus, but clearly derived from Artemis on a Roman denarius (**321**). We may also have two-headed or two-faced gods. There are bearded and beardless Janus types, facing both ways, from the Danube as well as from Belgic Gaul and Britain (**153**, **277–8**, **481**); they may be compared with the Janus heads on Roman Republican silver and bronze, and with the many three- and two-headed monuments of Roman Gaul. There are also two heads in profile, bearded in Britain (**482**) and beardless from other regions (**77**), which no doubt are another different mode of representing the same deities as the Janus gods. Indeed there is a beardless tricephalus, arranged similarly, in profile, on the coins of the Remi (**373**, **374**).

Bearded heads are in a minority. It might be expected from ancient descriptions of the Celts (Diodorus Siculus 5.28.3) and their representation in Greek art that we should find the normal face to be beardless but moustached. There are moustaches without beards (**483**), but they are excessively rare. **484** shows almost the only one from Britain. But the vast majority of heads have neither beard nor moustache.

This is partly due to origins of so many coin heads in the beardless heads, male or female, of Apollo, Artemis, Persephone or other nymphs. One may recall Juno Moneta in Rome, whose head appears on many republican coins and is amongst the prototypes of some late Celtic coins. Sometimes surviving features of costume and adornment demonstrate a link with a prototype, but generally, in the absence of beard or moustache, the sex intended can only be guessed at. Mixed origins confuse the picture; coins ostensibly of gold philippus tradition, and hence with male head, may have borrowed ear-rings from the nymphs of Rhoda and Emporion (**485**). A torque belongs to either sex, but perhaps a collar of beads, a not uncommon feature, is exclusively female. Even if these heads were conceived as the tutelary deity of money or wealth in the involved cosmography of the Celts (if that is the right description) no one deity could claim a proprietary or exclusive interest. The sex will have been what in terms of his local mythology any one cared to make it.

The face is sometimes accompanied by ornaments or emblems. There is a notable group of coins mainly from Armorican Gaul on which there is a distinguishing mark actually in the hair, a boar, hippocamp, cross, whorl, wheel, sun, lyre or the like (**212–18**, **486**, **487**). In another case there is a boar upside down on the neck (**233**). We may compare the Boar god from Euffigneix, where the boar is carved vertically on the body. In all these cases the emblem must have been intended to give a recognisable identity to the otherwise anonymous head. There is also the case of the head with a horse walking in at one ear and out at the other (**194**).

More often, however, the ornaments are in front of or behind the head. The simplest case is the pair of dolphins (**488**, **489**), first seen on the coins of Syracuse, and then Emporion (**107**, **108**), but in their Celtic version these turn into cords or crescents issuing from the mouth (**490**) or sometimes into other forms of beast or ornament. These vary from a wolf eating a man, through birds and horses to suns and whorls. These symbols may provide a clue to the identity of the god, but it by no means follows that they always (or even often) have a meaningful connection with the head.

Figure 23. Osismian billon stater

A particularly striking use of the cords occurs in the west of Armorican Gaul. Here the head, in an elaborate hair style, is framed by a series of twisted strings. At the end of each string there is a small head echoing the main one. There may be two, three or four such echo heads (**218**). It looks as if we have an heroic head in the centre drawing its power or horror from the seething group of severed heads to which it is bound. It is very possible that many of the coin heads were thought of as severed; this is a dominant motif in Celtic art and could be expected on the coins copied from classical models where the head is conventionally truncated. Small severed heads occur as ornaments as far apart as Limousin and Transdanubia (**24**, **123**, **491**). In a few cases there are signs that the severed head (or perhaps an image of a head) was conceived as actually affixed to a standard for carrying. In one Gaulish and one British case a standing warrior or priest is carrying in his hand a severed head (**317**). The separate head is often used as a minor device in the field, as is also the separate hand (**120, 121, 210**); usually open, but once, in Britain, grasping a bunch of sticks.

Figure 24. Billon stater of the Veneti

Facing heads and busts occur, but they are rare. One Belgic type has the facing bust and raised arms of the gods and goddesses of the Gundestrup Cauldron (**413, 414**). I can see no reason why it has become customary in numismatic literature to identify these facing heads (and sometimes profiles) with the god Ogmios. The most striking facing head in Britain is plain Medusa, except that, like Sul on the Bath pediment, it may very well be moustachioed.

Towards the end of the coinage, under the influence of the coins of Rome, the types of head, especially on silver and bronze coins, launch out in new directions. We have many varieties of hair styles and of helmet, but by no means all are drawn from Roman models. Amongst later helmets for instance, we have both a simple bowl shape of Gallic origin (**204**), which was by far the commonest type there, and a more Roman fashion with crest and neck piece (**492**). In one case at least we have behind the head what Jacobsthal has called a leaf crown. Wings begin to appear in the hair or on the shoulders in the tradition of a Roman Mercury (**326, 327, 493**). A v-necked costume is often shown, with the material gathered in folds on the shoulder. Torques are commonly worn. Hair styles seem to show a few of the heads to be those of women, but most are sexless. A masculine knob or knot of hair behind the neck seems to be a British trait, so far as the coins are concerned (**493**), though something similar in style occurs on the Gallic bronzes of Germanus (**381**). Once again we do not have the means of identifying the persons, gods or heroes shown, but the engravers have given us many more individual features than on the earlier, more strictly traditional heads.

Portraits

Do any Celtic coins bear portraits? With the parallel of Roman Imperial portraiture the question is not far-fetched; and the emphasis on the personal name in the surrounding inscriptions could imply an intended identification. The answer must be probably never, and at best not proven. If we take an obvious candidate, the helmeted head coins of Vercingetorix (**204**), we see a clean-shaven heroic face; if one thing is certain about the appearance of Vercingetorix it is that he wore a moustache. One not uncommon silver coin of Cunobelin (**493**) has what certainly looks like a portrait head, but the bust, which is included, has a wing on the shoulder, and there are as many types of Cunobelin which show either a Julio-Claudian type of portrait or a wholely impersonalised clean-shaven face. Strange heads, for instance, on the British silver coins of *Bodvoc* (**494**) could be individual – they certainly bear the outward appearance of portraiture – but they could as well reproduce the accepted characteristics of a deity. And that, I fear, is in all cases the likely explanation. If one wants an actual portrait, one should turn rather to the Roman denarius of Hostilius, with the head that could well represent Bituitus (**495**); it may be compared with some Norican coins or the goatee beard on the coins of Andecombo (**476**).

Are Obverse and Reverse Related?

The tradition of Celtic coinage, derived from its models, was of a head on one side and some different device on the other. It would be attractive to see a connection in subject between the obverse and the reverse, as if the story began on one side and ended on the other. There are other examples where this could be so, especially in Britain, but I only know of one certain instance – the silver coin of Cunobelin on which the hunter goes off with bow and dog on one side and returns, staggering under the weight of the stag he has killed on the other (**497**, **498**). In Britain again we find coins with a fighter on each side, differently armed. We have no case of a coin with a human head on both sides – a coin could not perhaps be placed under the protection of rival deities.

Subsidiary Types

Heads apart, most of the interesting types on the coins occur on the reverses. Outstandingly the commonest device is the animal, although human figures also occur. Most of the animals do not stand alone; the main device is accompanied by one or more subsidiary ones such as a miniature animal or solar emblem, e.g. **233**, cf. **214–17**. The designs were presumably meant to be seen as a whole, but even this is uncertain; in many instances of two figures or devices they can only be understood if they were meant to be looked at from different angles. The secondary ornaments, often common emblems such as suns, whorls, tribrachs, wheels, lyres or boars, are often described in the literature as tribal badges; but when they are interchangeable on the same type this is clearly wrong. One suspects that the die-sinkers mostly chose a variety of symbols or devices from a recognised repertoire for reasons sometimes magical, sometimes decorative, and that not too much is to be read into the juxtapositions. But on some sophisticated types, as we shall see, this scepticism is not justified: the whole represents a carefully contrived composition.

Figure 25. Gold coin of the Aulerci Eburovices

Figures on the Reverse

There are a lot of representations of male figures, comparatively few of female. They are generally, but not always, incidental or subsidiary to the main type. One very large class consists of the charioteer on the reverse of philippus staters. Starting as a copy of a Greek charioteer, he very soon becomes Celticised. He is shown as a man with flowing hair (**499**), wearing a v-necked tunic with pleated skirt and belt. Sometimes he carries in his hand a torque, a sword, a spear or a standard with ship or boar emblem (e.g. **499–502**). Often he holds a twisted thong ending in a square object like a flag or kite (**503**), which I cannot explain but is, I think, also to be seen in sculptured trophies. Sometimes the charioteer becomes detached from his vehicle and floats in space (**504**), where he undergoes the usual kind of Celtic transformation into a pure pattern or into a running or climbing figure, nearly shedding his clothes in the process.

Figure 26. Coriosolites billon stater

Another large class of human figures is to be found underneath the horse on staters from north-west Gaul. There are figures with outstretched arms rising from the ground, winged figures kneeling or crawling, and figures of armed warriors with shield, spear and helmet (**212–15**). The costume, when shown, is essentially the same as that of the charioteers; there is no trace of the breeches that might be expected.

We have examples of winged figures, where the wings can replace arms. They occur on south German and Rhinelend staters, once with the man astride an arrow. We have other similar creatures from North Gaul on horseback (**122**). In Bohemia a centaur similarly has wings for arms (**84**). This was certainly a widely recognised monstrosity, to be distinguished from the normal classical winged Victory, which also occurs (**505**). Thus we have a variety of Victory types in Britain, male and female, including one slaughtering a bull (**506**, **507**, **521**); the female Victories are divisible between those with long costume, as in the Roman models, and those with the same short tunic and skirt as the charioteers. These Victories are almost the only women figures we have.

A great class of figures are the riders on horseback. These start with copies, as in the series of Danubian tetradrachms, but many are designs in their own right. The ordinary rider on a Celtic coin is shown naked just as he is described by Polybius (2.28) at the battle of Telamon, though on a number of British coins he is clearly wearing a cuirass. He rides bareback, without spur or stirrup; only occasionally does the horse have reins or bridle (**508**). He may have nothing in his hands, or he may carry throwing spear, lance, short sword, carnyx, boar or bird standard, bough, sceptre or even torque. The shield, if carried, is usually the long oval Celtic type with boss in the centre (**114**, **120**, **121**, **194**, **318**, **320**, **550**); but occasionally it is small and round (**478**). The helmet is optional, but if worn, there are often ribbons or streamers flowing from it. It is these that turn occasionally into horns. Riders of one sort or another occur practically throughout the area of the coinage, except on the Elbe. A special group of riders are those shown brandishing sword or spear and shield in a posture of ecstasy, the rider in most cases being undoubtedly naked and female (**195**, **255**, **509**). Yet, despite the multitude of riders, we have no certain representation of that best-known of Gallo-Roman goddesses, Epona, who is to be seen on so many monuments riding side-saddle; the only possible candidate is a British coin on which the 'horse' looks more like a fabulous lion and is a clear Roman copy.

Apart from the copies of Greek chariots, where the dividing line between the Greek and the Celtic cannot be drawn with conviction, we have comparatively few representations, but they do exist. The well-depicted chariot on the coins of the Remi with the legend *Remo* has been mentioned several times (**373**, **374**). There is also a coin of *Triccos Turonos* where a spearman is shown walking down the chariot pole (**510**). Contrary to earlier supposition, we can now add a British coin with a chariot. It is of Eppillus of Kent and is only known from two specimens, both poor. We still await one that will really show us what a British chariot and charioteer looked like.

There are also coins that show us fighters on foot. There is the fine group of Aeduan coins of the time of Caesar's wars and the coin of Epasnactus from immediately afterwards, which we have seen. They show the Celtic warrior in full panoply with spear, sword, carnyx, boar standard and shield. On the Aeduan coins he wears the tunic and skirt (**316**, **317**, cf. **318**). On the Epasnactus coin, he appears over-equipped, as if in parody of Roman accoutrement (**329**, **330**). This may be compared with the similarly over-dressed foot soldier of Cunobelin (**511**). The foot soldier with long shield and sword also occurs on the upper Danube and the Elbe, where the horseman is absent (**136**, **137**, **144–8**, **151**). The strange object on the right of **132** is in fact an enormous bird, as large as the mortal on the other side.

The remaining figures are not readily grouped. In Britain, we have a variety of seated figures, mostly sitting on thrones, sometimes winged (**512–14**). On the Continent, seated figures are much more scarce; those there are are often derived from the seated Zeus on tetradrachms of Alexander. The seat or throne was certainly a mark of high office, earthly or divine. Seated figures in Britain include two (**395**, **512**, **531**) where a smith holds a hammer. The hammer god was known on the Continent in some areas as Succellos. He also occurs on one early Armorican gold coin (**515**), carrying hammer and touchstone. Two remarkable potin types show a kneeling or running figure holding a torque in one hand (**412**, **516**). The kneeling or squatting figure is in the posture of the stone figure from Roquepertuse and the bronze one from Bouray.

Finally we may mention some of the more extravagant combinations that occur: a man leading a horse (**256**), a man apparently encouraging a bear to dance (**517**), a dancing figure beside an enormous sword and chain (**191**), another dancing beneath a horse (**518**), and more crudely, the several representations of a man being consumed by a beast, e.g. **536**. This list could be prolonged, but I have said enough to indicate the classes of human figure and activity depicted on the coins. Numerous though they are, relatively they play a small part in the coinage.

Animal Types

Animals easily outnumber men as subjects for the reverses of Celtic coins. They are as often as not fantastical beasts, composed of elements drawn from more than one animal, but in other cases plain, routine, representations of farmyard and forest animals. Often we find two animals on a different scale on the same side of the same coin, apparently bearing no relationship to one another.

Horses. Much the most common animal in all areas is the horse. Where one can tell, this is normally a mare, but stallions occur. The choice of the horse type in a sense derives from the origins of the coinage, but the original Macedonian types copied were no doubt chosen in part because they depicted a preferred animal; it was well within the powers of reinterpretation of a Celtic coin engraver to transform the original horse into any other beast to taste; that the horse remained the dominant type through some three centuries is a significant mark of where Celtic emphasis lay.

At different ends of the Celtic world the horse began as a chariot horse and as a riding pony. In both cases the animal was extremely small by our standards. Later, the horse more often is free; it may be shown standing, stepping, running, galloping or grazing. The tail is usually long and full and often in two or three strands (e.g. **241**); only occasionally on late coins is it docked (**310**, **311**); the mane is nearly always braided. Reins are often shown, and the rings of snaffle bits occasionally, at least in Britain. It is only in Britain and Noricum that we have the representation of horse trappings.

The formalisation of the horse in the most widely separated parts of the Celtic world has many features in common, for instance double legs and harp and pear-shaped heads. Some of these may owe something to the thongs and rings of the trappings. Thongs, too, are apt to emerge from the horse's mouth, like words in a cartoonist's caption. On one coin we have horse and foal (**519**), on several others two horses (**119**, **441**), but the upper horse here tends to lose its forelegs, perhaps by engraver's licence; the same thing happens when two horses are heraldically arranged front to front.

The horse was from an early stage subject to variations of fantasy. The most frequent and persistent was to give it a human head. This is the dominant type in north west Gaul, but it occurs sporadically all over Gaul. In Poitou the human head may wear a bowl-shaped helmet (**211**). The type is certainly related to the classical sphinx and centaur, both of which are also found, but more rearely. We have the sphinx in Spain, Gaul and Britain (**344**, **493**, **564**), the centaur, male or female, in Bohemia and Britain. The British centaurs (**520**) display the well-known taste of centaurs for music, playing pipes or a trumpet.

Similarly, the horse, normal or human-headed, is frequently winged in the manner of the classical Pegasus (**522**); but the early representations of winged horses are not reproduced by copying from a standard classical prototype (**110**, **127**, **128**). A Celtic horse has acquired its own Celtic wings. It is not always possible to distinguish the winged horse, in animal-headed version, from the winged gryphon, composed of an eagle's head and wings, with a lion's body, tail and talons. There are a great many gryphons of different types, more or less classical (**523–5**). Both pegasus and gryphon may be prancing or seated. One may recall that the original gryphons of classical antiquity, who lived in the Rhipaean mountains in the region of the Urals, and well outside our range, were guardians of the gold of the North, but the Celtic gryphon is not confined to gold coin; he is part of the borrowed Celtic phantasmagoria which turns up again, for instance, on the Gundestrup cauldron.

Horses undergo other variations. One is to grow horns, so as to acquire the aspect, rather than the essence, of an antelope (**525**). Another is to acquire a tail instead of hindquarters, so as to become a sea serpent or hippocamp (**217**, **284**). This occurs in many forms and from an early date in Spain, Gaul and Britain. Other deformations of horses are found too, especially when the horse is a subsidiary ornament or part of an heraldic arrangement.

A feature repeated in many parts is the association of horse with bird, the latter usually seated on the horse's back (**526**). We meet it on the silver of Tótfalu and Simmering (**62**), widely in Gaul and again in Britain (**527**). The bird is sometimes an eagle, often a crow or raven. We are much more likely to be right if we interpret it as akin to Badb Catha, the Irish goddess of war, who used to appear in the form of a raven – the

Raven of Badb – than as an observation of nature.

Boars. After the horse, the most widespread animal is certainly the boar. It is almost entirely absent from the Danube basin, but we find it in Germany and throughout Gaul. As a main type its distribution is fairly limited. We have it on the gold coins of the Elbe, on silver coins of the centre and south west of Gaul, on the bronze coins of north-east Gaul and on a very large class of potin coins that spread from east France into Germany (**104, 144, 145, 214–19, 220, 313, 314, 347, 348, 376, 387, 388, 393, 408, 409, 411, 431, 484, 544, 552**). We have it also on some silver and bronze coins of Britain. However, as an ornament accompanying the horse or elsewhere, it is found in nearly every part of Gaul, usually in a somewhat stereotyped or formalised shape. We have one composite beast, the forepart of which is certainly a boar and the hind part a sea-serpent tail.

Figure 27. British boar (Icenian silver coin)

Where sex can be determined, the animal is usually correctly described as a boar, but sows occur (as in **481** and **492** from Britain). The boar is sometimes a real one, charging, standing or sitting; but, as often as not, what is represented is not a boar, but a boar-standard – that is to say an image of a boar erected on a pole for carrying into battle. In some cases this is absolutely clear, alike in Gaul, in Spain and in Britain (**218, 233, 303, 316, 408, 409, 476, 528–30**); in others where the representation is more artificial, one can be less dogmatic, but where the boar's trotters are firmly attached to a horizontal line of ground, this is probable, since most animals are not so attached. Boar standards are a common feature of Roman sculptured trophies.

Bulls. Next in line comes the bull. Here we have two distinct forms, the short-horn animal, similar to contemporary cattle, and the tall-horned *bos primigenius* (**531, 532**). Butting bulls are of Massilian origin, standing bulls of Roman, but the Celtic engravers gave some spirited versions of their own, of which the Gallic coins reading *Ateula Vlatos* (**326, 327**) are the best. There are also similar bulls on British coins, for instance the Dubnovellaunus silver (**532**). The bucranium is an important decorative element, on occasions used as a type alone (**458, 533, 534**). A moon between the horns seems a common adjunct (**533, 534**). Bulls occasionally undergo transformations; the quadruped on the common potin coins of central Gaul, which led to our tin coins, started as a butting bull (**535**).

Beasts. Other beasts are sporadic in their appearance. In some cases it is plain that the engravers had not seen in the flesh the animals they sought to represent; in others that they were merely copying coin prototypes. Amongst the occasional animals with which the engravers were clearly familiar are rams, goats and antelopes. Their rarity seems to show that they had in their true forms little ritual or religious significance to the Celts. Bears, of which there are several examples, certainly look as if they were as familiar as one could expect in Bohemia, Central Gaul and even Britain (**412, 532–4**). Wolves likewise occur, though they are nearly as rare as bears (**118, 129, 536, 537**). They or something like them are not infrequently shown chewing up a human being (**537**). Dogs also are found, but rarely, and they are then rather nondescript beasts. There are no cats, but possible hares. Lions are another matter. They are fairly common and spread from Spain to Britain but are of wildly improbable aspect (**6–10, 81, 112, 115, 253, 257, 275–8, 303, 340, 403, 446, 485, 538**). They owe their origin in nearly every case to the coins of Massilia, but at several removes. They were certainly sought after as the archetype of the ferocious beast, so dear to later Celtic mythology. It is sometimes difficult to say where lion ends and gryphon begins. Prominent also amongst the animals known only from coin prototypes was the elephant, borrowed from the coins of Rome, which occurs in Belgic Gaul (**383, 384**). One must also include in the same class, I think, the dolphins, which are frequent ornaments in one way or another; but they can also be confused with the carnyx having a dolphin head.

Birds. Of the remaining creatures, birds predominate. We have eagles, cranes or storks (**542**), ravens or crows, ducks and cocks, together with a mass of unrecognisable birds, large and small, and sometimes combined on the same coins. The eagles have clear Roman antecedents in most cases (**539–41**). The cock's body often incorporates a human face in the breast (**543**). A bird may have a snake in its beak or talons (**202, 369, 545**). Snakes, too, occur on their own. In Bohemia we have a striking group of silver coins with harpies, human-headed birds, but all the coins come from one obverse die in three states (**83**).

Figure 28. Arvernian gold stater

Of reptiles we have fine examples not only of the snake but also of the lizard (**370**). Perhaps the most typical form of snake is a composite beast, usually with a horned ram's head (**323**, **351**, **544–6**); this monstrosity is mentioned in the Irish sagas and an example of it heads the procession of soldiers on the Gundestrup cauldron (plate 41). This important creature turns up as a free type or as an ornament. Sometimes the body has added legs or fins or tails (**544**). There are examples where the body has a head at each end. In its simplest form, this is the beast we met in the Scythian designs on the Bohemian Coiled Serpent staters (**154**). But though snakes were clearly important in this context, fishes do not seem to occur at all. We do, however, have some most remarkable sea serpents (**547–9**).

Plants and Trees

The representations of inanimate nature are fairly common, but very formalised; they offer evidence for the spread of decorative fashions in foliage rather than for the presence of the plants, flowers or trees themselves. Leaves, usually as borders to the design, are frequent in Britain and in Bohemia, but there are few examples in Gaul. Vine leaves are distinguishable amongst them (**550**). Wreaths of leaves in the hair occur everywhere. Formal trees are used to fill in the background behind an animal. A number of types show a horseman or standing figure carrying a palm or other branch. Ears of corn, sometimes highly formalised, are used as the main or subsidiary design (**551**). Flowers are formalised beyond recognition (**113**, **122**, **302**, **327**, **366**, **367**); but in a small number of types there appears to be a flower in the hair of the head on the obverse. **552** shows a British coin of Epatticus, which displays an excellent tree behind the boar.

The impression conveyed by these types is that the Celts with whom we are dealing still attached a great deal more importance to hunting and the care and culture of domestic animals than they did to arable farming. The plough does not appear on the coins and there is but little emphasis on corn and wine as sources of wealth; but there are, as we shall see, plenty of wine jars.

Material Objects

It is seldom that a material object is the central subject of any Celtic coin type, but a great variety of such objects are to be found in a subsidiary or incidental role. I shall indicate the main classes and significant absentees.

Weapons. We have already met the arms of warriors on horseback and on foot, and occasionally in chariots. In addition to the spears, swords, trumpets, shields and standards they carry, we have separate representations of these arms, as also of bows, axes, arrows and clubs (**96**, **146**, **133**, **261**). Some of these tend to be concentrated in particular areas. The single axe is characteristic of Aquitaine; the axe, single or double with the bow, is also found in Germany and on the Danube. Elsewhere they scarcely occur.

Perhaps the most characteristic weapon we have is, however, the short Celtic sword of the type whose hilt is in the form of a man with outstretched arms (**191**, **502**). Swords of this type are common as main or subsidiary features of the design in Normandy and Limousin; once, as we have seen, there is a chain attached. Longer swords are shown on coins of the Aedui. The carnyx (**553–5**) and the boar standard are very widespread; we have a fine picture of a carnyx-blower's head at ground level with his carnyx erect as a background to a horse (**555**). In addition to the boar standard, which occurs in the hands of riders and foot soldiers as an ornament, and as a type in its own right, we have on the Romanising coins of Espasnactus an adopted Roman standard (**329**, **330**).

Costume. We have few representations of costumes as such but as we have seen many show us the normal wear of the Celtic soldier – a tunic with a v-neck, usually drawn in with a belt at the waist. There are occasional instances of chain mail. A mantle is fairly common, usually flying in the wind. Helmets are shown, generally bowl shaped (**204**), but sometimes with neck protection and once or twice perhaps with face mask attached; a particular example is the Kentish coin showing a trophy (**556**). Helmets were often adorned with crest or streamer, which we see formalised on an exaggerated scale on the Danube but present equally in Gaul and Britain (**120**, **403**).

The almost total absence of Celtic breeches is one of the most inexplicable features of these coins. The loose drapery that we see on a number of British coins when the subject is active or at work, for instance on our Cunobelin smith type (**512**), is noticeably rare on the continent. There is a fine example of a fibula on a coin of Belgic Gaul (**250**) and some possible examples elsewhere. We see many torques worn or carried in the hand and a few as coin types (**121**, **222**, **236**, **310**, **311**, **350**, **351**); it was clearly a symbol indicating the wealth or importance of the holder. Earrings are often shown in the ear, but it is sometimes difficult to distinguish them from the tattoos on the cheek which some coins certainly seem to show; the extreme form is a band across the whole cheek on the coins of the Aulerci Eburovices (**234**). However there is no means of knowing with marks on the relatively blank spaces of the cheek (e.g. triskeles, suns or lyres, **557–60**) where realism ends and symbolic association begins.

Figure 29. Gold coin of the Aulerci Eburovices

We may say generally that the coins give us a consistent picture of how the Celts visualised the human figure and its adornment, which does not vary greatly from one end to the other of the Celtic world. But it by no means coincides with the classical representation of the same Celts in Hellenistic and Roman art. Truth probably lies somewhere between the two; there is no doubt that critical use of the evidence of coinage, seeking to exclude at one extreme that which is no more than copying of other coins, and at the other that which consciously apes Roman novelty, can materially supplement the visual record from excavation finds as to the actual appearance of the Celts.

Temples, Thrones, Statues. Coins are less effective in giving us representations of the outward circumstances of Celtic life. We are not shown human beings in their context. We have no houses as such. If we have temples on the coins of *Durat Iulios* (**325**) and *Viriciu*, which is probable, then the representation is purely formal, a cella with pediment (see bibliography). We do however, have two instances, on late bronze of *Roveca* and *Ratumacos* respectively, of what appear to be temple columns with capitals; these certainly do not comply with any normal Vitruvian canons (**561**). A coin of *Bienos* gives a house within a shrine (**562**, cf. **563**). Of temple furniture we have altars on coins of Cunobelin, one square with flames emerging (**564**), one round without, and what is probably an altar on coins of Verulamium in the form of a post with a crescent-shaped bowl above. On a very striking silver coin of *Arus Segusiaus* (**335**, **336**) we are shown what is obviously a primitive wooden idol, if I may so describe it, to be contrasted with the Herculean figure standing beside it.

Comparatively rare also are representations of homely objects. The chairs or 'thrones' we have seen do not fall into that class; the domestic seat will normally have been a stone, or log, but we are shown various pots or vessels such as the hanging cauldron (**565–7**) or the cup of plenty (**568**). A bull may be accompanied by a regular amphora (cf. **203**, **205**). A smith is beating out a cauldron with an L-shaped hammer on **395**. Lyres, usually four-stringed, abound in formal representation, and we have more modest breeds of horn beside the carnyx (**443**). One has the impression that it was no part of the aim of the Celtic engraver to represent that which was simple and homely, but only that which was bizarre or heroic. Nearly all the few scenes (as opposed to figures) depicted, are in this class, from the priestly figures with severed head, to the hunter struggling home with his slaughtered prey on his back. When we have an apparently simple scene, such as a groom leading a horse by a cord, we should certainly reckon that it has some legendary meaning that we are most unlikely ever to unravel.

Symbolism

This need to look behind the surface of Celtic coin types has made a happy hunting ground for the crankish interpreter in pursuit of devious religious symbolism. The difficulty is to distinguish between the reality of the Celtic pursuit of the bizarre or heroic and what I may call the clichés of the coinage. While demonstrably the highlights represent significant and carefully thought-out patterns, at the opposite end of the scale we have any number of crude and primitive copies, which have little or no intellectual content. Indeed it is only the mid-twentieth-century turn of taste that has transformed such objects as potin coins into works of art at all. Even the best are liable to contain a great variety of minor fill-in ornaments to many of which not too much serious meaning need be attributed. To a minor degree similar ornaments are found on the contemporary down-to-earth and practical coins of Rome.

The most common of these ornaments are rings, wheels and rosettes; these are certainly meant in general as sun symbols. We have similarly a number of crescent moons, though not nearly so many (**569**). Sun and lyre ornaments (**557**) go together, both originally aspects of Apollo. We may also have stars (**115**, **158**), mostly, I think, in an ornamental rather than symbolic role. Ovals, starting as compressed chariot wheels, may become shields or eyes if they must have a meaning; but we have many four-, six- and eight-spoked wheels, which are probably at once themselves and sun-ornaments. Other marks have no clear meaning. S's, V's and O's are ornaments, not letters, used to fill in blanks; so are points and other more nondescript marks. Some of them are displaced elements drawn from a disintegrated head; this is characteristic of Belgic Gaul and Britain, where these elements are used to form the basis of elaborate geometrical patterns. Patterns follow a three- or four-armed construction. Division into three is particularly characteristic, and tribrachs or triquetras are found in all areas; those on the coins of our Coritani (**570**) have an exact parallel on the bronze decorations of the Celtic chariot in Copenhagen, on many of the Danube tetradrachms and on Aeduan staters. There is also a fair number of pure pentacles (**124**, **326**, **510**). Many other standard patterns occur, such as zig-zags and meanders, some of which we know to have been usable for magical purposes. But, as I have said, too much is not to be read into the use of such traditional stock-in-trade ornaments, which were the common property of all Celtic smiths of the time.

In fact we have in these coins an astonishing number of all that was best and worst in Celtic production of the period. There is little if anything to the art gallery of the Gundestrup cauldron that cannot be paralleled somewhere in the coinage of Gaul; and almost as much is to be found on Roman representations of Trophies in the Uffizzi in Florence. Even some of the monstrosities and fantasies of the Irish tales are foreshadowed in it. At the same time, there is no denying that much of it was primitive, imitative and repetitive. The highest expressions are certainly those of north-west or Armorican Gaul, the most advanced representations those of Britain. What I have been able to show you here will, I hope, point the way towards the exploration of this still largely unknown repository of Celtic art.

Conclusion

This brings us to the end of what I wish to say. In the course of this book, my first aim has been to set before you as simply as I can the known or ascertainable facts about the enormous coinage of the Celts. They are not easily come by from the standard literature and are worth retelling in a new arrangement. I have tried to eliminate most of the trappings of speculation and local prejudice with which they are all too often decked. I have sought not to enter into learned controversy but from time to time have suggested new theories. I hope that I have sufficiently distinguished between facts and my interpretations of them. I have inevitably wandered much in time and space, but it has been a part of my aim to show the continuity of common ideas, common nomenclature and common treatment of themes in the different parts of the Celtic world. Each part has something in common, which may be illustrated by pairs of types each from widely separated origins (**571**, **572** rev; **572**, **573** obv; **574**, **575**; **576–8**). In particular, without repeating the well-known story of Celtic coinage in Britain, I have tried to bring out the extent to which Celtic Britain was indissolubly bound with the continental Europe in which its origins lay; and also to illustrate that these bonds were not confined to the nearer parts of northern Gaul.

I hope that what I have been able to show you is new to many of you and that, small and remote though much of my material is, you will have found some fascination in it. Some of the coins are surprisingly common; others of excessive rarity. The basis of study is and will long remain the superb collection in Paris, the publication of which in the last century has provided the foundation of so much that has followed. Nevertheless the collections of Great Britain – not least of Scotland – provide a worthy cross-section of the coinage except, perhaps, that of Germany and the Elbe. The British Museum collection, based on the Morel collection, which was acquired early in this century, together with the resources of the Universities of Oxford, Cambridge and Glasgow, provides an excellent foundation, which can be supplemented by the coins in Edinburgh, Aberdeen, Cardiff and Leeds. Most of the coins I have used to illustrate this book have been drawn from one or other of these collections.

8

Select Bibliography of Celtic Numismatics

In the absence of any comprehensive and up-to-date study, there is no easy route to the understanding of Celtic coinage. The literature is vast and scattered, and it is in many languages. It consists mainly of short articles published in a variety of journals, numismatic and archaeological. Even when the relevant articles are found, any inexperienced reader has difficulty in evaluating them. For a variety of reasons many of the views expressed are not to be taken at face value, and even the identifications of the coins, referred to often by out-of-date trade names, can be troublesome. What is required is not a simple bibliography, which would itself be vast, but a guide to steer the reader through the literature most likely to help him, whether he be numismatist, archaeologist or general reader.

The select bibliography that follows takes the place of notes in justification of the text. In a number of cases comments are added on the nature or importance of the publication. The reader who wishes to test the validity of statements made on subjects that are often controversial will find references to literature that should enable him to make up his own mind.

The bibliography is arranged in the same order as the first five chapters in the text, and is based on geographical divisions. No special section is devoted to coin legends or types, literature on which may be found under the sections dealing with the coins in question. An important problem has been to decide how much to rely on general articles, from which references to earlier literature can be found, and where to refer to actual sources, such as original excavation or hoard reports. No firm policy has been adopted, decisions being taken on the basis of what is likely, in regard to any one subject, to be of interest to English-speaking readers. Even if an article is not specifically mentioned, there will not be much that has been written on the subject of Celtic coins to which an indirect route has not been provided. It will be obvious that the references to literature in the languages of western Europe are fuller than those for eastern Europe. Most readers of a book in English will be familiar with the main western European languages, but will have to rely, in the case of publications from eastern Europe, on summaries in western languages and on the accompanying illustrations and figures. This has been taken into account in the selection.

Although this book is concerned to some extent with the relationship of Celtic coins to contemporary art, archaeology and history, no attempt is made here to offer a guide to the extensive literature on these subjects. Anyone with sufficient interest to follow up the literature on coins will either know, or readily find, bibliographies of the related subjects.

I hope that, in the form now offered, this bibliography will save the reader much of the time and effort that has gone into acquiring an acquaintance with this massive documentation. I hope, too, that it will encourage an intelligent use of the numismatic evidence in the wider study of Celtic and la Tène problems.

> [Editorial note: for a bibliography of D.F. Allen's own writings published by 1976 see R.H. Thompson's compilation in *NC* 1976, 259–71. I would particularly like to thank Dr Karel Castelin for his help with, and suggestions for, the bibliography on central and eastern Europe, and Mr C. Haselgrove for help with the bibliography on Britain. D.N.]

List of Abbreviations used in the Bibliography

AB	*Annales de Bretagne* (Rennes)
ANE	*Alliance numismatique européenne* (Brussels)
Ann.	*Annali dell'Instituto italiano di Numismatica* (Rome)
ANSMN	*American Numismatic Society Museum Notes* (New York)
A.Vestnik	*Arheoloski Vestnik* (Ljubljana)
BAR	British Archaeological Reports
BIAB	*Bulletin de l'Institut archéologique de l'Académie des Sciences de Bulgarie* (Sofia)
BM	*Berliner Münzblatter*, neue Folge (Berlin)
BfM	*Blätter für Münzfreunde* (Lübeck)
BNJ	*British Numismatic Journal* (London)
BSFN	*Bulletin de la Société française de Numismatique* (Paris)
BSNR	*Buletinul Societăţii numismatice române* (Bucharest)
BSPF	*Bulletin de la Société préhistorique française* (Paris)
CEN	*Cercle d'Etudes numismatiques, Bulletin trimestriel* (Brussels)

EC	*Etudes celtiques* (Paris)
INC	International Numismatic Congress
JBHM	*Jahrbuch des Bernischen Historischen Museums* (Bern)
JNG	*Jahrbuch für Numismatik und Geldgeschichte* (Munich)
JRS	*Journal of Roman Studies* (London)
MNZ	*Moravské numismatické zprávy* (Brno)
MONG	*Mitteilungen der österreichischen numismatischen Gesellschaft* (Vienna)
NC	*Numismatic Chronicle* (London)
NCCs	*Numismatický časopis československý* (Prague)
N.Circ.	Spink's *Numismatic Circular* (London)
NK	*Numizmatikai Közlöny* (Budapest)
N.Listy	*Numismatické listy* (Prague)
N.Sbornik	*Numismatický sborník* (Prague)
N.Vijesti	*Numizmatičke Vijesti* (Zagreb)
NZ	*Numismatische Zeitschrift* (Vienna)
PPS	*Proceedings of the Prehistoric Society* (London)
PZ	*Prähistorische Zeitschrift* (Berlin)
RAC	*Revue archéologique du Centre* (Vichy)
RAE	*Revue archéologique de l'Est et du Centre-Est* (Dijon)
RBN	*Revue belge de Numismatique* (Brussels)
RC	*Revue celtique* (Paris)
RGK	Römisch-Germanische Kommission (des deutschen archäologischen Instituts, Frankfurt am Main)
RIN	*Rivista italiana di Numismatica* (Milan)
RN	*Revue numismatique* (Paris)
SCIV	*Studii şi Cercetări de istorie veche* (Bucharest)
SCN	*Studii şi Cercetări de numismatică* (Bucharest)
SM	*Schweizer Münzblatter* (Basel)
SNR	*Schweizerischer numismatischer Rundschau* (*Revue Suisse de Numismatique*) (Zurich)
SZ	*Slovenská zem*
WPZ	*Weiner Prähistorische Zeitschrift* (Vienna)
Wiad.Num.	*Wiadomości Numizmatyczne* (Warsaw)
ZN	*Zeitschrift für Numismatik* (Berlin)

List of Works referred to by Short Titles

Allen D. F. Allen 'Monnaies-à-la-croix' *NC* 1969, 33–78

Blanchet A. Blanchet *Traité des Monnaies Gauloises* (Paris 1905, repr. Bologna 1971)

BN E. Muret and A. Chabouillet *Catalogue des Monnaies Gauloises de la Bibliothèque Nationale* (Paris 1889)

Castelin K. Castelin *Die Goldprägung der Kelten in den Böhmischen Ländern* (Graz 1965)

Colbert de Beaulieu J-B. Colbert de Beaulieu *Traité de Numismatique Celtique* (Paris 1973)

Crawford M. H. Crawford *Roman Republican Coinage* (Cambridge 1974)

CRE C. H. V. Sutherland and C. M. Kraay *Catalogue of Coins of the Roman Empire in the Ashmolean Museum I: Augustus* (Oxford 1975)

de Guadan A. M. de Guadan *Numismática ibérica e ibero-romana* (Madrid 1969)

de la Tour H. de la Tour *Atlas des Monnaies Gauloises* (Paris 1892, repr. London 1965)

Dessewffy M. Dessewffy *Barbár Penzéi* (Budapest 1910–13)

Forrer R. Forrer *Keltische Numismatik der Rhein- und Donaulände* (Strassburg 1908, repr. Graz 1968). The Graz reprint is accompanied by a second volume (1969) containing up-to-date notes (see Bibliography, section 1.1); this is referred to as Forrer II.

Göbl, *Noricum* R. Göbl *Typologie und Chronologie der keltischen Münzprägung in Noricum* (Vienna 1973)

Göbl, *Typenatlas* R. Göbl *Ostkeltischer Typenatlas* (Braunschweig 1973)

Hill G. F. Hill 'Notes on the ancient coinage of Hispania Citerior' *ANSMN* 50 (1931)

Mack R. P. Mack *The Coinage of Ancient Britain* (3rd edn, London 1975)

Nash D. Nash *Settlement and Coinage in Central Gaul c.200–50 BC* (BAR S.39, Oxford 1978)

Paulsen R. Paulsen *Die Münzprägung der Boier* (Leipzig & Vienna 1933)

Pautasso A. Pautasso *Le Monete Preromane dell'Italia Settentrionale* (Varese 1966, 1970)

Pink, *Einführung* K. Pink *Einführung in die keltische Münzkunde* (Vienna 1939, 2nd edn Vienna 1960, 3rd edn ed. Göbl 1974)

Pink, *Münzprägung* K. Pink *Die Münzprägung der Ostkelten und ihrer Nachbarn* (Budapest 1939)

Preda C. Preda *Monedele Geto-Dacilor* (Bucharest 1973)

Scheers S. Scheers *Traité de Numismatique Celtique II: La Gaule Belgique* (Paris 1977)

SNG C. M. Kraay and D. Nash *Sylloge Nummorum Graecorum* vol. v, Ashmolean Museum, Oxford; part III, Macedonia (Oxford 1976)

Villaronga L. Villaronga *The Aes Coinage of Emporion* (BAR S.23, Oxford 1977)

1. *General Works*

1.1

The best comprehensive treatise on Celtic coinage remains Blanchet. For many years the author brought his information up to date by periodic reports in *RC* 28–32, 34, 39, 48; *EC* 1, 5; *RN* 1907, 1922, 1932. A simpler treatment of the Gaulish material by itself is in

A. Blanchet and A. Dieudonné *Manuel de Numismatique française* (Paris 1912) 1–91

The only competitor, as a comprehensive treatise, is Forrer, which lacks Blanchet's critical judgement, and is marred by several theories that even at the time appeared ridiculous, for instance on the Cimbri and Teutones. It is, however, useful, particularly for the east, and its utility has been much enhanced by the Graz reprint of 1968, accompanied by a second volume (1969) containing up-to-date notes by six authors, edited by K. Castelin, and including an invaluable bibliography (henceforth Forrer II).

A shorter introduction to Celtic coins is Pink, *Einführung*, which contains interesting views, but its dates are compressed into an impossibly narrow compass; moreover, too much prominence is given to a supposed connection between Bohemian and Iberian coinage. The third edition does not add to the list of coin finds.

Most recently published is Colbert de Beaulieu, which is the introductory volume to a projected series of extended treatments of particular Celtic coinages including, for instance, the Belgic and monnaie-à-la-croix coinages. It deals with the technical problems of Celtic numismatics, and offers a general interpretative framework for the study of Celtic coinage.

To obtain a general knowledge of the coins, rather than the literature, the best works to keep available for constant reference are *BN* and de la Tour, which are related. The latter, arranged in infuriating order, is nevertheless the vade-mecum of dealers and collectors (to whom its attributions are sacred), but it is only intelligible if read with the former. Together they provide a fairly comprehensive guide to Celtic coinage as a whole, and are the sources of most of the attributions currently used, but they are stronger on the west than on the east. For a concordance of Forrer and de la Tour references see Forrer II, pp.109–16.

Other works of interest exist, but none can be particularly recommended. The following is at least reasonably accessible:

B. Roth 'Ancient Gaulish coins, including those of the Channel Islands' *BNJ* IX (1912) 1–80

A few general articles aid comprehension of the subject, and the following are worth reading:

D. F. Allen 'Wealth, money and coinage in a Celtic society' in J. V. S. Megaw (ed.) *To Illustrate the Monuments, essays on archaeology presented to Stuart Piggott ... on the occasion of his sixty-fifth birthday* (London 1976) pp.199–208

A. Blanchet 'Réflexions sur les monnaies gauloises' *RN* 1951, 21–34

C-A. Moberg 'Om keltiska mynt och antik historia' *Fornvännen* 46 (1951) 1–20, 137–58

K. Castelin 'Zur Chronologie des keltischen Münzwesens in Mitteleuropa' *JNG* 12 (1962) 199–207

J-B. Colbert de Beaulieu 'Umlauf und Chronologie der gallokeltischen Münzen' *JNG* 16 (1966) 45–62 (cf. Colbert de Beaulieu pp.169ff)

K. Castelin 'Zum "Münzrecht" der Kelten in Böhmen' *JNG* 18 (1968) 119–25

D. Nash 'The chronology of Celtic coinage in Gaul: the Arvernian "hegemony" reconsidered' *NC* 1975, 204–18

D. F. Allen 'Temples or shrines on Gaulish coins' *The Antiquaries' Journal* LIII (1973) 71–4

K. Castelin 'Galliens Gold und Cäsar' *Money Trend* 10/1974, 11–12; cf. *RN* 1974, 160–2 (in French)

1.2. *Works Relating to Specific Geographical Regions*

There are now a number of important studies of the coinages of particular Celtic regions that may conveniently be brought together, since they form the basis for the study of those areas and will be referred to repeatedly in the following bibliography.

Cisalpine Gaul (Northern Italy). Pautasso

Eastern Europe. Pink, *Münzprägung*

Geto-Dacian region, especially Romania. Preda; see section 3.1 below

Hungary. Dessewffy, which describes a private collection, now broken

up, and includes material from outside Hungary; see section 3.1 below.
Noricum. Göbl, *Noricum*, which is valuable primarily as a pictorial guide to the Norican silver tetradrachm coinages (see section 3.1 below)
Bohemia. Castelin; see sections 3.1 and 5.1 below.
Central Gaul. Nash; see section 6.2 below
Belgic Gaul. Scheers
Spain. De Guadan
Britain. see section 6.6 below

1.3. *Catalogues*

Although the subject matter is limited in each case to specific collections, the group of catalogues that follows represent a very useful introduction to some aspects.

J-B. Colbert de Beaulieu, F. Blind and P-D. Labarrière *Catalogue des Collections archéologiques de Besançon IV: Les Monnaies gauloises* (Paris 1959, second edn 1967). In the second edition the illustrations are deplorable, but some extra information is given.

J-B. Colbert de Beaulieu, M. Dayet, F. Blind and P-D. Labarrière *Catalogue des Collections archéologiques de Montbéliard, Les Monnaies gauloises* (Paris 1960)

idem *Catalogue des Monnaies gauloises de Jura* (Paris 1962)

S. Scheers *Les Monnaies gauloises de la Collection A. Danicourt à Péronne* (C.E.N. Travaux no.7, Brussels 1975)

L. Reding *Les Monnaies gauloises du Tetelbierg* (Luxembourg 1972)

K. Castelin *Keltische Münzen, Katalog der Sammlung in Schweizerischen Landesmuseum Zürich* (Stäfa 1978). Commentary volume forthcoming.

Most of the research work done in recent years is to be found in a maze of articles. The principal contributors to the subject have been J-B. Colbert de Beaulieu, Karel Castelin, Hans-Jorg Kellner, Judita Winkler, Bucur Mitrea, Andrea Pautasso, D. F. Allen, Simone Scheers, M. Thirion, J. C. M. Richard and Constantin Preda. General summaries of recent work are published from time to time, recently in connection with the periodic International Numismatic Congresses, which now admit Celtic coins as a separate section. The following summaries are worth consulting:

K. Christ 'Ergebnisse und Probleme der keltischen Numismatik und Geldgeschichte' *Historia* VI (1957) 215–53

K. Castelin 'Die keltische Numismatik in der Jahren 1960–1965' in *A Survey of Numismatic Research 1960–1965* (INC,

Copenhagen 1967) pp. 119–49

J-B. Colbert de Beaulieu, bibliography for France, Italy and Czechoslovakia 1966–71, in *A Survey of Numismatic Research 1966–1971* (INC, New York 1973) pp.263–73

K. Castelin, bibliography for Switzerland, West Germany, East Germany and Austria 1966–71, ibid. pp.274–86

S. Scheers, bibliography for Belgium 1966–71, ibid. pp.287–9

L. Reding, bibliography for Luxembourg 1966–71, ibid. p.290

D. F. Allen, bibliography for Great Britain 1966–71, ibid. pp.248–51

G. Probszt (ed.) *Numismatische Literatur Osteuropas und des Balkans I* (Graz 1960), *II* (Graz 1963)

1.4. *Iron Currency Bars*

Although not numismatic in the ordinary sense, it is desirable to take account here of the literature on iron currency bars, a form of ingot currency that preceded coinage in Britain and the Rhineland. The most useful summary in English is

D. F. Allen 'Iron currency bars in Britain' *PPS* XXXIII (1967) 307–35

In addition, British hoards have been found at Danebury, Wiltshire, and Gretton, Northamptonshire.

2. *The Silver Belt: Central Sector*

2.1. *Massilia Imitations of the Po Valley: Gallia Cisalpina (Italy north of the Po)*

The standard work on this subject is Pautasso, which presents, with excellent enlarged illustrations, all the material on record. It does not draw all the conclusions possible from this material, territorial and chronological, and it is probable that in minor respects the chronology suggested needs amendment. Nevertheless, the material is there for study, including references to past literature of significance. Attention need only be drawn to the following works, which still have a value:

A. Blanchet 'Recherches sur l'influence commerciale de Massilia en Gaule et dans l'Italie septentrionale' *RBN* 1913, 291–328

H. Rolland 'L'Expansion du monnayage de Marseille dans le pays celto-ligure' *Revue des Etudes ligures* 15 (1949) 139–48

Of interest to British readers is

D. F. Allen 'The Paul (Penzance) hoard of imitation Massilia drachms' *NC* 1961, 91–106

The dating of the series depends on the crucial Capitol hoard from Rome:

C. Serafini 'Tesoretto di monete d'età reppublicana rinvenuto sul Campidoglio' *Bulletino della Commissione Archeologica Comunale de Roma* LXXI (1943–45) 109

There has been much interest in the legends in Italiot script on these and related coins. The principal discussions are in

J. Whatmough *The Prae-Italic Dialects of Italy II* (London 1933) pp. 121–46

which takes up Mommsen's discussions of the subject, and also

J-B. Colbert de Beaulieu 'Remarques sur les inscriptions monétaires nord-italiques en Gaule cisalpine et en Gaule transalpine' *Cong. Int. de Num.* Rome 1961, vol. II (1965) pp. 179–84

2.2. *A Ligurian Group? : The Maritime Alps*

This class of coin has not often been recorded, but most of the known varieties are to be found in Pautasso, which dates them too early. The evidence for the type comes mainly from the Serra Riccò hoard, of which the following is the original publication:

P. Barocelli 'Serra Riccò, ripostiglio de monete galliche' *Notizie degli Scavi di Antichità* (Rome 1926)

Another part of the hoard, which contains the evidence for dating, is published in

D. F. Allen 'New light on the Serra Riccò hoard of Cisalpine coins' *JNG* XXI (1971) 97–108

Further examples are illustrated in *N.Circ.* LXXIX (1971) 14, 15.

3. *The Silver Belt : Eastern Sector*

3.1.

The standard and indispensable work is Pink, *Münzprägung*. It is not easy, indeed sometimes perverse, and the map that accompanies it is deplorable. Yet the route to most information is there. The bizarre nomenclature by which the main types are known come from this work or from hoards. Pink is best read with Dessewffy, which provides as good or better illustration, though it makes no claims as a work of scholarship. Pink's study takes account of and gives references to preceding work, especially that of Ödön Gohl, which, being nearly all written in Hungarian, presents difficulties to British readers. For those who wish to consult it direct, the great majority of Gohl's work appeared in *NK* I (1902) to XXII (1922).

Accessible and still of interest are Blanchet's ideas in

A. Blanchet 'Recherches sur les monnaies celtiques de l'Europe centrale' *RN* 1902, 157–73 idem 'Nouvelles recherches sur les monnaies celtiques de l'Europe centrale' in his *Mémoires et Notes de Numismatique* (Paris 1909)

A useful bibliography is in

A. Barb 'Bibliographie der donaukeltischen Münzprägung, 1920–1930' *NK* 28 (1929–30) 65–6

The essential hoard evidence for dating the series comes from Romania and Yugoslavia; see Preda and

V. J. Hunter 'A third-century hoard from Serbia and its significance for Celtic history' *ANSMN* 13 (1967) 17–40

These are brought together in

C. Preda 'Über die Anfänge der "barbarischen" Münzprägung vom Typ Phillips II' *JNG* 20 (1970) 63–77

idem 'Einige Fragen der geto-dakischen Numismatik' *JNG* 16 (1966) 63–82

Other than these, the literature on coins of the eastern sector is mostly written country by country rather than subject by subject. The more important works, to the extent that I have encountered them, I have arranged by modern countries, which are not always the same as the countries at the time when the works were written. It will sometimes be worth referring also to the references given for gold coinages in section 4.

Romania. The literature here is particularly strong. The most useful publication from the point of view of the British reader is Preda, which provides detailed maps and copious illustrations of the Geto-Dacian coinages. Important articles include

C. Preda 'Einige Fragen der geto-dakischen Numismatik' *JNG* 16 (1966) 63–82

idem 'Triburile geto-dace şi circulaţia monedelor lui Filip al II-lea la nord de Dunăre' *SCIV* VII (1956) 267–88

idem 'Contribuţii la problema provenienţei argintului tezaurele geto-dace, în lumina descoperirii monetare de la Stăncuţa' *SCIV* VIII (1957) 115–24

idem 'Probleme de numismatică geto-dacică (Quelques questions de numismatique geto-dace)' *SCN* III (1960) 43–80, a text close to Preda in *JNG* 16 (1966)

idem 'Aspects de la circulation des drachmes d'Histria dans la plaine gétique et la datation des premières imitations de typ Philip II (trésor de Scărişoara, Olténie)' *Dacia* X (1966) 221–35

B. Mitrea 'Penetrazione commerciale e circulazione monetaria nella Dacia prima della conquistra' *Ephemeris Dacoromana*,

Annuario della Scuola Romana di Roma (1945) 1–154
J. Winkler 'Contribuţii numismatice la istoria Daciei' *Studii şi Cercetări ştiinţifice* III, Acad. Rep. Pop. Romîne, filiala Cluj VI (1955) 13–180

On the important series of facing head coins see Preda p.142ff and

C. Preda 'Monnaies imitant le type "Larissa" et à tête janiforme découvertes a Bugiuleşti (Olténie)' *Dacia* VIII (1964) 353–61
S. Dimitriu and O. Iliescu 'About the issues of the Apollo-Amphipolis type and their role in the currency history of the Geto-Dacians' *Dacia* III (1959) 260–310

The type being linked with the Janus head coins, reference should also be made to the evidence for date in

V. J. Hunter 'A third-century hoard from Serbia and its significance for Celtic history' *ANSMN* 13 (1967) 17–40

The following are well-reported hoards showing the main range of types:

N. Chidioşan, I. Ordentlich and N. Kiss *Der Münzhort von Şilindia* (Oradea 1972)
E. Chirilă 'Der dakische Münzschatz von Crişeni-Berchieş: Beiträge zur Typologie der dakischen Reitermünzen' *Dacia* IX (1965) 185–200
E. Chirilă and G. Mihăescu *Der Münzhort von Căprioru* (Muzeul Judeţean Dîmbroviţa 1969)
O. Floca 'Monnaies "daciques" du type Hunedoara, les trésors de monnaies de Răduleşti et de Sălaşul de Sus' *Dacia* XI–XII (1945–47) 71–104
idem 'Tezaurul monetar de la Cugir (reg. Hunedoara)' *SCN* II (1958) 95–110
idem 'Descoperirea monetară de la Sălaşul de Sus (reg. Hunedoara) şi unele consideraţii asupra monedelor romane republicane de imitaţie' *SCN* III (1960) 89–134
G. Severeanu 'Le trésor monétaire d'Inoteşti (Buzau)' *BSNR* 21 (1926) 7–10
D. Popescu 'Le trésor de monnaies "daces" de Tulgheş' *Dacia* IX–X (1941–44) 201–42
C. Preda 'Tezaurul de la Vovrieşti şi unele probleme privind monedele geto-dace din Moldova' *Arheologia Moldovei* IV (1966) 137–73
G. Severeanu 'Tezaurul din Gherghina. Contribuţiuni la începuturile numismaticei romane in ţinuturile dunărene şi ale Dobrogei de astăzi' *BSNR* 14 (1919) 45–138

idem 'Trésor de Huşi. Ornaments et monnaie daces de la région de Huşi' *Bucureşti* I (1935) 17–36

Bulgaria. The Bulgarian picture is defective. An old account of the hoards from Bulgaria is in

G. Seure 'Trésors des monnaies antiques en Bulgarie' *RN* 1923, 8–153

For authentic and more recent information it is best to turn to Preda, p.328ff, who discusses the type derived from tetradrachms of Philip III. See also:

Y. Youroukova *Coins of the Ancient Thracians* (BAR S.4, Oxford 1976)

Th. Gerassimov 'Kolektivni nahodki na moneti' *BIAB* XI (1937) onwards

Forrer II, map 14, is based on Gerassimov's reports.

Although the majority of the copies of Philip III, both tetradrachms and drachms, are believed to come from Bulgaria, they are not confined to that country; see, e.g.,

A. Metzulescu 'Un album cu fotografii de monede dacice' *Arta şi Arheologia* XIII–XIV (1937–38) 5–13 especially p.7 (find from Pieleşti)

None appear to have been found in hoards dated by Roman coins. For a coin of this class, but with legend ΚΑΥΑΡΟΥ ΒΑΣΙΛΕΩΣ, see *ZN* XXIV (1904) 46; Forrer 177, fig.340 from an example in Berlin. Cavarus is dated by Polybius IV.46.52 to the end of the third century B.C.

Yugoslavia. There is some useful recent literature on Celtic coins from Yugoslavia, in addition to the older

J. Klemenc 'Die Münzfünde in Jugoslavien 1910–1936' *Numismatika* II–IV (Zagreb 1934–36) 124–33

Most important are

V. J. Hunter 'A third-century hoard from Serbia and its significance for Celtic history' *ANSMN* 13 (1967) 17–40

V. Kolšek 'Keltski novci iz Celja' *A.Vestnik* XVII (1966) 409–11

P. Kos *Keltski novci Slovenije (Keltische Münzen Sloweniens)* (Situla, Ljubljana 1977)

V. Liščić 'Nalaz barbarskog novca u selu Ribnjačka' *N.Vijesti* IV (Zagreb 1957) 1–11

P. Popović 'Nalazi novca iz latenskog nacelja na Gomolavi 1970 godine' *Rad Vojvoćanskih Muzeja* 20 (Novi Sad 1971) 147–60 ('Discoveries of Money in the la Tène settlement of Gomolava in 1970')

idem 'Hoard of imitations of the Roman republican denars from the Belgrade National Museum' *NK* LXXII/LXXIII (1973/4) 7–13

K. Castelin 'Bemerkungen zum Schatzfund von Bački Obrovac 1956' *Actes du symposium 'Frappe et ateliers monétaires dans l'antiquité et moyen age'* Jan.–Feb. 1975 (Belgrade 1976) pp.19–27

Hungary. The literature, other than Pink, *Münzprägung*, is mainly in Hungarian. See Gohl's articles in *NK* I (1902) to XXII (1922), the individual articles being listed in Forrer II, pp.335–87. There is also

K. Bíró Sey 'Ket Kelta éremlelet a Nemzeti Múzeumban' *Folia Arch.* XXIII (1973) 29–42

The following, however, are in English, French or German:

Ö. Gohl 'Note sur les monnaies barbares de la Hongrie' *Procès verbaux et mémoires du Cong. Int. de Num. à Bruxelles* (1910) 645–63

idem 'Usine monétaire et fonderie celtique à Szalacska (Hongrie)' *RN* 1907, 170–83

A. Alföldi 'Zur Geschichte des Karpatenbeckens im I. Jahrhundert v. Chr.' (Ostmitteleuropäische Bibliothek no.37, Budapest 1942) vol.1–2

K. Bíró Sey 'The question of the chronology of the transdanubian Celtic bronze coins' *Acta Archaeologica* XXIV.4 (1972) 359–63

K. Castelin 'Keltische Kleinsilbermünzen von Brigetio' *NK* LXVIII/LXIX (1969/70) 3–12

Of particular interest because it included the dies of 'Kaposthal' coins found at Szalacska is

Ö. Gohl 'A szalacskai kelta pénzverö és bronzöntö mühely' *NK* VI (1907) 47–64

Compare the find of dies from Tilişca:

N. Lupu 'Die Münze in der dakischen Burg von Tilişca' *Forschungen zur Volks- und Landeskunde* VI (Bucharest 1964) 5–31

Austria, northern Yugoslavia and Czechoslovakia (Noricum and Bohemia). The most important works for Noricum include Pink, *Einführung*, and Göbl, *Noricum*. The latter does not discuss coin hoards, and is perfunctory on small silver. Others are:

M. Mackensen 'The state of research on the "Norican" silver coinage' *World Archaeology* 6.3 (1975) 249–75

G. Dembski 'Die keltischen Fundmünzen Oesterreichs' *NZ* 1972, 37–73

idem 'Die keltischen Fundmünzen von Aguntum' *NZ* 1971, 43–50
idem 'Die Keltenmünzen des Bodensee Gebietes unter besonderer Berücksichtigung Vorarlbergs' *Jahrb. d. Vorarlberger Museums-Vereins* (Bregenz 1973) 107–25
idem 'Die antiken Münzschatzfunde aus Österreich' *NZ* 1977, 3–11, gives inventories of hoards
K. Castelin 'Wann endete der keltische Münzumlauf in Oesterreich' *MONG* XVII.2 (1971) 10–13
M. Mackensen and E. Wankmüller 'Ein Depotfund norischen Kleinsilbers aus Celje' *JNG* 23 (1973) 77–85
J. Todorović *Skordisci: istorija i kultura* (Novi Sad & Belgrade 1974)

For the coins found on the Magdalensberg see

H. Bannert and G. Piccottini *Die Fundmünzen vom Magdalensberg* (Klagenfurt 1972)

A good summary of the Norican material by Kellner is in Forrer II, pp.61–3.

For the silver 'Biatec' series (Slovakia) the standard work, though not a very satisfactory one, is

V. Ondrouch *Keltské mince typu Biatec z Bratislavy* (Bratislava 1958)

This is basically an account of an important silver find at Bratislava, which is taken up in

J-B. Colbert de Beaulieu 'Notes d'épigraphie monétaire gauloise II: la monnaie celtique de l'Est à la légende MACCIVS' *EC* IX (1960) 106–11

The main collection of illustrations of these coins is in Paulsen. Another useful collection of material is in

J. Eisner 'Mince typu Biatec, nalezené v Bratislavě r. 1923' *NCCs* I (1925) 87–120

The relationship of silver to gold Biatec coinage is discussed in Castelin, and in the articles in Czech that preceded it, e.g. *N.Listy* XII (1957) 157–68.

A useful general summary is in

E. Kolníková 'The finds of Celtic coins in Slovakia and the main problems of the East Celtic coinage' *Actes du 8-ème Cong. Int. de Num.* New York 1973 (Paris 1976) pp.181–7

Amongst the types antecedent to the coins of Noricum, but also related to the Biatec series, are those found in the hoards of Simmering and Tótfalu. See Paulsen and

G. Aldor 'A totfalusi kelta éremlelet' *NK* III (1903) 55–61
idem *La Trouvaille de Monnaies Celtiques de Tótfalú* (Budapest 1904)

For a unique tetradrachm with legend GESATORIX RE / ECRITVSIRI REGI F (or H, 11.98 g) see

K. Pink 'Die Münze des Gesatorix' *WPZ* XXIII (1936) 74–6

and commentary in Forrer II, p.64.

Castelin, *contra* Pink, considers the coin genuine. Kritasiros is known from Strabo 7.304, 313 as a king of the Boii and Taurisci (in Noricum) *c.*60 B.C. The prototypes for the 'Biatec' series of silver coins are discussed in

Ö. Gohl 'A Biatec-csoportbeli barbár pénzek prototipusai' *NK* XX (1921) 9–17 and 63–4

See also

idem 'A Biatec-csoportbeli barbár pénzek' *NK* XII (1913) 41–51

and Castelin in Forrer II, pp.46–7.

Particular attention has also been given to the small silver coins of this region, e.g.

A. Luschin von Ebengreuth 'Keltenmünzen von der Gerlitzenalpe und aus Moggio' *Jahrb. d. k. k. Zentralkommission f. Kunst- u. historische Denkmäler* II (1904) 73–102

Important finds of both large and small size coins are in

H. Bannert and G. Piccottini *Die Fundmünzen vom Magdalensberg* (Klagenfurt 1972)
W. Šmíd 'Die Keltenmünzen des Rudolfinums. Landesmus' *Rudolfinum in Laibach Bericht f. d. j. 1906* (Laibach 1907) 37–49 (including association of fibula and coin in a grave at Mihovo bei St Barthelmä)

Castelin has turned his attention increasingly to this field:

K. Castelin 'K mincovnictví norických Keltů' *N.Listy* XX (1965) 1–9
idem 'Zur datierung der spätnorischen Kleinsilbermünzen' *SM* 21 (1971) 33–7

Transitional small silver coins, also relevant to Bohemia, have antecedents in the Simmering and Tótfalu hoards. See Paulsen and

G. Aldor *La Trouvaille de Monnaies Celtique de Tótfalú* (Budapest 1904)

For the Karlstein type from Magdalensberg see

M. Menke 'Schrötlingsformen für keltisches Silbergeld aus Karlstein, Ldkr. Berchtesgaden' *Germania* 46 (1968) 27–35

The standard works for silver finds from Bohemia and Moravia are as follows (for small silver finds see above, and for gold finds see section 5.1 and Castelin):

P. Radoměrský 'Nálezy keltských mincí' in E.Nohejlová-Prátová (ed.) *Nálezy Mincí v Čechách na Moravě a ve Slezsku* (Prague 1955) pp.1–84

K. Castelin 'Keltské mince z Hrazan' *N.Listy* XXII (1967) 33–9

idem 'Zum "Münzrecht" der Kelten in Böhmen' *JNG* 18 (1968) 119–25

idem 'Znovu o konci keltské mincovny na Hradišti u Stradonic' *N.Listy* XXVI (1971) 65–70

idem 'Stradonice a Závist v numismatické chronologii' *N. Listy* XXXI (1976) 33–44

idem 'Oboly mrtvých u středoevropských keltů' *N.Sbornik* 15 (1978)

On Celtic minting technique and mints in Bohemia-Moravia see

K. Castelin 'Keltische Münzformen aus Böhmen' *Germania* 38 (1960) 32–42

idem 'Keltská mincovna na Kladensku?' *N.Listy* XVI (1961) 41–4

idem 'Moravské duhovky' *N.Listy* XIV (1959) 129–33

The similar work for finds from Slovakia is

V. Ondrouch *Nálezy Keltských antických a byzantských mincí na Slovensku* (Bratislava 1964)

See also *SZ* 9 (1962) 169–86 and earlier work in

idem 'Mince Keltov a Dáko-Getov na Slovensku' *MNZ* 8 (1961) 5–55

For silver of Prague type see section 4.4.

Poland. Although the number of Celtic coins found in Poland is small, it has attracted a large literature, of which the following is only a selection.

Z. Zakrzewski 'O monetach celtyckich znajdowanych w Polsce (Sur les monnaies celtiques trouvées en Pologne)' *Przegląd archeologiczny* III (1927) 216–21

L. Piotrowicz 'Les trouvailles de monnaies celtiques en Pologne' *Eos. Comment. Philol.* XXIV (Lwów 1932–33) 415f

A. Záki 'Celtowie na ziemach Polski' *Rocznik Bibliotheki PAN w Krakowie* 4 (1958) 21–35

idem 'Les Celtes sur les terres de Pologne' *Bericht über d. V. Int. Kongr. f. Vor- und Frühgeschichte* Hamburg 1958 (Berlin 1961) pp.869–73

Z. Woźniak 'Monety celtyckie w Polsce' *Sprawozdania z prac*

Naukowych Wydz. I PAN (1966) 66–72
idem 'Monety celtyckie z Ziem Polskich' *Wiad.Num.* XI (1967) 201–31. This contains the best map of find-spots.
A. Krzyżanowska 'Złota moneta Celtów Śląskich w Muzeum Narodowym w Warszawie' *Wiad.Num.* X (1966) 173. This records the find of a Celtic gold coin in Poland.
K. Castelin 'Złote monety celtyckie w Czechosłowacji i w Polsce' *Wiad.Num.* X (1966) 163–72
idem 'Keltenmünzen in Schlesien' *Arbeits- und Forschungsberichte z. Sächs. Bodenkmalpflege* 20/21 (Berlin 1976) 221–77. This is an important publication.
idem 'Nová Cerekev (Nowa Cerekwia) a Karlstein' *Slezský numismatik* 6/7 (June 1971) 21–2

3.2. *Danubian Tetradrachms in the West*

Evidence for coins from Danubian countries penetrating the western Celtic world is scarce, but it exists. See

M. Thirion 'Tétradrachmes celtiques trouvées en Belgique:
(a) tétradrachme celtique trouvé à Moerbeke-Waas'
(b) tétradrachme celtique trouvé à Torhout' *ANE* 13 (1963) 140–2, 156–7
D. F. Allen 'A hoard of Danubian tetradrachms from England' *JNG* 18 (1968) 113–18
idem 'William Stukeley as a numismatist' *NC* 1970, 117–32

3.3. *Thasos Imitations: The Black Sea Hinterland*

The most recent contribution is

Y. Youroukova *Coins of the Ancient Thracians* (BAR S.4, Oxford 1976)

An important publication, which also includes imitations of the coins of Macedon under the Romans, is

C. Moisil 'Les tétradrachmes de Thasos et de Macedoine I-ère et leur circulation en Dacie' *Balcania* VII (1944) 3–22

An important hoard of art treasures from Transylvania, also containing 'good' imitations of Thasos is in

D. Popescu 'Nouveaux trésors géto-daces en argent, Trésor de Herăstrău' *Dacia* XI–XII (1945–47) 35–69

Other Transylvanian finds are recorded in Bucur Mitrea's annual reports,

'Découvertes récentes des monnaies antiques ... sur le territoire de la République Populaire Roumaine' in *Dacia* II (1958) onwards.

The key country for 'bad' imitations of Thasos is Bulgaria. See

Th. Gerassimov 'Novi trakijski tetradrahmi ot I. v. pr. n. e' *Izvestija na archeologičeskoto družestvo gr. Varna* x (1956) 79–86

and Forrer II, p.85 map 14.

Finds are not confined to Romania and Bulgaria, but to a limited degree occur in other Danubian countries: see Forrer II, p.13 n.22 (Czechoslovakia and Poland, for instance). But the imitations do not occur in Moldavia or Benarabia (Forrer II, p.84 n.321), and they have ceased before the Augustan period (ibid., p.85 n.325). For hoards mixed with Roman coins see Crawford, from which it transpires that Transylvanian finds belong to the bracket 78–49 B.C. (nos 320, 331, 347, cf. 295, 322, 325) and to the brackets 49–45 B.C. (no.457) or 27–2 B.C. (no.490). In other words, as would be expected, 'bad' Bulgarian copies in what became Moesia are later than the 'good' Dacian copies of Transylvania.

For coins on which ΘΑΣΙΩΝ of the original legend is replaced by ΘΡΑΚΙΩΝ see Forrer p.232; also for coins with the name ΚΟΤΥΟΣ ΧΑΡΑΚΤΗΡ. Forrer, p.233, appears to be the only publication of a coin in the British Museum with the legend ΔΗΜΗΤ, on which the Heracles of the reverse is replaced by a rider.

3.4. *Imitations of Roman Denarii (Hungary)*

Again a much studied subject. The basic work, including information on republican and imperial prototypes, is

A. Alföldi 'Materialien zur Klassifizierung der gleichzeitigen Nachamungen von römischen Münzen aus Ungarn und den Nachbarländern' I: *NK* XXV (1926) 37–48; II: *NK* XXVI–XXVII (1928–29) 59–72; III: *NK* XXVIII–XXIX (1929–30) 10–25

This takes up earlier work, including

Ö. Gohl 'A budapesti eraviszkus éremlelet' *NK* I (1902) 17–45

The coinages lasted down to post-Augustan times:

Ö. Gohl 'Eraviszkus pénzek a Lágymányoson' *Budapest Régiségei* VIII (1904) 181–3. (The latest coin was Augustus Imp XII; cf. Bia 1846 hoard, *Archiv für Oesterreichische Geschichte* 24 (1860) 349, where the latest coin was of Caesar, 45 B.C.)

This issue must lie near the date of the Roman conquest of Pannonia, if not after:

W. Kubitschek 'Denare der Aravisker' *Anzieger d. Akad d. Wiss. in Wien* LXVI (1929) 9–15

For a find of dies for Roman denarii from Tilişca (Romania), which should be compared, see

N. Lupu 'Die Münze in der dakischen Burg von Tilişca'

Forschungen zur Volks- und Landeskunde VII (Bucharest 1964) 5–31

P. Popović 'Hoard of imitations of the Roman republican denars from the Belgrade National Museum' *NK* LXXII/LXXIII (1973/4) 7–13

On the import of Roman coins into the Danube basin see

M. H. Crawford 'Republican denarii in Romania: the suppression of piracy and the slave trade' *JRS* 1977, 117–24

4. *The Silver Belt : Western Sector*

4.1. *Rhoda Imitations : The Garonne Basin (South-west France)*

The standard collection of material for monnaies-à-la-croix is

P. C. Robert 'Numismatique de la province de Languedoc, période antique' in *Histoire générale de Languedoc II* (1875) 475–520, and *XVI* (1900) pl. I–IV

A more recent collection of material, whose organisation and interpretation leave room for improvement, is

G. Savès *Les Monnaies Gauloises "à la croix" et Assimilées* (Toulouse 1976)

The principal value of this book is its full illustrations. The archaeological background, which is important, is to be found in

G. Fabre *Les Civilisations Protohistorique de l'Aquitaine, suivi du répertoire des découvertes protohistoriques faites dans les départements des Landes, B + Htes Pyrs, Gers, L + G* (Paris 1952) 146–52

J. Guilaine (ed.) *La Préhistoire Française* II (Nice 1976)

A. Soutou 'L'Aspect numismatique des relations transpyrénéens aux deux premiers siècles av. J-C.' *BSFN* June 1963, 266–7

Monnaies-à-la-croix found in Spain are listed, and coins from the hoards of Valera and Drieves illustrated, in

J. C. M. Richard 'Monnaies gauloises du Cabinet Numismatique de Catalogne: contribution à l'étude de la circulation monétaire dans la péninsule ibérique antérieurement à l'époque d'Auguste' *Mélanges de la Casa de Velasquez* 8 (1972) 51–87

For the prototypes of the Cross series see the important work of

A. M. de Guadan 'Las monedas de plata de Emporion y Rhode' *Annales y Boletin de los Museos de Arte de Barcelona* XII (1955–56, published Barcelona 1968)

For the earliest series of copies see

J. C. M. Richard 'Les imitations de la drachme de Rhodé (Rosas, España) en Gaule de Sud' *Acta Numismatica* I (1971) 39–44

Some legends are discussed by Richard in *BSFN* 1975, 151–3. For the legends UNTIKIA and KEREKONTONA see

A. Soutou 'Deux monnaies volques à légende en caractères ibériques' *Revue des Etudes ligures* XXVIII (1962) 1–4, 252ff

The subject as a whole has attracted modern writers. Two independent studies were in preparation at the same time, both of which give references to the literature: see Allen and

A. Soutou 'Remarques sur les monnaies gauloises à la croix' *Ogam* XX (1968) 101–27, continued in *Ogam* XXI (1969) 155–69 (including a response to Allen)

Both have attracted criticism; see Colbert de Beaulieu, pp.278–95, and

J. C. M. Richard 'Les monnaies gauloises à la croix et le trésor de Lattes (Hérault, France)' *JNG* 20 (1970) 49–62

J-B. Colbert de Beaulieu 'La limite septentrionale des monnaies à la croix et la politique de Rome' *RBN* 1971, 115–31

The main bone of contention relates to the dating of these coins. The studies of Soutou and Allen place faith in the presence of coins of this class in Spanish hoards, of which the best published is

M. A. Basch and M. A. Gorbea 'El tesorillo de Valeria – nuevas aportaciones' *Numisma* XIV/71 (1964) 25–42

There is no comparable publication of the Drieves hoard. Since the only two places in Spain from which these coins are recorded in any number are the sites of two well-dated hoards, it is difficult to disregard this evidence, even if the implications conflict with currently held views on chronology.

For the hoard from Moussan (Aude), with types similar to the relatively early Béziers hoard, see the important publication by

J. C. M. Richard 'Découverte de monnaies gauloises à la croix faite à Moussan (Aude) en 1967' *Bull. Comm. Arch. de Narbonne* 30 (1968) 1–10. Cf. *BSFN* 1968, 245–6 for a summary.

For the Lattes hoard, which is particularly important for the Volcae Arecomici and is fully recorded, see

R. Majurel, J. Arnal and H. Pradès 'Deux nouveaux trésors de Lattes (Hérault)' *Ogam* XIX (1967) 397–433

For finds from Nages (Gard), also important for this group, see

M. Aliger 'Notes sur les monnaies gauloises à la croix recueilles à Nages (Gard)' *Ogam* XVII (1965) 235–41, continued in ibid. XX (1968) 345–50 and XXI (1969) 171–7 and *Celticum* XVI (1967) 42–8

For the coins of Vieille-Toulouse, which are important in relation to the

Volcae Tectosages, see

M. Labrousse 'Monnaies gauloises de la collection Azéma au Musée du vieux Toulouse' *Pallas* IX (1960) 197–202

For the Bompas (Pyrenées Orientales) hoard, which contains dating evidence from Roman coins (to 77 B.C.) for the series of the Volcae Tectosages, see

A. Blanchet 'Chronique: trouvailles' *RN* 1911, 259–60; *Bull. de la Soc. des Antiquaires de France* (1911) 132

For the Saint-Frichoux (Aude) hoard, which contains similar evidence (down to 44–42 B.C.) see

J. C. M. Richard 'Le trésor de monnaies gauloises à la croix et de monnaies de la république romaine découvert à Saint-Frichoux (Aude) en 1856' *BFSN* 24 (1969) 391–2

For monnaies-à-la-croix in the British Museum see

J. C. M. Richard 'Les monnaies à la croix du British Museum' *NC* 1975, 46–55

4.2. *Emporion Imitations: Towards the Loire (West-central France)*

There is very little on this subject. Much has been written on the coins of Emporion in Spain as well as on their local imitations, often with pseudo-legends in Celt-Iberian characters. But on the imitations in Gaul the literature is slight. For the coins of Spain see, for instance, de Guadan, Hill, Villaronga, and

J. Amoros *Les Dracmes Empuritanes* (Barcelona 1933)

idem 'Monedas griegas y derivadas en Hispania' *Cong. Int. de Num.* I (Rome 1961) pp.121–44

A. M. de Guadan *Las Leyendas Ibéricas en las Dracmas de Imitación Emporitana* (Madrid 1956)

J. C. M. Richard and L. Villaronga 'Recherches sur les étalons monétaires en Espagne et en Gaule du Sud antérieurement à l'époque d'Auguste' *Mélanges de la Casa de Velasquez* 1973, 81–131; cf. *8-ème Cong. Int. de Num.* New York 1973 (Paris 1976) pp.135–7

For an imitation found in Languedoc see

M. Labrousse 'Imitation gauloise de drachme ampuritaine trouvée dans l'Avreyon sur la site de Cosa (Tarn-et-Garonne)' *Celticum* (3) 1961, 185–93

For Gaulish silver types derived from Emporiae coins, especially types found in the Bridiers (Creuse) hoard, see Nash pp.22–40.

The common silver coins attributed to the Elusates or the Sotiates (BN 3587; the latter attribution is more probable since the bronze versions bear the legend *Sotiota*) have a typological ancestry deriving from an early type of Emporion, which has not been adequately published. Interesting intermediary stages exist, for example a coin in the Hunterian collection in Glasgow (**126**), but the full story has not been brought together.

An important early group is of silver coins found in Poitou, particularly from the departments of Indre and Deux-Sèvres. For an account of this silver coinage as a whole see Nash, pp.41–59 and 250–5. For an important hoard of the latest variety see

J-B. Colbert de Beaulieu 'La trouvaille de monnaies gauloises de Saint-Pierre-de-Maillé' *Gallia* XXIX (1971) 3–16

The hoard is of particular interest because of the chronological correlation established by the single gold coin it contained.

4.3. *The Impact of Rome : The Rhône Valley (South-east France)*

The background is to be found in

H. Rolland 'L'Expansion du monnayage de Marseille dans le pays celto-ligure' *Revue des Etudes ligures* 15 (1949) 139–48

idem 'Monnaies gallo-grecques' *Cong. Int. de Num.* I (Rome 1961) pp.111–19

idem 'Monnaies de la république romaine trouvées en Gaule' *Actes du XXVII–XXVIIIe Congrès de la Fédération historique du Languedoc* 1953–54 (Montpellier 1956) pp.31–50

For the early Rhône valley coinages Blanchet remains relevant. Almost from the start most of the coins were inscribed; some in Italiot legends, which have been carefully studied. See

J. Whatmough *The Prae-Italic Dialects of Italy II* (London 1933) pp.121–46, which takes up what Mommsen wrote on the subject

J-B. Colbert de Beaulieu 'Remarques sur les inscriptions monétaires nord-italiques en Gaule cisalpine et en Gaule transalpine' *Cong. Int. de Num.* Rome 1961 (1965) vol.II, pp.179–84

idem 'Note d'épigraphie monétaire gauloise' *EC* XI (1964/5) 46–69

Some of the types with Italiot legends (Iailkovesi, Kasios, Iazus) have been discussed in

J-B. Colbert de Beaulieu 'Légendes monétaires de Gaule en caractères dérivés de l'Etrusque' *Actes du 90e Congrès nat. des Sociétés Savants* (Nice 1965) pp.445–50

Later distributions have been studied in

S. Scheers *Les Monnaies de la Gaule inspirées de celles de la République Romaine* (Leuven 1969)

This work, being confined to those coinages where there is a detected Roman prototype, excludes several important types relevant here. The maps need to be used with caution, as they do not distinguish hoards from isolated finds. Nevertheless, this book is one of the most valuable collections of source material yet published. There has been no recent literature on the excluded types, most of which are amongst the earlier ones. It is still worth consulting the Moirans hoard, which provides evidence of the transition from early to late:

G. Vallier *Découverte de médailles gauloises à Moirans (Isère) 1879* (Grenoble 1879); see Blanchet, p. 570, for further bibliography

The most important recent hoard for the study of the later coins of the Rhône valley, all with horseman reverses, and buried *c.*45 B.C, is

H. Müller 'Le trésor de deniers consulaires et de quinaires gaulois de Villette' *Bull. de l'Acad. Delphinale* 1922, no.144, 32

The horseman coins (Vocontii) were the starting point for a large number of other equally important series of 'quinarii', or reduced denarii, found in the centre and centre-east of Gaul, running down to the Roman conquest and after. These have attracted much recent study. Here is the principal literature, which, since most are inscribed, can be arranged under the legends:

ΚΑΛΕΤΕΔΟΥ

J-B. Colbert de Beaulieu 'La Légende ΚΑΛΕΤΕΔΟΥ et ses variétés' *EC* 13 (1966/7) 327f (I do not think it is sound)

idem 'La monnaie de Caletedu et les zones du statère et du denier en Gaule' *RAC* 5 (1966) 101–29. (Cf. Colbert de Beaulieu pp.138–9)

idem 'Les monnaies de Caletedu, sont-elles vraiment éduennes?' *RAE* 16 (1964) 285–94

M. Dayet 'Les monnaies de ΚΑΛΕΤΕΔΟΥ' *RAE* 9 (1960) 134–54

D. F. Allen 'The coins found at la Tène' *EC* XIII (1973) 477–521

idem 'The Houssen hoard at Colmar' *RBN* CXXII (1976) 79–85

Q DOCI / Q DOCI SAM F

M. Dayet 'Les deniers à la légende Q DOCI SAM F et les bronzes qui les accompagnaient' *RAE* 15 (1964) 254–75

TOGIRIX / TOGIRIX and Q IVLIVS TOGIRIX

M. Dayet and J-B. Colbert de Beaulieu 'Qui était Togirix?; les monnaies gauloises au nom de Togirix' *RAE* 13 (1962) 82–118

The denomination thus established in one area became the chief silver constituent of the overlay of later coinages in central and northern Gaul, further literature on which is described in section 8.

For silver coins of Armorica see section 6.4 below, and for silver of Britain see section 6.6.

4.4. *The Western Influence on Silver Coins of the East*

In parallel with the development of the quinarius small money denomination in Gaul, there were subsidiary silver coinages in Germany and the east. Excellent studies have been done of several of these subsidiary currencies, but no thorough study has been made of their relationship with the basic gold coinages of the area. In the main their types have western origins, or these origins are obscure. For the very limited circulation of Roman coins in the area see

S. Bolin 'Die Funde römischer und byzantinischer Münzen im freien Germanien' *Bericht RGK* 19 (1929) 86–145

C. Rodewald *Money in the Age of Tiberius* (Manchester 1976)

The following are the types of Celtic coins that have been studied:

The Torque-Man Type

J. Cahn 'Wangionen, Mattiaker oder Ubier? *Mitt. für Münzsammler* 6 (Frankfurt 1929) 321–4, 339–40

H. Schönberger 'Zu den Keltenmünzen Forrer 352' *Germania* 30 (1952) 383–8 (see also *Germania* 34 (1956) 152–4)

E. Schubert 'Eine neue Münze vom Typus Forrer 352' in O.H. Frey (ed.) *Marburger Beiträge zur Archäologie der Kelten*, Festschrift für Wolfgang Dehn zum 60. Geburtstag (Bonn 1969) pp.206–9

G. Behrens 'Keltenmünzen in Rheingebiet' *PZ* 34–5 (1949–50) 345–6

D. F. Allen, review of S. Scheers (op. cit., section 4.3) *NC* 1971 352–6 (for the stages of development from a Roman denarius prototype)

K. Castelin 'Zu den keltischen Silbermünzen vom "Nauheimer Typus"' *JNG* 25 (1975) 1–15, on the same subject in greater detail

The Sitting-Man Type

K. Castelin 'Die keltischen Quinare mit dem sitzenden Männlein (der Typus vom Marberg)' *Money Trend* 12/74 (1974) 7–11

The 'Prague' Type (though its real home appears to lie towards central Germany)

K. Castelin 'Ein kleiner keltischer Münzfund aus Prag' *MONG* XII (XXVIII) 1962, 114–16

H-J. Kellner 'Die keltischen Silbermünzen vom "Prager Typus", zur Silberprägung der Boier' *JNG* 15 (1965) 195–207

D. F. Allen 'More on the Prague type' *JNG* 17 (1967) 95–9

The 'Bushel' Type

G. Behrens 'Keltenmünzen in Rheingebiet' *PZ* 34–5 (1949–50) 344–5

H-J. Kellner 'Die keltischen Münzen von der Engehalbinsel bei Bern' *JBHM* 41/2 (1962) 259–74, especially 270

D. F. Allen 'The coins from the oppidum of Altenburg and the bushel series' *Germania* 56.1 (1978) 190–229

U. Friedländer 'Ein Fund keltischer Silbermünzen aus Fränken *SM* 110 (1978) 21–38, for a hoard of Bushel and Manching type small silver

German Coins with Cross Reverses (west Germany, Rhaeti and Alauni?)

K. Castelin 'Die Kreuzmünzen in Süddeutschland' *SNR* 49 (1970) 77–108

idem 'Die süddeutschen Kreuzmünzen und die Helvetier' *SNR* 54 (1975) 79–96

idem 'Die Kreuzmünzen bei den Rätern und Alaunen' *SNR* 50 (1971) 92–124

idem 'Zu den süddeutschen Kreuzmünzen' *Hamburger Beiträge zur Num.* 22/3 (1968/9, published 1972) 529–37

Remarks on the proposed connection between German and Gallic cross coins are made in Allen 1969 and Soutou 1969 (section 4.1 above).

The Vangiones Types. The coins, of which there are several types all of quinarius denomination (e.g. Forrer 349, 350, 351, de la Tour 9408) belong to the Rhineland, especially the western bank. They scarcely stand apart from the main Gaulish series, but are perhaps relevant here. They have not been thoroughly studied recently, though Kellner comments in Forrer II, p.72. See also

G. Behrens 'Keltenmünzen in Rheingebiet' *PZ* 34–5 (1949–50) 345–8

idem, in H. V. Petrikovits and A. Steeger (eds) *Festschrift für August Oxé* (Dormstadt 1938) pp.160–3

H. Schönberger 'Zu den Keltenmünzen Forrer 352' *Germania* 30 (1952) 383–8

5. *The Gold Belt : Eastern Sector*

5.1. *Alexander III and Philip V of Macedon : The Elbe Basin (Czechoslovakia and central Germany)*

Bohemian Staters and Fractions. The basic collection of material in relation to the gold and silver coinages of Bohemia (but by no means all of this derivation) is in Paulsen, but the treatment is not as scientific as the collection is thorough. The basic historical and metrological analysis of the gold coinages of Bohemia is in Castelin. This is in effect the assembly in book form and in the German language of work done over many years and published in article form in the Czech language, mostly in *N.Listy*, the details of which are therefore not listed here. The same material is summarised conveniently for those who do not wish to go into the details in

K. Castelin 'Le monnayage d'or celtique dans les pays tcheques' *RN* 1965, 69–78

This supersedes parts of the following work, still often quoted:

K. Pink 'Die Goldprägung der Ostkelten' *WPZ* XXIII (1936) 8–41

It is worth referring to some of the more important finds of this class of coin outside Czechoslovakia:

E. Fiala 'Der Podmokler Goldfund' *NZ* 34 (1902) 149–56

K. Castelin 'Münzen aus dem Fund von Podmokly in Münzkabinett Dresden' *Beiträge und Berichte der Staatlichen Kunstsammlungen Dresden* 1972–75, 161–70

A. J-B. Changarnier-Moissenet *Monnaies des Boiens de la Germanie, Trésor de Siauges-Saint-Romain (Haute-Loire)* (Dijon 1914)

Ö. Gohl 'La trouvaille de Nagy-Biszterecz (Hongrie): essai sur le monnayage des Cotini celtiques' *Méms du Cong. Int. de Num. de 1900* (Paris 1900) pp.90–8 (gold with silver)

K. Castelin 'Oro celtico in Italia settentrionale' *Cong. Int. de Num.* II (Rome 1961) pp.185–94

F. Panvini-Rosati 'Ripostiglio de monete celtiche al Museo archeologico di Firenze' *Ann.* 2 (1955) 59–61. Others are in the British Museum.

Z. Nemeškalová-Jiroudková 'Keltische Goldprägungen aus böhmischen Münzstätten in Mittelitalien' *Památky archeologické* LXVI (1975) 383–416

idem 'Zur Frage des keltischen Münzschatzfunds von Campiglia Marittima' *Actes 8-ème Cong. Int. de Num.* New York 1973 (Paris 1976) pp.181–8

K. Castelin 'Der vindelizische Stater aus dem Oppidum "La Cloche" bei Marseille' *JNG* XXVII (1977) 7–19

D. Nony, *BSFN* 1977, 169–72, discusses a hoard from Courcoury (Charente Maritime) in France

See also Forrer II, pp.56–9 for other references and pl.14 for a picture of the Nagy-Biszterecz hoard. For a 'unicum' in the same series see

D.F. Allen 'Nový keltský čtvrstatér z Prahy' *N.Listy* XXII (1967) 65–7; summary in English p.67 'A new Celtic quarter-stater from Prague'.

For a hoard containing several types see

K. Castelin 'Bemerkungen zum Schatzfund von Bački Obrovac 1956', in *Frappe et Ateliers Monétaires dans l'Antiquité et Moyen Age* (Belgrade 1976) pp.19–27

Central German Finds. Some relevant finds, together with other material from the area, are in

K. Schirwitz 'Griechische, keltische und römische Münzen aus Mitteldeutschland' *Germania* 30 (1952) 46–55

H-J. Kellner and G. Neumann 'Die keltischen Münzfunde in Mitteldeutschland' *Ausgrabungen und Funde* 11 (1966) 253–60

5.2. *Derivatives to North, West and South-West*

North (Nebenreihe). The references for what are called by Castelin 'Nebenreihe', i.e. coins of the weight standards of Bohemian staters and fractions, but of varied types, are to be found under Bohemian staters above.

West (Curled Beast or Rolltier staters). A derivative, which itself represents the start of the Rainbow cup (Regenbogenschüsselchen) series is discussed in

K. Castelin 'Le statère BN 8744, une frappe "Ménapienne"?' *RBN* 117 (1970) 91–6

idem 'Der böhmische Rolltierstater und die süddeutschen Regenbogenschüsselchen' *JNG* 14 (1964) 117–45

South ('Salasses' on both sides of the Swiss-Italian Alps). The coins attributed to the Salasses, which derive from the Bohemian corruption of the Alexander stater, are most fully discussed in Pautasso, pp.137–53, but the older publications are still worth consulting. The uninscribed varieties belong to the Swiss side of the Alps, the inscribed ones to the Italian side, where alone the Salassi are recorded as living.

A.M. de Longpérier 'Monnaies de Salasses' *RN* 1861, 333–47

R. Forrer 'Klassifikation der Salasser-Gepräge und eine unedierte Salasser-Variante' *BM* 4 (1911–13) 700–6

idem 'Fundkarte zur Verbreitung der Salasser-Gepräge' *BM* 5 (1914–16) 2–4

Some of the finds of 'rainbow cups' noted above, for instance those from Switzerland, also contained this class of coin and are relevant. For coins of the same system see section 5.3, under *Rainbow Cups in Switzerland.*

Other imitations of Alexander III. There are other imitations of staters of Alexander III that are not Celtic, and there are a few that do not fit into any regular pattern. The well-known series in Forrer fig.357–9, further illustrated in

G. Behrens *Keltische Goldmünzen in der Sammlung des Römisch-Germanischen Zentralmuseums in Mainz* (Mainz 1955) pl.1, 3–5, and 2, 1–3

and discussed in

P. Lederer 'Westliche oder östliche Barbarenmünze?' *BM* 42 (1921) 252–4

is apparently an eastern non-Celtic barbarisation; see Kellner in Forrer II, p.73. Forrer 490 and 486 (on which see Forrer II, p.97) are apparently German; Forrer 356 (on which see Forrer II, p.73) is presumably Gaulish.

5.3. *The 'Rainbow Cup' Series of Vindelicia, Bavaria*

The standard classification of this very important and extensive series, which links east and west, is still the hundred-year-old

F. Streber 'Über die Sogenannten Regenbogenschüsselchen' *Abhandlung d. Köningl. bayer. Akad. d. Wissenschaften* I (Munich 1860) II (1862)

It is difficult to gain access to this book in Britain, but the classification in it is reproduced in

A. M. de Longpérier 'Sur quelques monnaies celtiques' *RN* 14 (1869) 14–25

Also relevant, though out of date, is Pink, *Goldprägung*. The only recent review of the ensemble, soundly analytical but with no claim to be final, is by Castelin in Forrer II, pp.79–82. For a fuller treatment, with discussion of the chronology, see

K. Castelin 'Der Prägezeit der süddeutschen Regenbogenschüsselchen' *JNG* 23 (1973) 53–76

idem 'L'epoca di coniazione delle "Regenbogenschüsselchen" della Germania meridionale' *RIN* 1975, 67–96

The Curled Beast or Rolltierstater (transition from Bohemia to Bavaria)

K. Castelin 'Der böhmische Rolltierstater und die süddeutschen Regenbogenschüsselchen' *JNG* 14 (1964) 117–45. An important introduction.

The Shadow of Rome. Indirectly relevant to the Rainbow cups, though of distinct derivation (weight standard Bohemian, obverse Roman, reverse Gaulish), are certain small gold coins, on which see

H-J. Kellner 'Die älteste keltische Fundmünze aus dem Oppidum von Manching' *Germania* 39 (1961) 299–305

Mainstream (Bavaria: Vindelicia). Apart from the discovery of a very late variety at Manching, which was conceivably a mint, on which see
W. Krämer 'The oppidum of Manching' *Antiquity* 34 (1960) 191–200 (see also *Germania* 35 (1957) 32–3; 40 (1962) 297–317)
virtually nothing has been written on this subject recently.
'Smooth Staters' (Upper Tauher – middle Neckar, north of main stream).
K. Castelin and H-J. Kellner 'Die glatten Regenbogenschüsselchen' *JNG* 13 (1963) 105–30
Rainbow Cups in Switzerland (relevant also to Bohemian coins).
B. Reber 'In der Schweiz aufgefundene Regenbogenschüsseln und verwandte Goldmünzen' *Anzeiger f. Schweiz. Altertumskunde* NF II.3 (1900) 157–66 (interpretation out of date, but some useful information)
K. Castelin 'Ein keltische Goldstater aus dem Funde von St. Louis' *SM* 9 (1959) 37–40
idem 'Zur Sogenannten "Basler Gruppe" keltischer Goldstatere' *SM* II (1961) 35–7
idem 'Zur Vergrabungszeit des keltischen Münzschatzes von St. Louis 1883' *SM* 15 (1965) 133–7
Württemburg Finds. Some relevant finds, together with other material from the area, are in
W. Nestle *Funde antiker Münzen im Königreich Württemberg* (Stuttgart 1893); cf. *Fundberichte aus Schwaben* I (1893) VI (1898) XV (1907)
G. Sixt 'Regenbogenschüsselchen und andere keltische Münzen aus Württemberg und Hohenzollern' *Fundberichte aus Schwaben* VI (1898) 37–41
Central German finds. There is some material in
K. Schirwitz 'Griechische, keltische und römische Münzen aus Mitteldeutschland' *Germania* 30 (1952) 46–55
H-J. Kellner and G. Neuman 'Die keltischen Münzfunde in Mitteldeutschland' *Ausgrabungen und Funde* II (1966) 253–60
Italian Finds, including inscribed coins.
K. Castelin 'Oro celtico in Italia settentrionale' *Cong. Int. de Num.* II (Rome 1961) 185–94
Z. Nemeškalová-Jiroudková 'Zur Frage des keltischen Münzschatzfunds von Campiglia Marittima' *Actes 8-ème Cong. Int. de Num.* New York 1973 (Paris 1976) pp.181–8
Rhineland Staters, triquetra marked. Apart from Castelin in Forrer II, p.82, nothing significant has been written on the north German variety,

marked with a triquetra, found east of the Rhine. In addition to gold, it occurs also in good silver and in base silver or bronze. The principal hoard of gold coins is from Mardorf (examples at Kassel), recently published in

I. Kappel 'Der Münzfund von Mardorf und andere keltische Münzen aus Nordhessen' *Germania* 54 (1976) 75–101

A large hoard of base coins, of which there are examples in many museums, is adequately described in

H. Buchenau 'Ein Fund von Regenbogenschüsselchen in Bochum' *BfM* 43 (1908) 3935–6

Examples are among the few Celtic coins that have been found in Holland.

5.4. *Lysimachus of Thrace : The Pontic Hinterland*

The only article of note on these pieces, which have occasionally been found in the Baltic area, is

W. Schwabacher 'Antik barbarmynting belyst av svenskt material' *Fornwännen* 47 (1952) 263–75

But the head of Lysimachus is copied on some Gaulish staters; see

J-B. Colbert de Beaulieu, F. Blind and P-D. Labarrière *Catalogue des Collections archéologiques de Besançon IV : Les Monnaies gauloises* (Paris 1959, second edn 1967) p.23

D. F. Allen 'The early coinage of the Treveri' *Germania* 49 (1971) 102

6. *The Gold Belt : Western Sector*

6.1. *Philip II of Macedon : The First Phase in Gaul*

Very little has been written for many years on the first phase of the 'philippus' in Gaul. Blanchet is still the principal source, though more material has since been found. Brooke's bold attempt to depress the date of the start of these coins (*NC* 1933, 88–138), though supported by Pink, was from the first doomed; see Milne, *JRS* 30 (1940) 11–15. Serious work has concentrated on the second phase, that is on individual series associated with particular regions. A thorough study of the earliest philippus coins, both as regards find-spots and die sequences, is the most keenly felt desideratum in Celtic numismatics. On one aspect of the background see

J-B. Colbert de Beaulieu and P. R. Giot 'Un statère d'or cyrénaique découvert sur une plage bretonne et la route atlantique de l'étain' *BSPF* LVIII (1961) 324–31

which discusses actual finds of Greek coins in Gaul (almost negligible in number).

Of particular importance, both for itself and for the myths it dispels, is

H-J. Kellner 'Der Fund von Tayac, ein Zeugnis des Cimbernzuges?' *JNG* 20 (1970) 13–47

On the subject of the early gold coinages of central Gaul see Nash, pp.63ff, and on early philippus coinages of the Rhineland see

D. F. Allen 'The philippus in Switzerland and the Rhineland' *SNR* LIII (1974) 42–74

6.2. *Regional Developments : The Arvernian Centre*

History and geography should point to the Arverni in the Auvergne as the fulcrum for the spread of the philippus in different directions. In fact the story of the coinage of the Arverni and its neighbouring tribes is defective.

On historical grounds the early staters and quarter staters (i.e. those over 8.0 g or its equivalent) are often called Arvernian. They tend to be found, however, not in the territory of the Arverni but nearer the Loire and the Rhine. It is no longer permissible to attribute to the Arverni the corruptions of the Macedonian monogram of Apella, which eventually becomes a triskeles. For coins derived from the Macedonian head of Helios mint mark, and found to the west of central Gaul, see Nash, pp.90ff, and

J-B. Colbert de Beaulieu 'Origine, évolution et mutation d'un différent monétaire en Gaule celtique' *RBN* 1952, 31–9

The first coins clearly established by find-spots as those of the Arverni are those found in hoards, as shown by Nash, pp.138ff, and

A. Blanchet 'Les monnayages des Arvernes à propos des trouvailles récentes' *RN* 1938, 121–31

For another series of gold coins that has been attributed to the Arverni see

J-B. Colbert de Beaulieu 'Une suite de statères d'or attribués aux Arvernes' *RBN* 1958, 63–73

This should be read with

K. Castelin 'Les statères Arvernes à la lyre' *RBN* 108 (1961) 71–81

It is at the end of the series, with the coins of Vercingetorix in gold and in bronze, that the coinage of the Arverni is on surer ground. This has been studied in detail in the following articles, which take up the earlier literature:

J-B. Colbert de Beaulieu and G. Lefèvre 'Les monnaies de Vercingétorix' *Gallia* 1963, 11–75; 1966, 21–8; 1970, 1–9

Little recent literature can be named regarding the gold coins of the

Bituriges Cubi or Lemovices; for an overall treatment see Nash, pp.202–7. For gold of the Pictones and those once wrongly attributed to the Santones see

J-B. Colbert de Beaulieu 'Remarques sur le monnayage celtique des Pictones' *Actes du 87e Cong. nat. des Soc. Savants* (Poitiers 1962) pp.153–70

For a summary in English see Nash, pp.246–50.

6.3. *Regional Developments to the East: The Swiss and Rhineland Group*

Switzerland. Switzerland is the meeting point of the coinages of east and west. Most of the literature, none of which is exhaustive, covers more than one stream of coins. It is the coinage of the west that is relevant here. The hundred-year-old standard work is

H. Meyer 'Beschreibung der in der Schweiz aufgefundenen gallischen Münzen' *Mitt. der Antiquarischen Gesellschaft in Zürich* XV (1863), also published as a separate book (Zürich 1863).

Other attempts to cover the ground are

D. F. Allen 'The philippus in Switzerland and the Rhineland' *SNR* LIII (1974) 42–74

E. Vogt 'Zur gallischen Numismatik der Schweiz' *41. Jahresber. (1932) d. Schweizerischen Landesmuseums in Zürich* (Winterthur 1933) 91–101

R. Forrer 'Die sechs keltisch-gallischen Münzströmungen der vorrömischen Schweiz' *Anzeiger für Schweizer Altertumskunde* 40 (1938) 192–200

G. Wüthrich 'Celtic numismatics in Switzerland' *NC* 1945, 1–33 (an excellent collection presented without understanding)

An attempt to place the gold coins found at la Tène in their historical context is made by

D. F. Allen 'The coins found at la Tène' *EC* XIII (1973) 477–521

For a coin type, an example of which comes from la Tène, see

H-J. Kellner 'Zur Goldprägung der Helvetier: die Viertelstatere vom typ Unterentfelden' in E. Schmid, L. Berger and P. Bürgin (eds) *Provincialia* (Festschrift für R. Laur-Belart) (Basel & Stuttgart 1968) pp.588–602

Numismatically the borderline between Switzerland (Helvetii) on the one hand and Doubs and Jura (Sequani) on the other is not distinct, and material in the catalogues of the coins of Besançon, Montbéliard and Jura (section 1.3 above) contain related material. Along the Rhine the following are relevant to this section:

Alsace

R. Forrer *Les Monnaies Gauloises ou Celtiques trouvées en Alsace* (Mulhouse 1925)

Baden and South-west Germany

K. Christ 'Antike Münzfunde Südwestdeutschlands. Münzfunde, Geldwirtschaft und Geschichte im Raume Baden-Württembergs von keltischer bis in alamannischer Zeit' *Vestigia* 3.1–2 (Heidelberg 1960)

F. Wielandt 'Keltische Fundmünzen aus Baden' *JNG* 14 (1964) 97–115

The Rhineland Generally

G. Behrens 'Keltenmünzen im Rheingebiet' *PZ* XXXIV–XXXV (1949–50) 336–54

This is an especially important study, but has to be used with some care as a lot of coins not of identical types are lumped together in some of the maps. But the references by which to test the results are there.

Treveri (Trier). For coins of the Treveri see Scheers and

D. F. Allen 'The early coins of the Treveri' *Germania* 49 (1971) 91–110

K. Castelin 'Zu den Treverer-stateren "à l'oeil" vom Tetelbierg' *SM* 24 (1974) 73–7; cf. L. Reding *Les Monnaies Gauloises du Tetelbierg* (Luxembourg 1972) pp. 17–89

S. Scheers 'La circulation des monnaies gauloises sur le territoire Trévire' *Bull. des Antiquités luxembourgeoises* 8 (1977) 15–55

6.4. *Regional Developments to the North-West: The Armorican Group (Brittany)*

The richest area of Gaul for Celtic coins, especially those of gold, is Armorica, and the literature is almost equally rich. It is on this region that Colbert de Beaulieu's early work concentrated. On the early phase, especially countermarked coins, see

J-B. Colbert de Beaulieu 'La contremarque dans le monnayage d'or gaulois' *Gallia* 12 (1954) 55–72

Of the regular gold coins of the Armorican tribes, Colbert de Beaulieu's central study is that devoted to the Veneti:

idem 'Une énigme de la numismatique armoricaine: les monnaies celtiques des Vénètes I: le billon' *Mém. de la Soc. d'Hist. et Arch. de Bretagne* 33 (1953) 5–52; II 'l'or' ibid. 34 (1954) 5–38

It is impracticable to list all the individual notes and articles that he has written on Armorican coins; regular contributions are to be found in

Ogam V (1953) to VIII (1956)

AB LXVII (1960) to LXXII (1965)
RBN XCIV (1948) to CIV (1958)

and there is some discussion of the coinage of the Coriosolites in Colbert de Beaulieu, pp.65ff. On the Coriosolites see also

idem 'Le monnayage coriosolite' *N.Circ.* July 1951, 321–4

On other types of Armorican coinage see

idem 'L'attribution controuvée d'un monnayage gaulois aux Abrincatui' *RBN* XCVI (1950) 27–33 (Redones coinage)

idem 'La trouvaille de monnaies celtiques de Saint-Jacques-de-la-Lande' *RBN* XCIV (1948) 15–76; further lots from this hoard of Redones coins are published in *RBN* XCVII (1951) 105–16; *AB* LXX (1963) 42–52

idem 'La trouvaille de monnaies Vénètes du Pipriac' *RBN* IC (1953) 31–62

Of particular interest in Britain are Colbert de Beaulieu's articles bearing on the important Channel Islands finds of Armorican billon coinage. These occur in several places throughout his flow of articles, but the most important articles are

idem 'Trésors de monnaies celtiques de l'île de Jersey et la circulation des monnaies gauloises' *Bull. de la Soc. nat. des Antiquaires de France* 29.5 (1957)

idem 'Le trésor de Jersey-II et la numismatique celtique des deux Bretagnes' *RBN* 103 (1957) 47–88

idem 'Un troisième lot de la récolte de Jersey-II' *RBN* 105 (1959) 49–57

A shorter version in English is given in

idem 'Armorican coin hoards in the Channel Islands' *PPS* XXIV (1958) 201–10

Minor corrections are to be found in

D.F. Allen 'The origins of coinage in Britain: a reappraisal' in S.S. Frere (ed.) *Problems of the Iron Age in Southern Britain*, papers given at a C.B.A. conference, London 1958 (1961) pp.297–308

Although the drawings are perhaps more relevant to Celtic art than to numismatics, the following book illustrates the full range of Channel Islands types from the Marquanderie hoard, and gives references to earlier literature:

N.V.L. Rybot *Armorican Art* (Jersey 1952)

An important article on a type of Armorican coin, almost only known from a single hoard, is

J-B. Colbert de Beaulieu 'Les petites monnaies du Nord-Ouest de la Gaule' *Ogam* (6) 1954, 119–26

on which see also

Y. Rollando *La Préhistoire du Morbihan* (Vannes 1971) pp.112–13 and plate facing p.97

For thin silver coins of Armorica and Britain with origins in the head of Athena on gold coins of Alexander the Great, see Scheers and

D. F. Allen 'Les pièces d'argent minces du comté de Hampshire: nouveau lien entre la Gaule celtique et la Grande-Bretagne' *RN* 1965, 79–93

6.5. *Regional Developments to the North-East : The Belgic Group (From the Seine to the Marne and the Moselle)*

Apart from work incidental to studies of the origins of coinage in Britain, the principal recent research has been by Simone Scheers, and the most comprehensive work on Belgic coins is Scheers. Publications on specific subjects of major importance are

S. Scheers 'Le premier monnayage des Ambiani' *RBN* 114 (1968) 43–73

idem 'Un monnayage Ambien attribué aux Bellovaci' *RBN* 115 (1969) 5–56

K. Castelin 'Die Schönen Ambiani-statere mit "breitem Schrötling"' *Money Trend* 3/1978, 8–11, which presents a later date for the type than Scheers

S. Scheers 'Un monnayage gaulois non attribué de la Côte maritime Belge' *RBN* 116 (1970) 5–90

idem 'L'histoire monétaire des Suessiones avant l'arrivée de César' *Ancient Society* 1 (1970) 135–61

idem 'Coinage and currency of the Belgic tribes during the Gallic War' *BNJ* 1972, 1–6

J-B. Colbert de Beaulieu *Les Monnaies Gauloises de Parisii* (Paris 1970)

L. Reding *Les Monnaies Gauloises du Tetelbierg* (Luxembourg 1972) for a major collection of site finds of Belgic coins

For articles on the coins of the Treveri see section 6.3 above.

6.6. *Britain*

The following literature should provide a general introduction to the Celtic coinages of Britain. The earliest extensive work, which is still of value, is

J. Evans *The Coins of the Ancient Britons* (London 1864)

The current standard catalogue of British coin types is Mack. A major landmark in the study of the coinage is D. F. Allen 'The origins ...'

(cited in section 6.5 above), which provided a gazetteer of find-spots for British coins. This has been brought up to date by

C. Haselgrove *Supplementary Gazetteer of Find-Spots of Celtic Coins in Britain, 1977* (Occasional paper no. 11a, Institute of Archaeology, London 1978)

For the Belgic antecedents of the British coinage see the articles by Scheers in *RBN* 115 (1969) and *RBN* 116 (1970), cited in section 6.5 above (the coins in the 1970 article are perhaps more of British than Belgic origin), and in general her work on Belgic gold coinage.

For iron currency bars see section 1.4 above.

Articles on specific topics of importance are

M. Mackensen 'Die älteste keltische Gold- und Silberprägung in England' *JNG* XXIV (1974) 7–63, but British B2 is now considered to be a group of modern forgeries

D. F. Allen 'The Belgic dynasties of Britain and their coins' *Archaeologia* XC (1944) 1–46

idem *Sylloge of the Coins of the British Isles 3: The Coins of the Coritani* (London 1963)

idem 'Cunobelin's gold' *Britannia* VI (1975) 1–19

idem 'British potin coins: a review' in M. Jesson and D. Hill (eds) *The Iron Age and its Hill Forts* (Southampton 1971) pp. 127–54

idem 'Les pièces d'argent minces du comté de Hampshire: nouveau lien entre la Gaule celtique et la Grande-Bretagne' *RN* 1965, 79–93

D. F. Allen and C. C. Haselgrove 'The gold coinage of Verica' *Britannia* 1979 (forthcoming)

W. J. Rodwell 'Coinage, oppida and the rise of Belgic power in south-eastern Britain' in B. W. Cunliffe and T. Rowley (eds) *Oppida in Barbarian Europe* (BAR S.11, Oxford 1976)

J. R. Collis 'Functional and theoretical interpretations of British coinage' *World Archaeology* 3 (1971) 71–84

G. C. Brooke 'The philippus in the west and the Belgic invasion of Britain ' *NC* 1933, 88–138

idem 'The distribution of Gaulish and British coins in Britain' *Antiquity* VII (1933) 268–89

R. R. Clarke 'The early iron age treasure from Snettisham, Norfolk' *PPS* XX (1954) 27–86

J. P. C. Kent 'Les relations entre le monnayage des Romains et ceux des peuples voisins de l'ouest' *CEN* 10 (1973) 2–11

M. Henig 'The origin of some ancient British coin types'

Britannia III (1972) 209–23

D. F. Allen 'The coins of the Iceni' *Britannia* I (1970) 1–33

idem 'The Celtic coins' in *Hod Hill volume II: Excavations carried out between 1951 and 1958 for the Trustees of the British Museum by Sir Ian Richmond* (British Museum, London 1968) pp.45–56; on coinage of the Durotriges

idem 'A study of the Dobunnic coinage' in E. M. Clifford et al. *Bagendon, a Celtic Oppidum: a record of the excavations of 1954–56* (London 1961) pp.75–149

idem 'Celtic coins from the Romano-British temple at Harlow, Essex' *BNJ* XXXIII (1964) 1–6; XXXVI (1967) 1–7; XXXVII (1968) 1–6

idem 'Did Adminius strike coins?' *Britannia* VII (1976) 96–100

idem, on previously unknown small silver coins found in Hampshire and Sussex, *BNJ* XXXIV (1965) 1–7; XXXVI (1967) 8–10; XXXVII (1968) 7–9

7. *Spanish and Celt-Iberian Coinage*

The following publications provide a brief introduction to the Celt-Iberian coinages of Spain and southern France, and the coinages of Emporion and Rhoda. Fuller bibliography may be found in

G. K. Jenkins 'Literaturüberblicke der griechischen Numismatik: Spain' *JNG* II (1961) 75–155

idem 'Spain' in *A Survey of Numismatic Research 1960–1965* (INC, Copenhagen 1967) pp.96–105

idem 'The Iberian peninsula' in *A Survey of Numismatic Research 1966–1971* (INC, New York 1973) pp.206–20

J. Amoros 'Monedas griegas y derivadas en Hispania' *Cong. Int. de Num.* I (Rome 1961) pp.121–44, which includes information on finds, and covers the early literature

J. C. M. Richard 'La Gaule narbonnaise et la péninsule ibérique' in *A Survey of Numismatic Research 1966–1971* (INC, New York 1973) pp.252–62

See also sections 4.1 (Rhoda imitations) and 4.2 (Emporion imitations). The most prominent older work in English is Hill. Other important works include

A. Vives *La Moneda Hispánica*, 2 vols (Madrid 1926)

O. Gil Farrés *La Moneda Hispanica en la Edad Antigua* (Madrid 1966)

K. Raddatz *Die Schatzfunde der iberischen Halbinsel* (Berlin 1969) provides a comprehensive account of hoards

G. K. Jenkins 'Problems of the Celtiberian coinage' *Cong. Int. de Num.* Rome 1961, vol. II (1965) pp. 219ff
J. Untermann 'Zur Gruppierung der Hispanischen "Reitermünzen" mit Legenden in iberischen Schrift' *Madrider Mitteilungen* v (1964) 91ff; an important article
idem 'Lengua gala y lengua iberica en la Galia narbonensis' *Archivo de Preistoria Levantina* 12 (Valencia 1969) 99–161, which discusses the linguistic frontier in southern France
J. C. M. Richard 'Une monnaie à la légende NERONCEN découverte en Corrèze et le monnayage ibérique de Narbonne' *Actes des 41e et 42e Cong. d'Etudes régionales, Fédération historique du Languedoc méditerranéen et du Rousillon et Fédération des Sociétés académiques et savantes de Languedoc-Pyrénées-Gascogne* (Carcassonne 1970) pp. 21–7
idem 'Les monnayages indigènes de Narbonne et sa région' *Féderation historique du Languedoc méditerranéen et du Roussillon* 1973, 135–49
A. Soutou 'Une monnaie gauloise à la légende "ibérique" controversée: NMY' *Ogam* 14 (1962) 131–42; 15 (1963) 328–30; 17 (1965) 79. Perhaps a coinage of Nemausus.

On Iberic denarii see

R. C. Knapp 'The date and purpose of the Iberian denarii' *NC* 1977, 1–18, which provides a guide to the earlier literature
J. S. Richardson 'The Spanish mines and the development of provincial taxation in the second century B.C.' *JRS* 1976, 139–52

8. *Subsidiary Coinages of Silver and Bronze*

For silver subsidiary coinages see section 4.3 above. There is no general work devoted to bronze coinages, which are normally treated together with the other coinages of their area. Blanchet contains much that is still very useful. The principal matter of debate in recent years has been the chronology of the bronze and potin coinages, especially their origins. The following books and articles provide reasonable coverage of the subject.

D. F. Allen 'British potin coins: a review' in M. Jesson and D. Hill (eds) *The Iron Age and its Hill Forts* (Southampton 1971) pp. 127–54

which provided good illustrations of the Continental series as well as the British.

J. B. Colbert de Beaulieu 'Chronologie des bronzes gaulois et

"British potin coins"' *RBN* 109 (1973) 5–41

contests Allen's chronology, which he believes presents too early an origin for potin coins. Cf. Colbert de Beaulieu.

D. F. Allen 'The Houssen hoard at Colmar' *RBN* CXXII (1976) 79–85

presents the principal evidence for Allen's early dating (cf. idem 'The coins found at la Tène' *EC* XIII (1973) 477–521), but most recently

K. Castelin 'Zur Chronologie der keltischen Fundmünzen von Basel-Gasfabrik und Basel-Münsterhügel' *Money Trend* 11/1977, 11–15

presents strong evidence in support of a late start for potins in Gaul.

For the bronze coinages of Belgic Gaul see Scheers; for bronzes of central Gaul see Nash; for Danubian bronzes see K. Bíró Sey 'The question of the chronology of the transdanubian Celtic bronze coins' cited in section 3.1 above, under Hungary; for British potin see D. F. Allen, op. cit. (1971) above. For Spanish and Celt-Iberian bronzes see section 7 above.

Key to the Plates

List of Abbreviations used in the Key
See also the list of short titles on p.153ff

A	Coin in the collection of the Heberden Coin Room, Ashmolean Museum, Oxford
ANS	Coin in the collection of the American Numismatic Society, New York
BM	Coin in the collection of the British Museum, London
BN	Coin in the collection of the Bibliothèque Nationale, Paris, with inventory number (see *BN*; cf. de la Tour)
G	Coin in the collection of the Musée de Guéret (Creuse, France) with inventory number
H	Coin in the Hunterian Collection, Glasgow, published by G. Macdonald *Catalogue of the coins in the Hunterian Collection, University of Glasgow*, vol. III (Glasgow 1905)
MAN	Coin in the collection of the Musée des Antiquités Nationales, Saint-Germain-en-Laye, with inventory number

PLATE I

			Production Techniques
1	AE	2.09	Remi: Slipped mould. BM
2	AR	1.84	Central Gaul, var. LITAVICCUS: bent coin. A
3	AV	1.94	Central Gaul: countermarked (Nash 192). BN 6425
4	AV	7.76	Rhineland: countermarked (Nash 216). BN 3657
			Silver of Cisalpine Gaul
5	AR	3.73	Massilia drachm. A
6	AR	3.16	Insubres (Pautasso pl.IX). BM
7	AR	3.72	Cenomani (Pautasso pl.XXIV). A
8	AR	3.15	Veneti (Pautasso pl.LIX–LX). A
9	AR	2.48	PIRUKOI (Pautasso pl.XLIV–XLV). A

10	AR	2.02	RIKOI (Pautasso pl.XXI–XXII, XLVI–XLVII). A
11	AR	0.66	Serra Riccò hoard fraction (Pautasso pl.X). A
12	AR	0.78	Serra Riccò hoard fraction (Pautasso pl.XIV). A

PLATE 2

Danubian Silver

13	AR	14.34	Phillip II tetradrachm (359–336 B.C.). A (*SNG* 2486)
14	AR	13.41	Early Philip copy (Preda pl.I–IV). A
15	AR	13.84	Early Philip copy (Preda pl.I–IV). A
16	AR	12.95	Patraos tetradrachm (*c.*340–315 B.C.). A (*SNG* 3354)
17	AR	12.74	Pannonia (Göbl, *Typenatlas* pl.38, 469). A
18	AR	12.73	Audoleon tetradrachm (*c.*315–286 B.C.). A (*SNG* 3369)
19	AR	17.14	Lysimachos tetradrachm (323–281 B.C.). A (*SNG* 3723)
20	AR	3.36	Tenos drachm (fourth century B.C.) BM
21	AR	13.56	Huşi-Vovrieşti type (Preda pl.XXI–XXVII). A
22	AR	3.12	RAVIS (BN 10103). BM

PLATE 3

Danubian Silver

23	AR	13.72	Arad-Banat area. BM
24	AR	13.72	Arad-Banat area, severed head type (Preda pl.XXXIV). BM
25	AR	11.65	Arad-Banat area, Ocniţa-Cărbuneşti type (Preda pl.XXXIII). BM
26	AR	11.94	Arad-Banat area, Ocniţa-Cărbuneşti type (Preda pl.XXXII). BM
27	AR	13.29	Criciova type (Preda pl. VIII). A
28	AR	13.56	Arad-Banat area, Crişeni-Berchiş type (Preda pl.XV). A
29	AR	12.27	Dacia, Cladovo-Saschiz type (Preda pl.LV). BM
30	AR	14.63	Dacia, Aninoasa-Dobreşti type (Preda pl.LVI–LVIII). A
31	AR	12.37	Dacia, Aninoasa-Dobreşti type (Preda pl.LVI–LVIII). A

PLATE 4

Danubian Silver

32	AR	10.55	Dacia, Petelea type (Preda pl.LXVIII). BM
33	AR	12.58	Dacia, Aiud-Cugir type (Preda pl. LXI). BM

34 AR 12.03 Dacia, Toc-Chereluş type (Preda pl.LXVI–LXVII). BM

35 AR 7.40 Cotini(?), Vîrteju-Bucuresti type (Preda pl.XLIII). BM, from Kustendje hoard

36 AR 8.35 Cotini(?), Adîncata-Mănăstirea type (Preda pl.XLI–XLII). BM

37 AR 12.42 Moesia (Preda pl.XXXVI no.11). BM, from Kustendje hoard

38 AR 10.57 Moesia, Tonciu-cu-sigla type (Preda pl.XIX). BM

39 AR 5.88 Larissa (395–344 B.C.). A (*SNG* 3875)

40 AR 13.79 Larissa type (Preda pl.XXVIII–XXIX). A

41 AR 12.46 Janus head type (Preda pl.XXXI). A

PLATE 5

Danubian Silver

42 AR 11.91 Pannonia, lake Balaton area (Göbl, *Typenatlas* pl.35, 436). BM

43 AR 3.29 Pannonia, lake Balaton area (Göbl, *Typenatlas* pl.33, 414). BM

44 AR 13.57 Kaposthal type (Göbl, *Typenatlas* pl.39, 484). A

45 AR 12.57 as last. A

46 AR 2.67 Kaposthal type (Göbl, *Typenatlas* pl.39, 500). A

47 AE 3.39 Dunaszecksö type (Göbl, *Typenatlas* p.39, 496). A

48 AR 12.40 SASTHIENI. BM

49 AR 12.53 Sasthieni type, var. Medieşul-Aurit (Preda pl.LIX). BM

50 AR 12.87 Audoleon type (Göbl, *Typenatlas* pl.32, 402). BM

51 AR 12.85 Audoleon type (Göbl, *Typenatlas* pl.35, 429). BM

52 AR 14.27 Audoleon type (Göbl, *Typenatlas* p.28, 332). BM

53 AR 4.27 Burgenland, Eravisci(?) (Göbl, *Typenatlas* pl.31, 385). BM

54 AR 12.09 Burgenland, Eravisci(?) (Göbl, *Typenatlas* pl.32, 396). BM

PLATE 6

Danubian Silver

55 AR 11.80 West Noricum (Göbl, *Noricum* pl.1,1). BN 9910

56 AR 10.69 East Noricum (Göbl, *Noricum* pl.20–21). H *Cent. Eur.* p.708, 7

57 AR 10.35 East Noricum (Göbl, *Noricum* pl.39–41). A

58 AR 10.17 East Noricum, overstruck (Göbl, *Noricum* pl.30–31). A

59	AR	9.59	ECCAIO (Göbl, *Noricum* pl.15–16). H *Cent. Eur.* p.707, 3.
60	AR	10.07	SVICCA (Göbl, *Noricum* pl.17–18). H *Cent. Eur.* p.707, 5.
61	AR	2.34	Simmering type (Forrer 299). BM
62	AR	2.57	Tótfalu type (Forrer 298). BM
63	AR	2.52	Tótfalu type (Forrer 300). A
64	AR	2.48	Tótfalu type (BN 9964). BM
65	AR	17.20	Alexander III tetradrachm (336–323 B.C.). A (*SNG* 2553)
66	AR	17.20	Philip III tetradrachm (323–316 B.C.). A (*SNG* 3206)
67	AR	16.59	Philip III type (Preda pl.LXXII). A (*SNG* 3242)
68	AR	13.25	Philip III type (Preda pl.LXXII). A
69	AR	3.39	Philip III type (Preda pl.LXXIV). A
70	AR	3.37	as last. A

Plate 7

Danubian Silver

71	AR	14.97	Thasos tetradrachm (after 146 B.C.). A (*SNG* 3681)
72	AR	15.07	Thasos type (BN 9674; Göbl, *Typenatlas* pl.46). A (*SNG* 3703)
73	AR	15.98	Thasos type (Göbl, *Typenatlas* pl.49; BN 9685). A (*SNG* 3711)
74	AR	16.11	Thasos type. BM
75	AR	3.78	Denarius, Kalenus and Cordus (Crawford 403/1) 70 B.C. A
76	AR	3.86	Denarius, M. Lepidus (Crawford 419/1) 61 B.C. A
77	AR	17.19	Boii, BIATEC (Paulsen pl.30–2, Forrer 17). BM
78	AR	17.21	Boii, NONNOS (Paulsen pl.32–3, Forrer 551). A
79	AR	9.80	ADNAMATI (Göbl, *Noricum* pl.7–10). A
80	AR	9.80	NEMET (Göbl, *Noricum* pl.10–13). A
81	AR	16.56	EVOIVRIX (Paulsen pl.35, Forrer p.128; BN 10160). BM
82	AR	17.18	DEVIL (var. BN 10164; Paulsen fig. 779–81, Forrer p.128) BM
83	AR	16.70	TITTO (Paulsen fig.811–13; BN 10159). BM
84	AR	16.91	BVSV (Paulsen fig.785–9; BN 10141). BM

Plate 8

Silver of the Rhône Valley and Garonne Basin

85	AR	17.21	Punic tetradrachm of Sicily (fourth century B.C.). A (*SNG* 2158)

86 AR 7.42 Roman didrachm, 280–276 B.C (Crawford 13/1). A
87 AR 2.51 IALIKOVESI (BN 2537–43). H *Rhône Valley* p.684 no.1
88 AR 2.31 KASIOS (BN 2524–36). BM
89 AR KASIOS (BN 2524–36). H
90 AR 4.55 Rhoda drachm, late third century B.C. A
91 AR 4.96 South-western Gaul, Rhoda type (BN 2337). A
92 AR 3.96 South-western Gaul, Rhoda type. A
93 AR 4.80 South-western Gaul, Rhoda type (BN 2325; Allen 2). BM
94 AR 3.59 Monnaie-à-la-croix (Allen 14 var.). A
95 AR 3.42 Monnaie-à-la-croix (Allen 14 var.). A
96 AR 3.46 Monnaie-à-la-croix (Allen 21 var,). A
97 AR 3.38 Monnaie-à-la-croix (Allen 41 var.). H *South-west Gaul* p.687 no.8.
98 AR 2.63 Monnaie-à-la-croix (Allen 37–41). A
99 AR 2.17 Monnaie-à-la-croix (Allen 123–4). A
100 AR 3.45 Monnaie-à-la-croix, UNTIKIA (Allen 125). BN 3558
101 AR 0.39 Monnaie-à-la-croix fraction (Allen 142). BM

PLATE 9

Silver of the Rhône Valley and the Garonne Basin

102 AR 1.33 Cadurci, LVXTERIOS. BN 4369A
103 AR 1.93 Northern monnaie-à-la-croix (Allen 147; BN 9284). H *Cent. Eur.* p.709,18
104 AR 2.18 Ruteni boar type (Allen 120). BM
105 AR 0.77 Magdalensberg type fraction (Göbl, *Noricum* pl.45). A
106 AR 4.74 Emporiae standing horse type (*c*.300–241 B.C). BM
107 AR 4.68 Emporiae pegasus type (*c*.241–195 B.C). A
108 AR 4.75 Emporiae pegasus Chrysaor type (218–195 B.C). MAN 3030
109 AR 4.63 South-western Gaul or Spain, Emporiae type (Nash 8). BM
110 AR 4.65 South-western Gaul or Spain, Emporiae type (Nash 5). BM
111 AR 4.39 Southern Gaul, Bridiers Emporiae type (Nash 23). BM
112 AR 4.32 Southern Gaul, Bridiers Massilia type (Nash 36). G 2736, from Bridiers hoard
113 AR 4.27 Southern Gaul, Bridiers Phillip II type (Nash 43). G 2746, from Bridiers hoard

114 AR 4.96 Southern Gaul, horseman type (Nash 47). BM
115 AR 4.35 Bridiers Massilia type (Nash 37). BN 2255
116 AR 3.85 Bridiers Emporiae type var. (Nash 63). BM
117 AR 4.09 Bridiers Emporiae type var. (Nash 61). BM

PLATE 10

Silver of the Rhône Valley and the Garonne Basin

118 AR 3.34 Poitou/Berry (Nash 124). BM
119 AR 3.29 Poitou/Berry (Nash 105). BM
120 AR 3.55 Poitou/Berry (Nash 76). BN 4433
121 AR 3.04 Poitou/Berry (Nash 85). BM
122 AR 2.64 Pictones (Nash 623). BM
123 AR 2.11 Limousin/Berry (Nash 661). A
124 AR 1.87 Limousin/Berry (Nash 500–2). A
125 AR 1.85 Limousin/Berry (Nash 513–14). MAN 3922, from Tendu hoard
126 AR 3.20 Elusates (Nash 70). H *South-west Gaul* p.687, 11
127 AR 3.17 Elusates. A
128 AR 2.64 Elusates. BM
129 AR 1.87 Sotiates: ADIETVANVS REX SOTIOTA. BN 3605

PLATE 11

Central European Gold

130 AV 8.60 Alexander III stater (336–323 BC). A (*SNG* 2520)
131 AV 7.22 Alexander type (Castelin fig.4). BM
132 AV 4.83 Alexander type (Forrer 486). BM
133 AV 5.72 Lake Constance type (Forrer 359). BM
134 AR 6.56 Roman didrachm (Crawford 22/1) 265–242 B.C. A
135 AR 16.70 Philip V tetradrachm (221–179 B.C). BM
136 AV 2.78 Alkis type (Castelin 35). BM
137 AV 2.75 Alkis type (Castelin 38). BM
138 AV 2.55 Alkis type (Castelin 47). BM
139 AV 2.39 Alkis type (Castelin 50). BM
140 AV 2.43 as last. BM
141 AV 6.97 Mussel type (Castelin 26). BM
142 AV 6.47 Mussel type with BIATEC legend (Castelin 31). BN 10165
143 AV 2.68 Alkis variant (Castelin 79). BN 9488
144 AV 7.95 Boar-warrior (Castelin 73). BN 9364
145 AV 2.74 Boar-warrior (Castelin 74). BN 9365

146 AV 7.82 Runner (Castelin 67). BN 9366
147 AV 2.50 Runner (Castelin 71). BN 9367
148 AV 0.90 Runner (Castelin 72). BN 9368

PLATE 12

Central European Gold

149 AV 0.98 Head-steer (Castelin 60). BN 9462A
150 AV 0.95 Head-horse (Castelin 86). BN 9462
151 AV 0.91 Runner variant (Castelin 83). BN 9373
152 AV 7.97 Thunderbolt type (Castelin 81). BN 9369
153 AV 0.37 Janus head type. BN 9464
154 AV 7.51 Rainbow-cup (Forrer 396). BM
155 AV 7.53 Rainbow-cup (Forrer 5). BM
156 AV 7.53 Rainbow-cup (Forrer 20). BM
157 AV 7.45 Rainbow-cup (Forrer 393, BN 9443). BM
158 AV 7.29 Rainbow-cup (BN 9434). BM
159 AV 7.30 Belgic bullet type, Suessiones(?) (Scheers fig.128). A
160 AV 7.16 Mardorf type (Forrer 399; Scheers fig.256). BM
161 AV 7.08 as last. BM
162 AE 5.26 Mardorf type, bronze version (BN 9441–2). A

PLATE 13

Gold of Gaul

163 AV 8.56 Philip II stater (359–336 B.C.). BM
164 AV 8.36 Rhineland Philip type (Nash 210). BM
165 AV 4.18 Rhineland Philip type. BM
166 AV 7.53 Rhineland Philip type (Nash 301). BN 3655A
167 AV 8.28 Rhineland type with cantharos. BM
168 AV 7.50 Central-western lyre type (Nash 230). BN 4541, found at Limoges
169 AV 7.68 Central-western lyre type (Nash 254). BN 6415
170 AV 1.92 Central-western lyre type (Nash 201). BN 6418
171 AV 8.55 Gironde area trident type (Nash 153). BM
172 AV 8.33 EIQITIVICO (Nash 169). BN 10289
173 AV 7.88 Philip type. BN 3627
174 AV 6.95 Burgundy (Nash 158–60). BM
175 AV 7.55 Rhineland(?) (Nash 305). BM
176 AV 7.08 Central Gaul, lyre type (Nash 266). BN 5951
177 AV 1.65 Central Gaul, lyre type (Nash 269). BN 5954
178 AV 7.11 Central Gaul, lyre type with KABAΛΛ. BN 5957

PLATE 14

Gold of Gaul

179	AV	6.77	Aedui, Chenôves type (Nash 166). H *Uncertain Gaulish* p.712, 8
180	AV	1.61	Aedui, Chenôves type (Nash 165). BN 4846
181	AV	7.00	Uncertain Gaulish. BM
182	AV	7.92	Central Gaul (Nash 239). BM
183	AV	7.82	Treveri (Scheers fig.130). BM
184	AV	1.87	Helvetic (Allen *Revue Suisse de Num.* (1974) pl.14). A
185	AV	1.77	Helvetic (ibid.). A
186	AV	1.95	Helvetic (ibid.). BM
187	AV	7.83	Aulerci Cenomani. BN 6829
188	AV	1.95	Rhineland. BM
189	AV	3.91	Early Armorican. H *North-west Gaul* p.692, 2
190	AV	3.95	Early Armorican. BN 6937
191	AV	2.01	Early Armorican (BN 6941). H *Armorica* p.691, 3
192	AV	8.56	Tarentum stater. BM
193	AV	1.93	Somme area (Scheers fig.8). H *North-east Gaul*, p.696, 10
194	AV	4.01	Somme area (Scheers fig.33). BM

PLATE 15

Gold of Gaul

195	AV	8.11	Armorica. BN 6756
196	AV	7.65	Belgic Gaul, Caleti(?) (Scheers fig.92). BM
197	AV	1.83	Belgic Gaul (Scheers fig.100). BM
198	AV	1.92	Belgic Gaul (Scheers fig.99). BM
199	AV	7.45	Somme area (Gallo-Belgic A; Scheers fig.63). BM
200	AV	1.77	Somme area (Gallo-Belgic A; Scheers fig.79). A, found in Marlborough forest
201	AV	7.60	Gironde area, Tayac type (Nash 156–7 var.). BN 3654A
202	AV	7.30	Arverni (Nash 363). BN 3766, Pionsat hoard
203	AV	7.44	Arverni, VERCINGETORIX (Nash 321). BN 3774, Pionsat hoard
204	AV	7.42	Arverni, VERCINGETORIX (Nash 326). BN 3775, Pionsat hoard
205	AV	7.31	Arverni, CAS (Nash 320). BN 3767
206	AV	6.79	Bituriges Cubi, ABVDOS (Nash 465). BM
207	AV	6.73	Bituriges Cubi, SOLIMA (Nash 472). BM
208	AE	2.04	Bituriges Cubi, ABVDOS (Nash 478). A

209 AE 3.25 Bituriges Cubi, ILAVSO (Nash 484–5). BN R.1271, Fondettes hoard

PLATE 16

Gold of Gaul

210 AV 6.38 Pictones (Nash 618). H *West Gaul* p.688, 8
211 AV 5.28 Pictones, SA. H *West Gaul* p.689, 13
212 AV 7.46 Namnetes. BN 6723, found at Candé, Maine-et-Loire
213 AV 7.25 Namnetes (BN 6723). A
214 AV 7.48 Veneti. BN 6881
215 AV 7.80 Veneti. BN 6879
216 AV 7.61 Osismi (BN 6768). BM
217 AV 2.00 Osismi (Nash 207). A
218 bill 6.44 Osismi (BN 6541). A
219 bill 6.55 Unelli / Baiocasses. A
220 bill 6.66 Coriosolites (BN 6614). A
221 bill 6.27 Coriosolites (BN 6703). A
222 AV 6.70 Andecavi / Aulerci Cenomani (BN 6493). BM
223 AV 6.17 Redones (BN 6774). BM

PLATE 17

Gold of Gaul

224 AV 7.30 Helvetii (BN 9302 var; Allen *Revue Suisse de Num.* (1974) pl.10). BM
225 AV 7.02 Leuci(?) (Scheers fig.261). BM
226 AV 6.56 Rhineland (Scheers fig.297). BM
227 AV 1.93 Rhineland (Scheers fig.280). BM
228 AV Rhineland (Scheers fig.283). Munich
229 AV 1.78 Rhineland (Scheers fig.289). BM
230 AV 1.81 Rhineland (Scheers fig.149) BM
231 AV 7.18 Parisii (BN 7782). BM
232 pot 3.79 Parisii (BN 7820). BM
233 AV 3.25 Aulerci Eburovices. BM, from Lens hoard
234 AV 1.54 Aulerci Eburovices. BM
235 AV 1.75 Belgic Gaul, Veliocasses(?) (Scheers fig.171). BM
236 AE 3.12 Veliocasses (Scheers fig.602). A
237 AV 6.54 Ambiani (Gallo-Belgic C; Scheers fig.86). A
238 AV 5.90 Ambiani (Gallo-Belgic E; Scheers fig.155). BM
239 AV 1.50 Belgic Gaul, Morini(?) (Gallo-Belgic DA; Scheers fig.124). BM
240 AV 1.26 Belgic Gaul, Morini(?) (Gallo-Belgic DC; Scheers fig.116). BM

PLATE 18

Gold of Gaul

241	AV	6.15	Suessiones (Gallo-Belgic F; Scheers fig.176). BM
242	AV	5.64	Nervii, Epsilon type (Scheers fig.217–18). BM
243	AV	5.62	Nervii, VIROS (Scheers fig.219). BM
244	AE	4.93	Nervii, VIROS (Scheers fig.220). BM
245	AV	5.42	Eburones (Scheers fig.254–5)
246	AV	5.66	Treveri (Scheers fig. 229). H *Northern Gaul* p.694, 10
247	AV	6.29	Treveri (Scheers fig.222). H *Northern Gaul* p.694, 8
248	AV	5.99	Treveri, LVCOTIO (Scheers fig.228). BM
249	AV	5.49	Treveri, POTTINA (Scheers fig.230–1). BM
250	AV	5.90	Suessiones, CRICIRV (Scheers fig.184). BN 7944A
251	AR	2.30	Suessiones, CRICIRV (Scheers fig.188). BN 7946
252	AE	3.43	Suessiones, CRICIRV (Scheers fig.193). BM
253	AE	3.13	Suessiones, CRICIRV (Scheers fig.192). A
254	AV	5.75	Suessiones, ROVECA (Scheers fig.194). BN 7632
255	AR	2.26	Suessiones, ROVECA (Scheers fig.197). BN 7633
256	AR	2.43	Suessiones, ROVECA (Scheers fig.201). BM
257	AE	3.64	Suessiones, ROVECA (Scheers fig.209a). BM
258	AE	2.74	Suessiones, ROVECA (Scheers fig.208a). A

PLATE 19

Spanish and Celt-Iberian Mints

259	AR	3.95	Bolscan (Osca) (de Guadan 348). A
260	AR	3.87	Iltirda (de Guadan 178–81). A
261	AR	3.99	Arsaos (de Guadan fig.370). A
262	AR	2.99	Turiaso (de Guadan 217–19). A
263	AR	3.23	Segobriga (de Guadan 391). A
264	AE	15.09	Cese (de Guadan 263–4). A
265	AE	11.30	Secaisa (de Guadan fig.280). A
266	AE	10.57	Saiti (Saetabis; de Guadan 125). A
267	AE	8.76	Beligiom (de Guadan 214). A
268	AE	13.87	Emporion (Villaronga pl.XIV). A
269	AE	6.09	Emporion (Villaronga pl.I, 8). A

PLATE 20

Spanish and Celt-Iberian Mints

270	AE	9.22	Narbo, NERONCEN (Hill pl.I, 1–4). A
271	AE	10.20	Narbo, NERONCEN (Hill pl.I, 5). A

272	AE	4.97	Narbo, NERONCEN (Hill pl.II, 5). A
273	AE	7.26	Spain, Secaisa (de Guadan pl.31). BM
274	AE	6.83	BHTAPPATIC (Hill pl.IV, 8). BM
275	AE	10.69	KAIANTOΛOY BAΣIΛ (Hill pl.V,2). H *South-west Gaul* p.686,2
276	AE	10.22	BITOYKOC BACIΛ (Hill pl. V, 5–6). BM
277	AE	10.27	BITOYIO BACIΛE (Hill pl.V, 5–6). H *South-west Gaul* p.686, 4
278	AE	11.28	PIΓANTIK (Hill pl.V, 7). H *South-west Gaul* p.686, 3
279	AE	9.18	Longostaletes, BωKIOC (Hill, pl.IV, 5). BM
280	AE	8.18	Longostaletes, ΛOYKOTINOC ΠVPΠ (Hill p.20). BM

Plate 21

Silver of Gaul

281	AR	2.31	IAZUS (BN 2904). H *Rhône Valley* p.684, 2
282	AR	2.09	VOL (BN 2621). A
283	AR	1.68	Allobroges, bouquetin type (BN 2879). A
284	AR	2.39	Allobroges, hippocamp type (BN 2917). A
285	AR	2.12	Rhône Valley, CN VOLVNT (BN 5895). A
286	AR	2.14	Rhône Valley, COMA (BN 5815–90). A
287	AR	2.21	Rhône Valley, BRIC (COMA) (BN 5807–14). A
288	AR	1.90	Rhône Valley, DVRNACOS AVSCRO (BN 5749). A
289	AR	1.93	Rhône Valley, DVRNACVS DONNVS (BN 5786). H *Rhône Valley* p.685, 10
290	AR	0.46	Rhône Valley fraction. BM
291	AR	1.85	Aedui or Lingones, KAΛETEΔOY SVLA (BN 8291 var.). H *East and central Gaul*, p.699, 1
292	AR	1.85	Aedui or Lingones, KAΛETEΔOY. H *East and central Gaul* p.699, 2
293	AR	1.96	KAΛETEΔOY variant. A
294	AR	1.00	as last. H *Uncertain* p.713, 17
295	AR	1.64	Sequani, Q DOCI SAM F (BN 5405). BM
296	AR	1.98	Sequani, Q DOCI / Q DOCI. BM
297	AR	1.82	Sequani, TOGIRIX (BN 5550). A
298	AR	1.75	as last. BM
299	AR	1.87	Sequani, Q IVLIVS TOGIRIX (BN 5632). BM
300	AR	1.77	Eastern Gaul, ARIVOS SANTONOS (BN 4525–34). BM
301	AR	1.81	Aedui, ORCETIRIX ATPILLI F (BN 4805). BM

Plate 22

Silver of Gaul

302	AR	2.32	Arverni, PICTILOS (Nash 430). BN 4012
303	AR	2.28	Auvergne, EPOMEDVOS (Nash 441). BN 4030
304	AR	2.38	Arverni, EPAD (Nash 420). BN 3884
305	AE	1.83	Arverni, CICIIDV.BRI IIPAD (Nash 422). BN 3894
306	AR	1.60	Rhineland, Pfalz type (Scheers fig.342). BM
307	AR	2.01	South-western Gaul (Nash 686). BN 4310A
308	AR	1.76	Leuci, SOLIMA / COΛIMA (BN 9025). BM
309	AR	1.95	Aedui, ANORBO DVBNORIX (BN 4945–5025). BM
310	AR	1.89	Aedui, DIASVLOS (BN 4870–84). BM
311	AR	1.92	Aedui, ΔOYBNO. BN 4886
312	AR	1.96	Aedui, ΔOYNO (BN 4926). BM
313	AR	1.94	Sequani, SEQVANOIOTVOS (BN 5351). BM
314	AR		Sequani, SEQVANOIOTVOS overstruck. BM
315	AR	2.30	Avenio drachm (BN 2513). BM
316	AR	1.61	Aedui, DVBNOCOV DVBNOREX (BN 5026). BM
317	AR	1.94	Aedui, DVBNOCOV DVBNORIX (BN 5044). BM
318	AR	1.84	Eastern Gaul, VIIPOTAL (BN 4484). BM
319	AR	1.91	Eastern Gaul, VIIPOTAL (BN 4495). A
320	AR	1.95	Eastern Gaul, LVCCIOS (BN 4336–43). A
321	AR	1.59	Aedui, LITAVICCVS (BN 5072). BM

Plate 23

Silver of Gaul

322	AR	1.88	Central or western Gaul, NERCOD (BN 4535–6). BM
323	AR	1.91	Belgic Gaul, CALEDV (Scheers fig.310). BM
324	AR	1.87	Western Gaul, BIINOS (BN 7050–3). BM
325	AR	1.89	Pictones, DVRAT IVLIOS (Nash 632). BM
326	AR	1.75	Belgic Gaul, ATEVLA VLATOS (Scheers fig.305). A
327	AR	1.60	as last (Scheers fig.306). BM
328	AR	1.69	Belgic Gaul, SENODON CALEDV (Scheers fig.309). BM
329	AR	1.92	Arverni, EPAD (Nash 423). BM
330	AE	2.47	Arverni, EPAD. A
331	AR	4.11	Denarius, C. Piso Frugi (Crawford 408/1) 67 B.C. A
332	AR	2.03	Aedui (BN 4858). BM

333 AR Aedui, EDVIS ORCETIR (BN 4822–31). H
334 AR 4.12 Denarius, C. Antius Restio (Crawford 455/1). 47 B.C. A
335 AR 1.62 Eastern Gaul, SEGVSIAVS ARVS (BN 4622). BM
336 AR 1.80 as last. A
337 AR 1.81 Bituriges Cubi, CAM (Nash 492). BN 4139
338 AR 1.91 Bituriges Cubi, IVRC (Nash 494). ANS
339 AR 1.91 Bituriges Cubi, CAMBOTRE (Nash 488). BM

PLATE 24

Western Gaulish Silver Fractions

340 AR 0.38 ESVIOS. BM, from Rozel hoard, Jersey
341 AR 0.30 BM
342 AR 0.26 BM
343 AR 0.36 BM

German Silver Types

344 AR 1.89 Bushel type. BM
345 AR 1.56 Bushel type. BM
346 AR 1.59 Bushel type, with MV. BM
347 AR 1.69 NINNO. BM
348 AR 1.62 MAV. BM
349 AR 1.91 Head/horse. H *East and central Gaul* p.701, 20
350 AR 1.97 Torque bearer. H *Northern Gaul* p.694, 13
351 AR 1.66 Torque man/horse. A

Late Silver and Bronze of Gaul

352 AR 1.21 Pallas head, Loire area (BN 5967). BM
353 AR 0.78 Rouen-Amiens type (Scheers fig.336). BM
354 AR 0.53 Hampshire type from le Catillon hoard. Allen *RN* 1965 no.30
355 AR 0.92 Belgic Gaul, Ambiani(?) (Scheers fig.337). BN 8514, found near Amiens
356 AR 0.52 Belgic Gaul. BN 10390
357 AR 0.47 Belgic Gaul. BN 10408
358 AV 1.25 Southern Britain, Selsey type (Mack 79). BM
359 AR 2.40 Aisne area, NIDE ΛABROΔIIOS (Scheers fig.322). BM

PLATE 25

Late Silver and Bronze of Gaul

360 AR 1.61 Atrebates, CARSICIOS COMMIOS (Scheers fig.319). BN 8687

361	AR	1.68	Atrebates, GARMANOS COMMIOS (Scheers fig.313–14). BM
362	AE	3.77	Atrebates, ANDOBRV GARMANOS (Scheers fig.315–16). BM
363	AE	5.57	Bituriges or Carnutes, VANDIILOS. BN 8073, found in Paris
364	AE	2.89	Bituriges or Carnutes, CALIAGIIIS (BN 8000). BM
365	AE	1.05	Arverni, DCANAVNOS (Nash 427). BN 3873
366	AR	2.32	Arverni, PICTILOS (Nash 430). BN 4012
367	AE	1.55	Arverni, CALEDV (Nash 425). BN 3932
368	AE	2.07	Carnutes, EΛKESOOYIZ TASGIITIOS. H *North-west Gaul* p.692, 3
369	AE	2.97	Carnutes (BN 6088). A
370	AE	4.16	Carnutes (BN 6322). BM
371	AE	3.05	Carnutes, YLLYCCI (BN 7493). BM
372	AE	3.42	Carnutes, GIAMILOS SIINV (BN 7565). A
373	AE	3.16	Remi, REMO/REMO (Scheers fig.519–20). A
374	AE	2.65	as last. A
375	AE	2.57	Eastern Gaul. BN 5093

PLATE 26

Late Silver and Bronze of Gaul

376	AE	1.61	Western Gaul, ANNICOIOS (Nash 638). BM
377	AE	1.44	Western Gaul, CONTOVTOS (Nash 637). BM
378	AE	1.45	Western Gaul, ATECTORI (Nash 636). BM
379	AE	3.32	Western Gaul, VIREDIOS (Nash 633). BN 4473
380	AE	3.82	Western Gaul, SACTNOS (Nash 635). BN 4514
381	AE	2.59	Northern Gaul, GERMANVS INDVTILLI L. A (*CRE* 460)
382	AR	3.90	Denarius, Julius Caesar (Crawford 443/1) 49/8 B.C. A
383	AE	3.05	Treveri, A HIRTIV (Scheers fig.564). BN 9235
384	AE	2.43	Treveri, A HIRTIV variant (Scheers fig.565). H *Northern Gaul* p.697,18
385	AE	1.87	Southern Gaul, T POM SEX F (BN 4353–62). BM
386	AE	2.21	Amiens area, VACIICO (Scheers fig.397). BM
387	AE	2.99	Ambiani (Scheers fig.404). BM
388	AE	2.45	Ambiani(?) (Scheers fig.416). BN 8518
389	AE	3.50	Oise area (Scheers fig.483). BN 8495
390	AE	2.67	Ambiani (Scheers fig.422). BN 8505
391	AE	2.28	Ambiani (Scheers fig.421 var.). BM

PLATE 27

Late Silver and Bronze of Gaul

392	AE	1.01	Britain, Tasciovanus (Mack 181). BM
393	AE	1.63	Britain, Tasciovanus, Verulamium mint (Mack 179). A
394	AE	1.01	Britain, Tasciovanus (Mack 182). BM
395	AE	2.55	Britain, Cunobelin (Mack 248). BM
396	AR	2.57	Britain, Cunobelin (Mack 249). A
397	AE	1.23	Britain, Cunobelin (Mack 256). BM
398	pot	1.47	British class I potin (Mack 17a). BM
399	pot	1.67	British class I potin, showing graining (Mack 9). A
400	pot	1.40	British class II potin (Mack 23). BM
401	pot	3.98	Sequani, Q DOCI (BN 5508). BM
402	pot	3.18	Sequani, TOC (BN 5611). BM
403	pot	2.54	Sequani TOC/TOC (BN 5620–30). BM
404	pot	3.95	Central or eastern Gaul, TVRONOS CANTORIX (BN 7002–14). BM
405	AE	9.99	Massilia bronze. A
406	pot	3.97	Central Gaul, early potin with MA. BN 5311
407	pot	4.69	Alesia type potin. BN 7434
408	pot	3.83	Leuci potin (Scheers fig.658). A
409	pot	3.45	Leuci potin (Scheers fig.667). A

PLATE 28

Late Silver and Bronze of Gaul

410	pot	3.86	Lingones potin (BN 8329). A
411	pot	5.10	Bellovaci potin (Scheers fig.655). BM
412	pot	4.48	Remi potin (Scheers fig.684). BM
413	pot		Remi potin (Scheers fig.689). BM
414	pot	4.12	Remi potin (Scheers fig.689). A
415	pot	3.75	Remi type variant (Scheers fig.688). BN 8135
416	pot	2.48	Senones(?) potin (BN 7388). BM
			Legends on Coins
417	AV	6.81	Northern Gaul (Scheers fig.147; Nash 306). BN 10190B
418	AR	3.88	Roscius Fabatus denarius (Crawford 412/1), 64 B.C. A
419	AR	3.56	Danubian imitation of Fabatus denarius. A
420	AE	13.67	Iberic inscription UNTIKESCEN (Emporiae) (Villaronga pl.VII, 58). A
421	AE	12.10	Duumviri at Calagurris under Tiberius:

			L.FVL.SPARSO and L.SATVRNINO (de Guadan p.205). A
422	AR	4.05	SESARS/BOLSCAN (de Guadan fig.368). A
423	AR	2.07	Caenicenses, ΚΑΙΝΙΚΗΤΩΝ. BN 2245
424	AR	2.22	Glanum, ΓΛΑΝΙΚΩΝ. BN 2247
425	AE	2.18	Samnagetes, Castico. BN 2263, found at Orange

Plate 29

Legends on Coins

426	AV	7.30	Salassi. BN 9270
427	AR	1.94	Aedui, ΔΟΥΝΟ (BN 4926–40). A
428	AV	6.98	ΘΙΟΛΕ, Marne region. BN 8944
429	AE	1.51	Southern or western Gaul, CMEP. BN 4363
430	pot	5.15	Bellovaci, ΑΓΙΙΔ (Scheers fig.654–5). BN 7467
431	pot	3.11	Eastern Gaul, ΔSS, corruption of ΟΥΙΝΔΙΑ. BN 8326
432	AE	3.35	Paris area, ΔΕΙΟΥΙGΙΙΑGΟC (Scheers fig.550). BN 7729
433	AE	3.97	Treveri, ΑΡΔΑ (Scheers fig.243–4). BM
434	AE	1.93	Treveri, ARDA (Scheers fig.246). BM
435	AE	3.82	Paris area, VENEXETOS (Scheers fig.643–4). A
436	AV	1.35	British with CAMUL (Cunobelin, Camulodunum; Mack 202). BM
437	AE	1.70	Poitou, VRIDO.RVF. BN 4333, found at Poitiers
438	AV	5.12	British, Iceni, ANTEDI (Mack 418). BM
439	AR	1.20	British, Iceni, ANTED (Mack 420). A

Plate 30

Legends on Coins

440	AV	0.99	British, Tincommius COM F (Mack 104). BM
441	AV	5.30	British, Verica CO F (Mack 125). A
442	AV	5.42	British, Eppillus COM F (Mack 301). BM
443	AE	1.47	British, Cunobelin TASCIOVANI F (Mack 242). BM
444	AE	1.68	British, Cunobelin TASC. FIL (Mack 245). BM
445	AV	5.28	British, Epaticcus TASCI F (Mack 262). BM
446	AE	5.50	Remi, ATISIOS REMOS (Scheers fig.521–4). A
447	AE	5.66	as last. BM
448	AR	1.79	Aedui, EDVIS ORGET. BN 4824
449	AR	1.14	British, Eppillus (Mack 108). BM
450	AV	5.32	British, Verica (Mack 121). BM
451	AE	2.42	British, Cunobelin (Mack 246). BM

452	AV	5.44	British, TASCI RIGONI (Mack 184). H p.721, 2
453	AE	6.92	Lexovii, SIMISSOS PVBLICOS LIXOVIO / CISIAMBOS. CATTOS VERGOBRETO. A
454	AE	5.64	as last. H *North-western Gaul*, p.691, 1
455	AE	9.45	Lexovii, CISIAMBOS / ARCANTODAN. BN 7158

PLATE 31

Legends on Coins

456	AE	3.33	Mediomatrici, ARC AMBACT (Scheers fig.500–1). BM
457	AE	3.56	as last. H *East Gaul* p.699, 34
458	AE	2.27	Mediomatrici, AMBACTVS (Scheers fig.503–4). BM
459	AV	5.38	Britain, Coritani VOLISIOS / DVMNOCOVER (Mack 463). BM
460	AV	5.32	Britain, Coritani VEP CORF (Mack 459). BM
461	AV	5.40	Britain, Coritani DVMN / TIGIR SENO (Mack 461). BM
462	AV	4.49	Britain, Dobunni ANTEDRIG (Mack 386). BM
463	AV	5.37	Britain, Dobunni CATTIO (Mack 391). BM
464	AE	2.80	Northern Gaul, AΘIIDIAC / A HIR IMP. BN 8087
465	AV	1.02	Britain, Eppillus CALLEV (Mack 107). BM
466	AE	1.74	Britain, Tasciovanus VER (Mack 177). BM
467	AV	5.51	Britain, Cunobelin CAMUL (Mack 201). BM
468	AE	2.08	Volcae Arecomici, AREC (BN 2677). A
469	AE	2.27	Mediomatrici, MEDIOMA (Scheers fig.499). BM
470	AR	1.22	Britain, Iceni, ECE (Mack 419). BM

PLATE 32

Coin Types and Motifs

471	bill	6.78	Armorica. BM, from le Catillon hoard
472	AV	7.23	Central Gaul (Nash 291). BN 10231A
473	AR	1.17	Britain, ANDOCO (Mack 199). BM
474	AR	1.02	Britain, Tasciovanus (Mack 158). BM
475	AE	1.01	Britain, Tasciovanus (Mack 182). BM
476	AR	1.83	Carnutes(?) ANDECOMBO (BN 6342). BM
477	AE	1.95	Britain, Cunobelin (Mack 253). BM, Colchester excavations
478	AE	2.64	Britain, Cunobelin (Mack 251). BM, found near Boulogne
479	AR	12.57	Hungarian antlered rider. BN 9723
480	AR	13.90	as last. BN 9807
481	AE	3.18	Britain, Cunobelin (Mack 252). BM

482	AE	1.77	Britain, Tasciovanus (Mack 167). BM, found at Braughing
483	AR	3.43	Western-Central Gaul (Nash 108). A
484	AR	2.12	Britain, Cunobelin (Mack 223). BM
485	AR	4.52	South-western Gaul (Nash 33). BN 2250, from Bridiers hoard
486	AV	7.50	Armorica, Aulerci Cenomani(?) (BN 6830). A
487	AV	7.23	Armorica. BM
488	AR	4.45	South-western Gaul (Nash 48). BN 2305B
489	AR	4.54	South-western Gaul (Nash 55). H p.712, 11

Plate 33

Coin Types and Motifs

490	bill	6.95	Armorica, Redones(?) (BN 6793). BM
491	AR	4.61	South-western Gaul (Nash 14). H p.712, 10
492	AE	2.54	Britain, Cunobelin (Mack 243). BM
493	AR	1.24	Britain, Cunobelin (Mack 237). BM
494	AR	1.02	Britain, Dobunni, BODVOC (Mack 396). BM
495	AR	3.84	Denarius, L. Hostilius Saserna (Crawford 448/2) 48 B.C. A
496	AR	3.77	Denarius, L. Hostilius Saserna (Crawford 448/3) 48 B.C. A
497	AR	1.06	Britain, Cunobelin (Mack 240). BM
498	AR	1.27	Britain, Cunobelin (Mack 240). A
499	AV	4.03	Amiens area, third century B.C. (Scheers fig.13). BM
500	AV	4.05	Normandy, third century B.C. BN 6927
501	AV	3.73	as last. BN 6928
502	AV	3.80	as last. BM
503	AV	7.94	Touraine, third or second century B.C. BN 6421A
504	AV	1.89	Normandy, third century B.C. BM
505	AR	4.75	South-western Gaul (Nash 26). BN 2276
506	AE	3.11	Britain, Cunobelin (Mack 221). BM
507	AR	1.28	Britain, Cunobelin (Mack 215). BM

Plate 34

Coin Types and Motifs

508	AE	2.00	Britain, Tasciovanus (Mack 171). BM
509	AE	3.31	Carnutes, PIXTILOS. H *Northern Gaul* p.693, 9
510	AE	3.03	Northern Gaul, TVRONOS TRICCOS. BN 6996
511	AE	2.21	Britain, Cunobelin (Mack 244). BM
512	AR	1.15	Britain, Cunobelin (Mack 238). BM

513	AR	1.31	Britain, Verica (Mack 130). BM
514	AR	0.92	Britain, Verica (Mack 126). BM
515	AV	2.12	Lower Loire. BN 6721, found near Ancenis
516	pot	4.85	Belgic, Remi(?) (Scheers fig.687). BN 8143, found near Troyes
517	AR	16.82	Pannonia, COISA (Paulsen fig.798–801). BN 10163
518	AE	2.73	Northern Gaul, ECCAIOS (BN 7471). BM
519	AV	7.95	Central Gaul. BN 6901
520	AE	1.54	Britain, Tasciovanus (Mack 192). BM
521	AE	2.49	Britain, Cunobelin (Mack 249). BM
522	AR	1.19	Britain, Cunobelin (Mack 235). BM, found at Sandy
523	AV	2.04	Rhineland. BN 4614A
524	AR	1.10	Britain, Cunobelin (Mack 234). BM
525	AR	1.23	Britain, Tasciovanus (Mack 165). BM

Plate 35

Coin Types and Motifs

526	AV	8.25	Western Gaul(?). BN 6422
527	AR	1.15	Britain, east Midlands (Mack 435). BM
528	bill	0.45	Armorica. BM
529	AV	3.25	Aulerci Eburovices. BM, from the Lens hoard
530	bill	6.44	Armorica. BM
531	AR	0.89	Britain, Dubnovellaunos (Mack 287). BM, found at Canterbury
532	AE	2.12	Britain, British LY7 (Kent; Mack 296). BM
533	pot	6.01	Northern or eastern Gaul (BN 8351). BM
534	pot	3.43	as last. BM
535	pot	2.51	Middle Loire. BM
536	AE	2.13	Carnutes (Blanchet fig.244 var.). A
537	AE	3.97	Carnutes, PIXTILOS (BN 7095). A
538	AR	0.88	Britain, Verica (Mack 123). BM
539	AE	3.53	Carnutes or Bituriges. A
540	AE	3.62	Carnutes. A
541	AR	1.28	Britain, Epaticcus (Mack 263). BM

Plate 36

Coin Types and Motifs

542	AV	4.57	Limousin. BN 4072
543	AE	2.87	Bellovaci (Scheers fig.474). BN 8584
544	AR	1.14	Britain, east midlands (Mack 445). BM
545	AE	3.12	Carnutes (BN 6077). A

546	AR	0.84	Britain, Cunobelin (Mack 214). BM, Colchester excavations
547	bill	6.62	Armorica, Redones(?). BN 6811
548	bill	6.96	as last. BN 6804
549	AV	7.49	as last. BN 6769C
550	AV	5.34	Britain, Verica (Mack 125). BM
551	AV	5.05	Britain, Cunobelin (Mack 206). A
552	AR	1.13	Britain, Epatticus (Mack 263a). BM, Chichester excavations
553	AV	5.42	Britain, Tasciovanus TASCIO SEGO (Mack 194). BM
554	AV	7.22	Western Gaul. BN 4511.2
555	AR	2.27	Western Gaul. BN 4553
556	AV	1.33	South-eastern Britain (Mack 36). Canterbury Museum

PLATE 37

Coin Types and Motifs

557	bill	6.09	Western Armorica (de la Tour J13). BM
558	AV	7.75	Sequani. BN 5318
559	AV	6.99	Central Gaul/Armorica. BN 6913
560	AV	1.90	Rhineland. BN 3670
561	AE	3.04	Veliocasses, SVTICOS (Scheers fig.614). BM
562	AR		Western Gaul, BIIINOS (BN 7050–4). MAN 2998
563	AE	2.94	Carnutes PIXTILOS (BN 7100). BM
564	AE	2.13	Britain, Cunobelin (Mack 260a). BM
565	AV	1.98	Lower Loire (BN 6950–1). H *Armorica* p.691, 2
566	AV	4.15	as last. BN 6950, found near Caen
567	AV	1.90	as last. A
568	AR	1.12	Britain, Verica (Mack 129). BM
569	AV	7.49	Arverni (BN 3711). BM
570	AV	5.54	Britain, Coritani (Mack 447). BM

PLATE 38

Coin Types and Motifs

571	=	42	
572	=	199	
573	=	55	
574	=	225	
575	AV	5.38	Britain, Dobunni EISV (Mack 388). BM
576	AR	2.38	Rhône Valley VOL. BN 2630

577 = **61**
578 = **62**

PLATE 39

Dies. Positive impressions are shown with **580** and **581**.

579 Reverse die for Bituriges Cubi silver coins, found on Puy de Corent (Puy-de-Dôme) in 1845. Bronze, originally in an iron shaft. MAN 12273. (Allen 'Wealth, money and coinage in a Celtic society', in J. V. S. Megaw (ed.) *To Illustrate the Monuments, Essays … Stuart Piggott* (1976) p.205).

580 Reverse die for TOGIRIX silver coins, found at Camp Sainte-Germaine, Bar-sur-Aube (Aube). Bronze, originally in an iron shaft. BN. (Ibid.)

581 Impressions from a bronze cast in MAN (25836) of a reverse die for Rhône Valley silver coins inscribed VOL; original in the Bibliothèque municipale, Grenoble. Probably found at Moirans, Isère. (Ibid.)

PLATE 40

Coin Moulds from Verulamium
(a) Belgic mint mould plate, approx. half size;
(b) Baked clay mould fragments from the Belgic mint, approx. half size

PLATE 41

The Gundestrup Cauldron
Silver cauldron with decorative panels in relief, middle la Tène culture, first-second century B.C, votive deposit in bog at Gundestrup, Jutland, Denmark. (Photos Nationalmuseet, Copenhagen)
(a) General view; (b) detail of internal panel.

The Plates

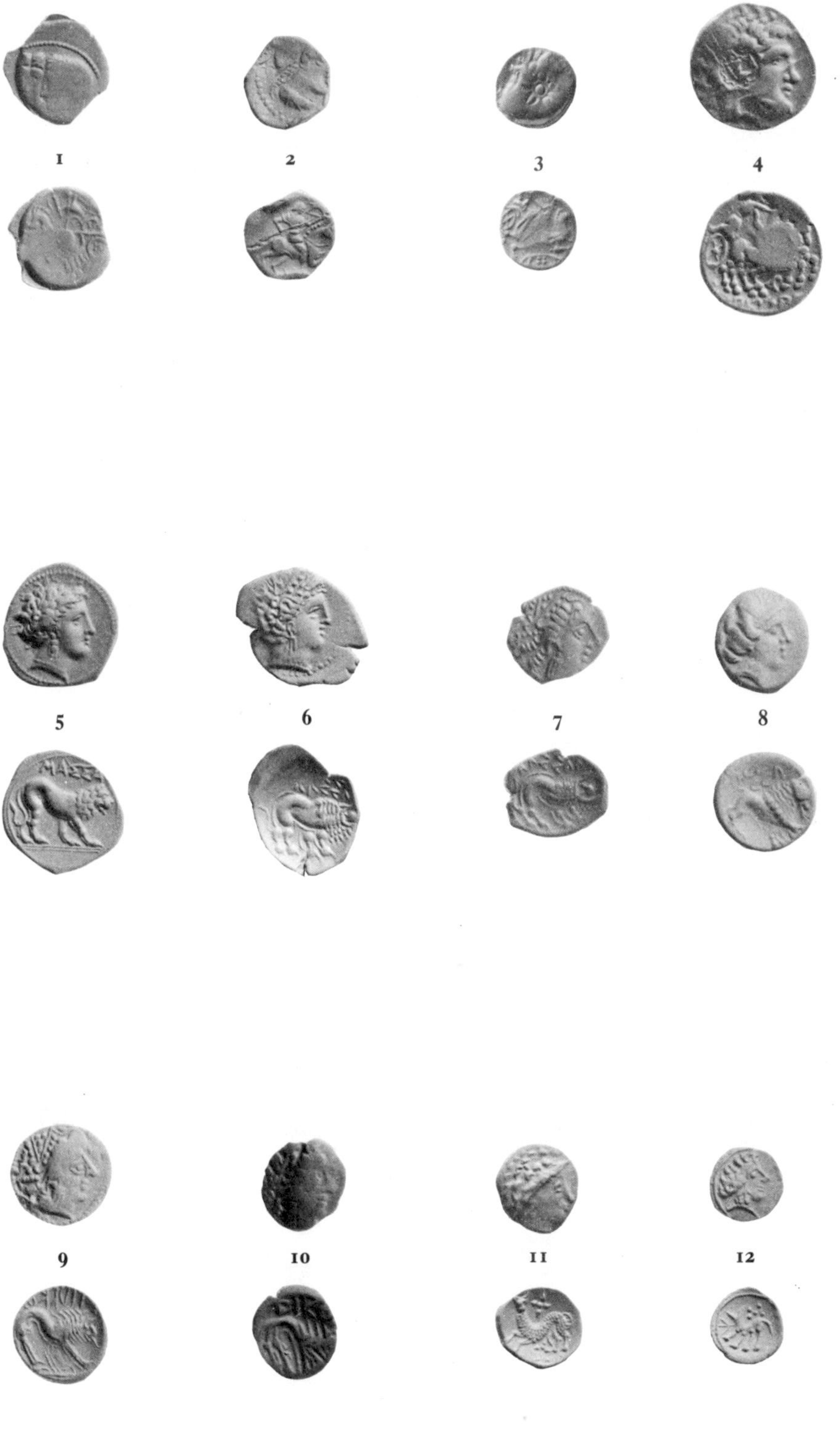

PLATE I

13

14

15

16

17

18

19

20

21

22

PLATE 2

23 24 25

26 27 28

29 30 31

PLATE 3

32 33 34

35 36 37 38

39 40 41

PLATE 4

PLATE 5

55 56 57 58 59

60 61 62 63 64

65 66 67 68

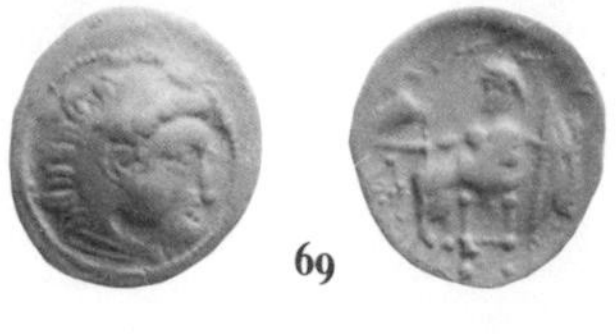

69

70

PLATE 6

71 72 73 74

75 76 77 78 79

80 81 82 83 84

PLATE 7

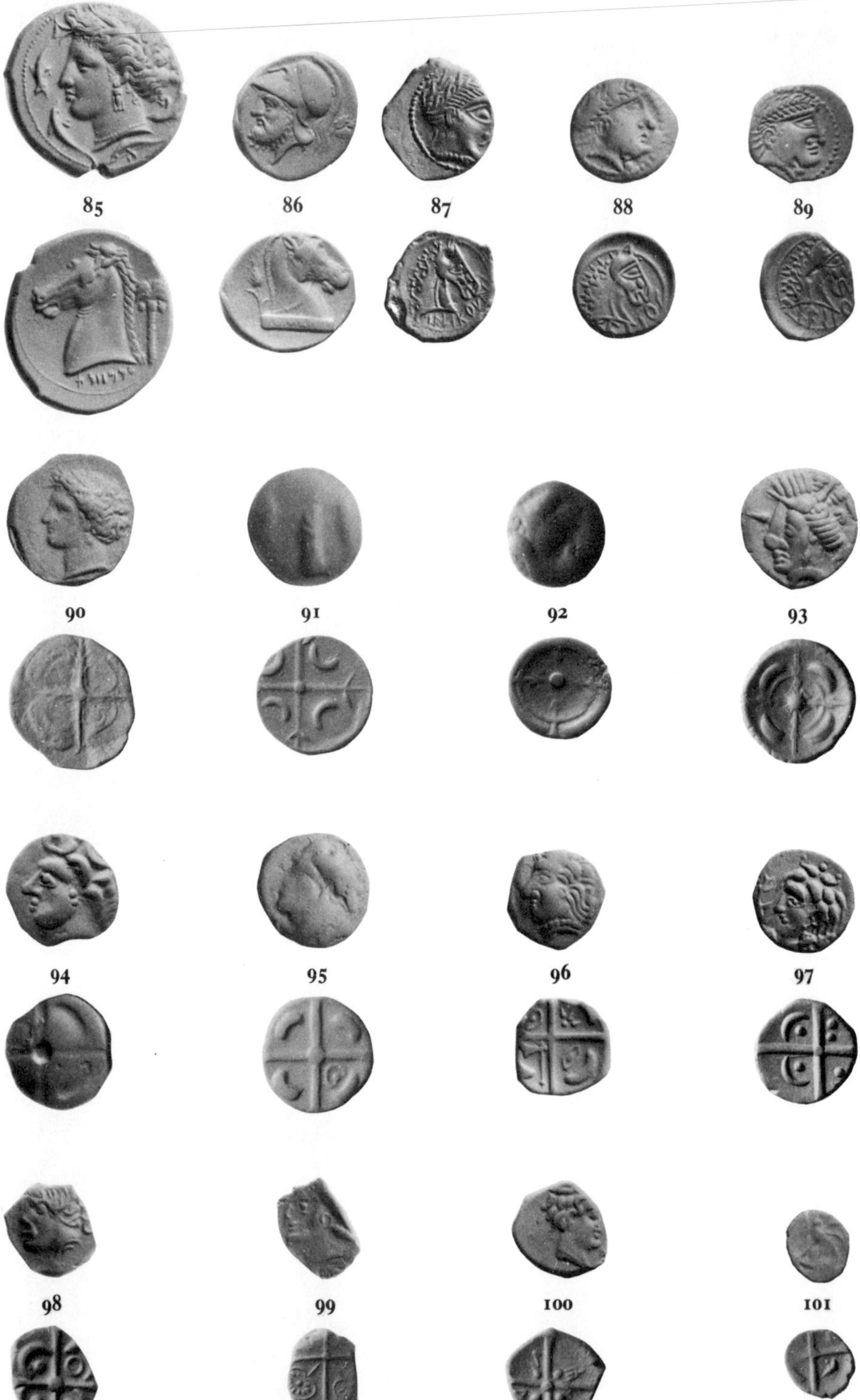

85 86 87 88 89

90 91 92 93

94 95 96 97

98 99 100 101

PLATE 8

102 103 104 105

106 107 108 109

110 111 112 113

114 115 116 117

PLATE 9

118

119

120

121

122

123

124

125

126

127

128

129

PLATE 10

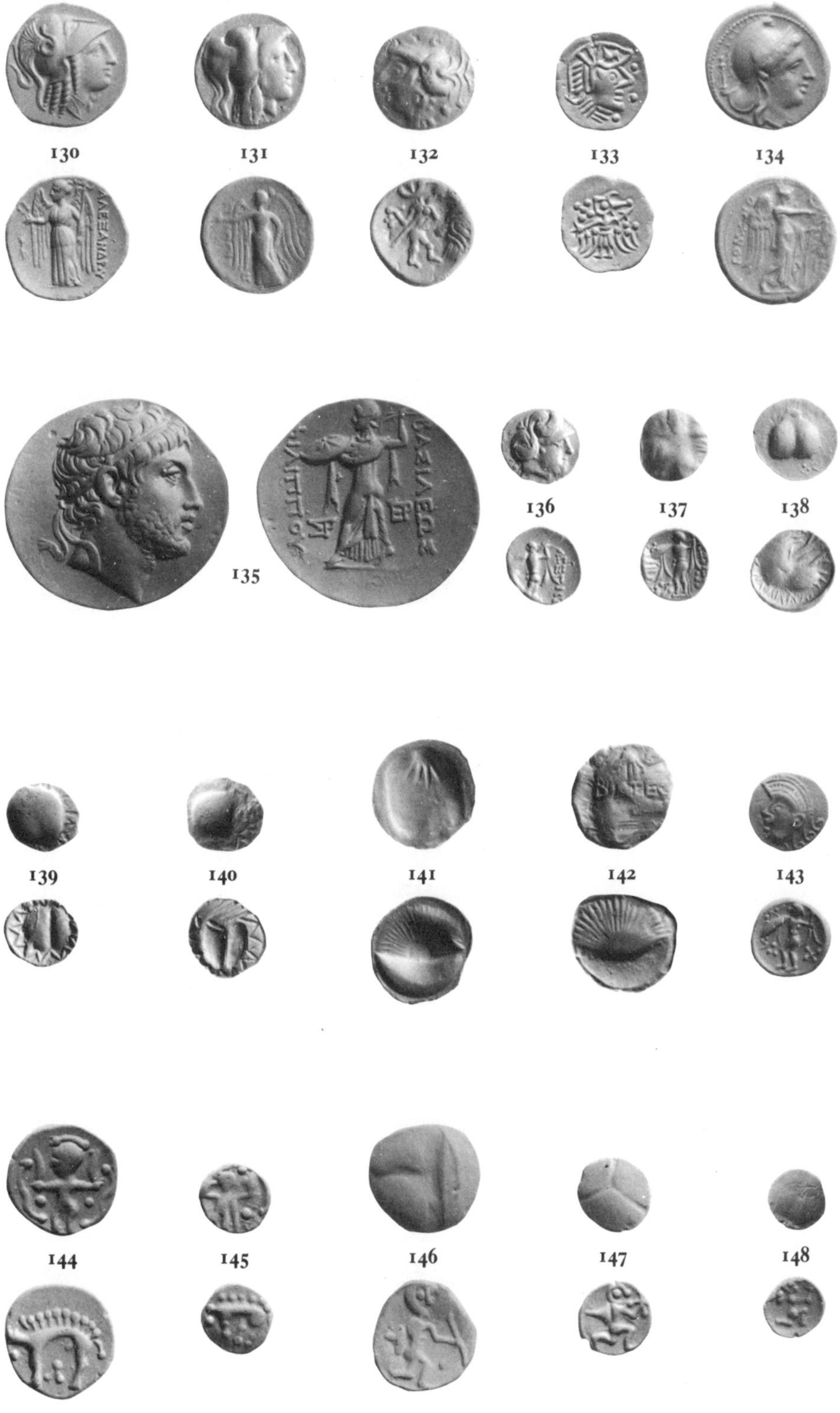
130
131
132
133
134
135
136
137
138
139
140
141
142
143
144
145
146
147
148

PLATE II

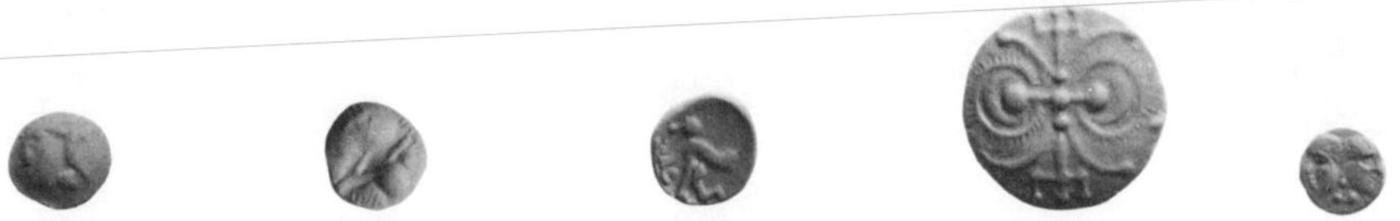

149 150 151 152 153

154 155 156

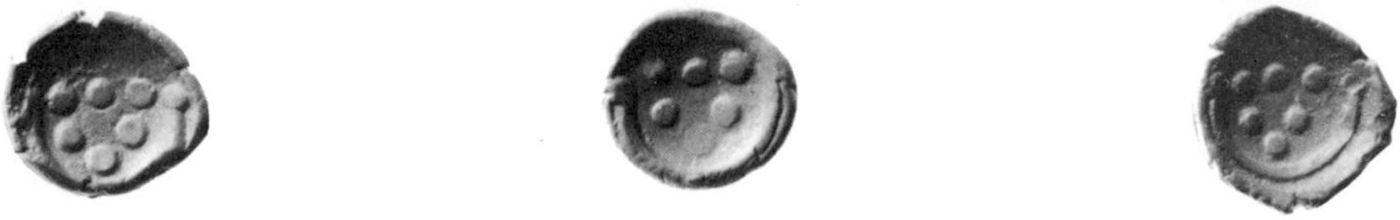

157 158 159

160 161 162

PLATE 12

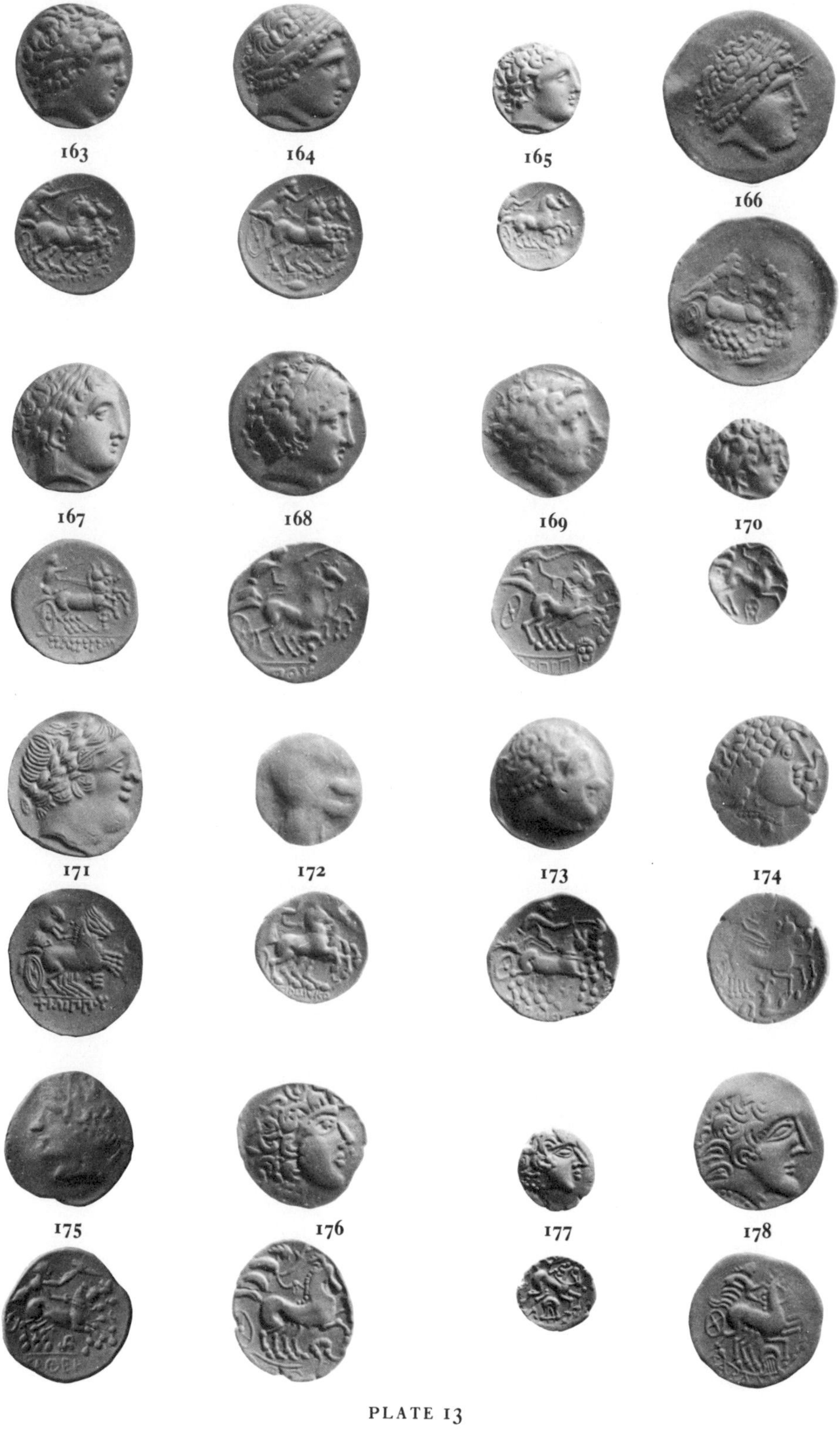

163 164 165 166 167 168 169 170 171 172 173 174 175 176 177 178

PLATE 13

179 180 181 182

183 184 185 186

187 188 189 190

191 192 193 194

PLATE 14

195

196

197

198

199

200

201

202

203

204

205

206

207

208

209

PLATE 15

210 211 212 213

214 215 216 217

218 219 220 221

222

223

PLATE 16

224 225 226

227 228 229 230

231 232 233 234 235

236 237 238 239 240

PLATE 17

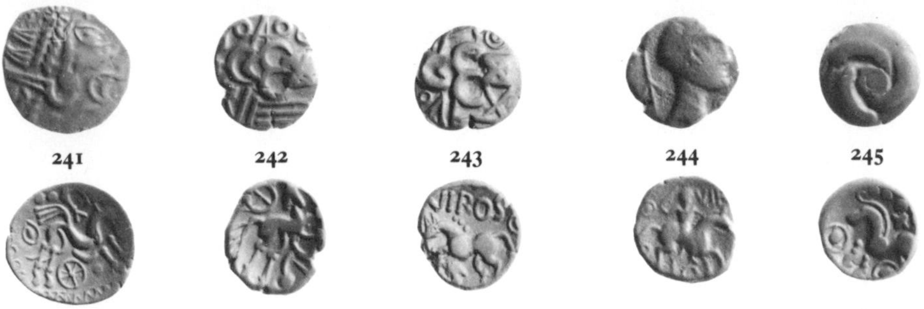

241 242 243 244 245

246 247 248 249

250 251 252 253

254 255 256 257 258

PLATE 18

259 260 261 262

263 264 265

266 267 268 269

PLATE 19

270 271 272

273 274 275 276

277 278 279 280

PLATE 20

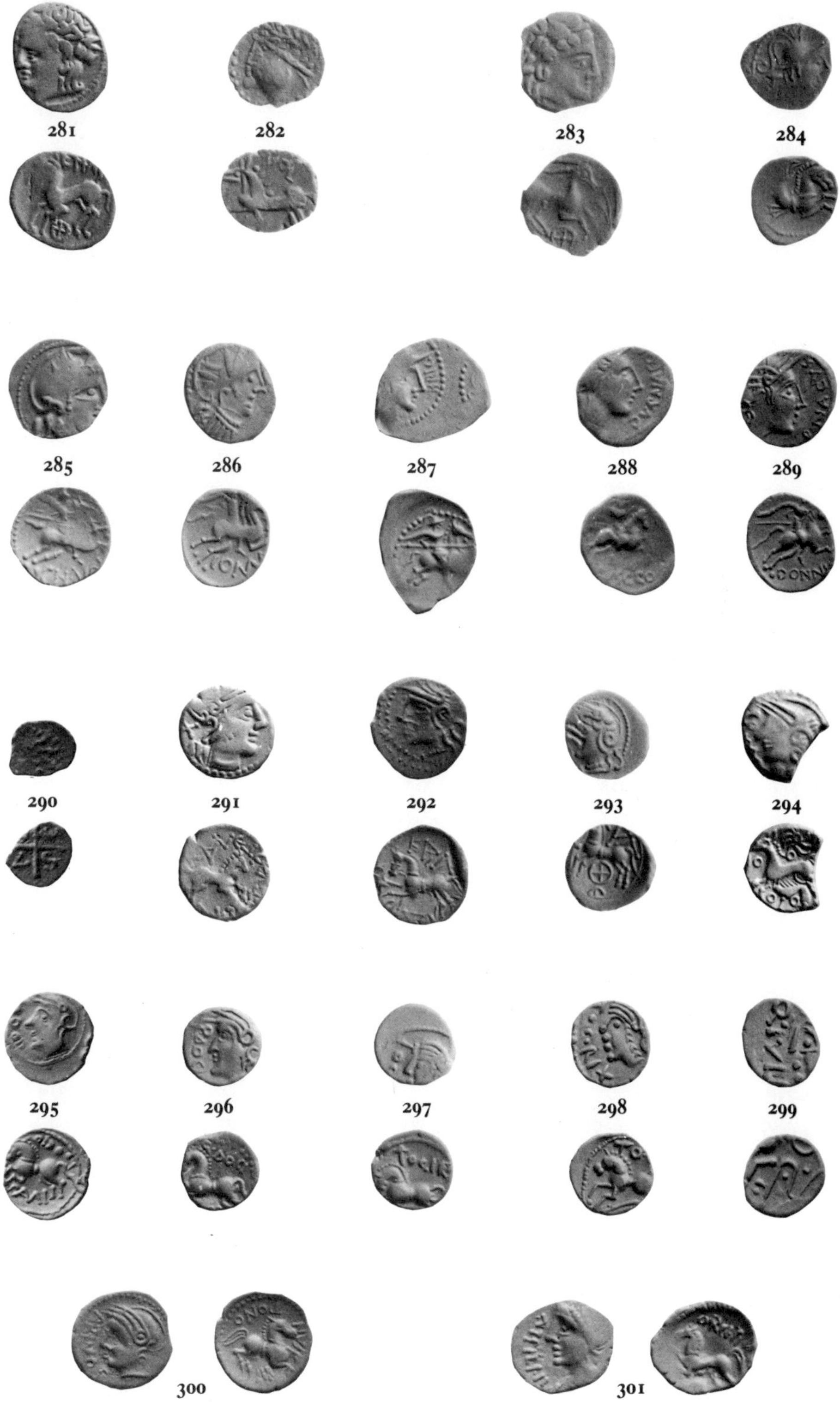
281
282
283
284
285
286
287
288
289
290
291
292
293
294
295
296
297
298
299
300
301

PLATE 21

302 303 304 305

306 307 308 309 310

311 312 313 314 315

316 317 318 319

320

321

PLATE 22

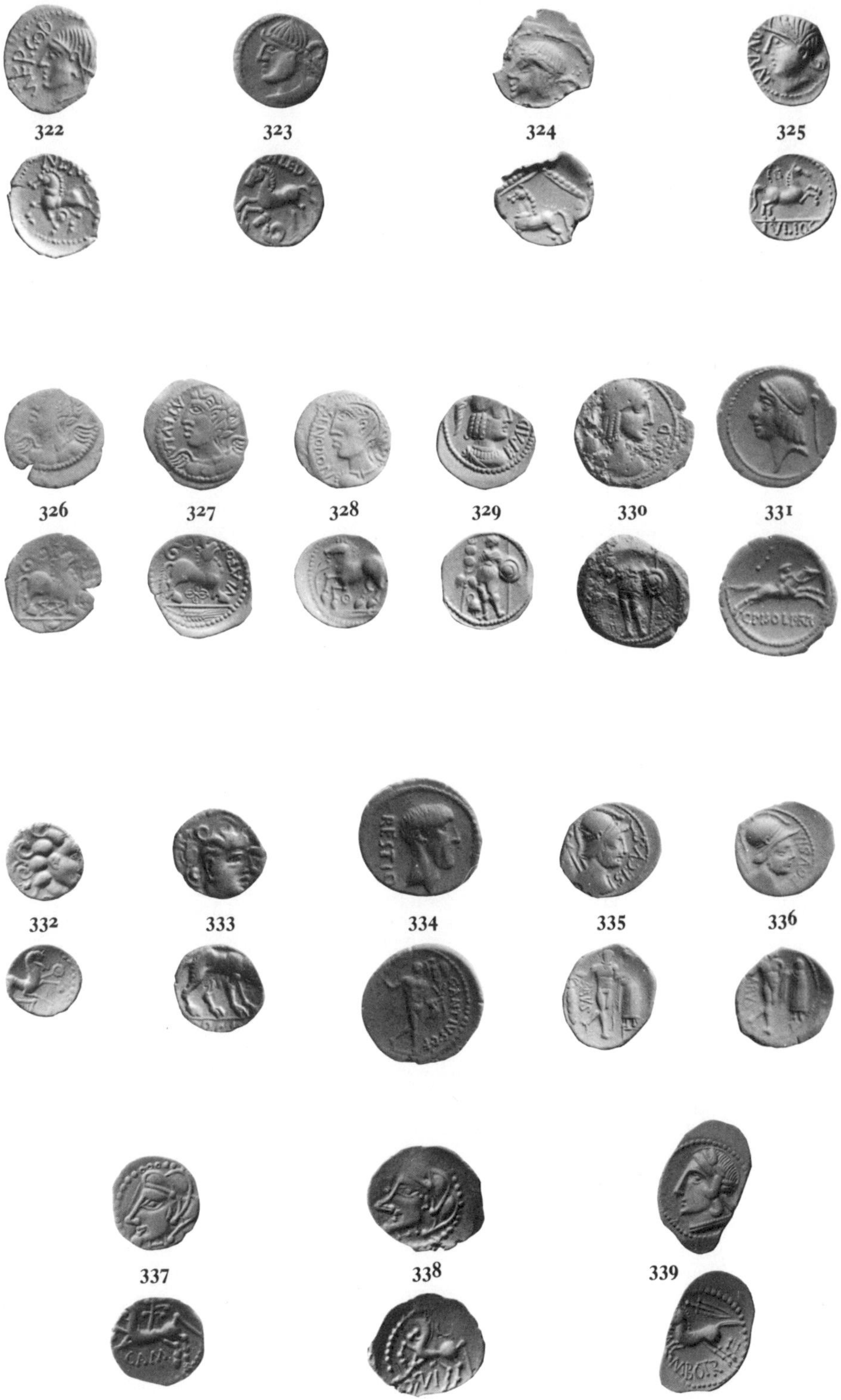

322 323 324 325

326 327 328 329 330 331

332 333 334 335 336

337 338 339

PLATE 23

340

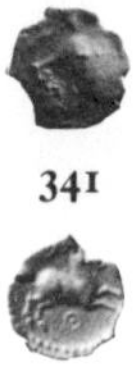
341

342

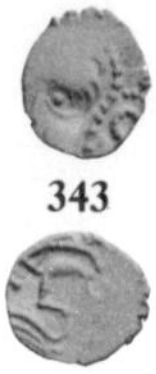
343

344

345

346

347

348

349

350

351

352

353

354

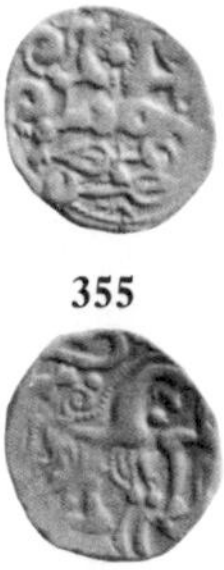
355

356

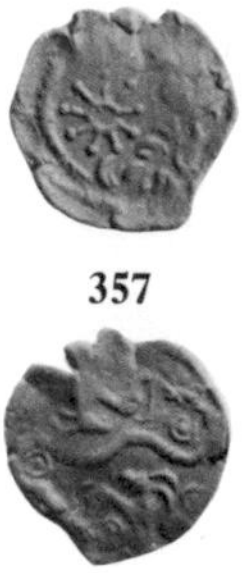
357

358

359

PLATE 24

360 361 362

363 364 365 366 367

368 369 370 371 372

373 374 375

PLATE 25

376 377 378 379 380

381 382 383 384

385 386 387

388 389 390 391

PLATE 26

392 393 394 395 396 397

398 399 400

401 402 403 404

405 406 407 408 409

PLATE 27

410 411 412 413 414

415 416 417 418 419

420

421

422 423 424 425

PLATE 28

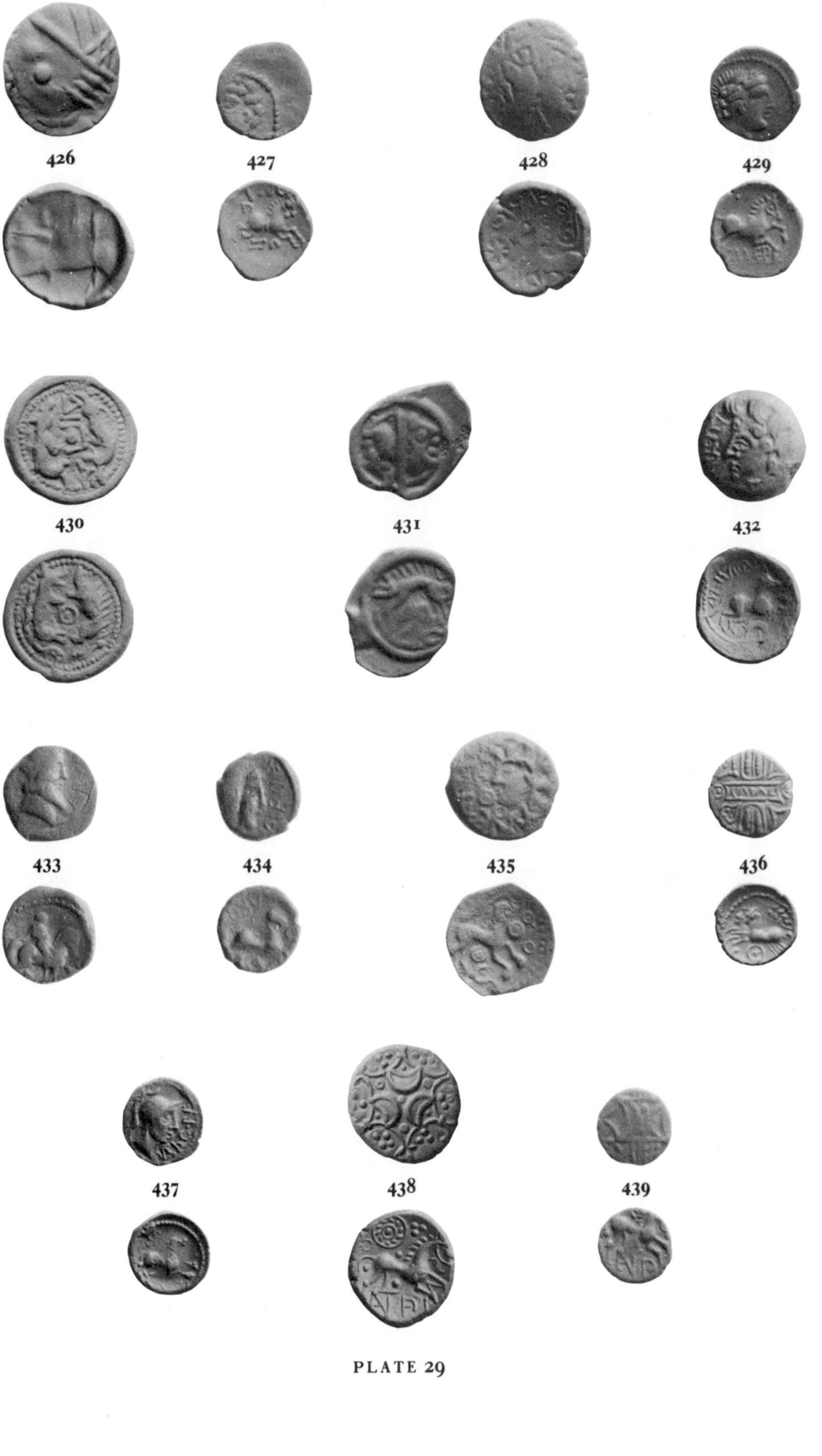

PLATE 29

440 441 442 443 444 445

446 447 448

449 450 451 452

453 454 455

PLATE 30

456

457

458

459

460

461

462

463

464

465

466

467

468

469

470

PLATE 31

471 472 473 474 475

476 477 478 479 480

481 482 483 484

485 486 487 488 489

PLATE 32

490 491 492 493 494

495 496 497 498

499 500 501 502

503 504 505 506 507

PLATE 33

508 509 510 511

512 513 514 515 516

517 518 519 520

521 522 523 524 525

PLATE 34

526

527

528

529

530

531

532

533

534

535

536

537

538

539

540

541

PLATE 35

542

543

544

545

546

547

548

549

550

551

552

553

554

555

556

PLATE 36

557

558

559

560

561

562

563

564

565

566

567

568

569

570

PLATE 37

571

572

573

574

575

576

577

578

PLATE 38

579

580

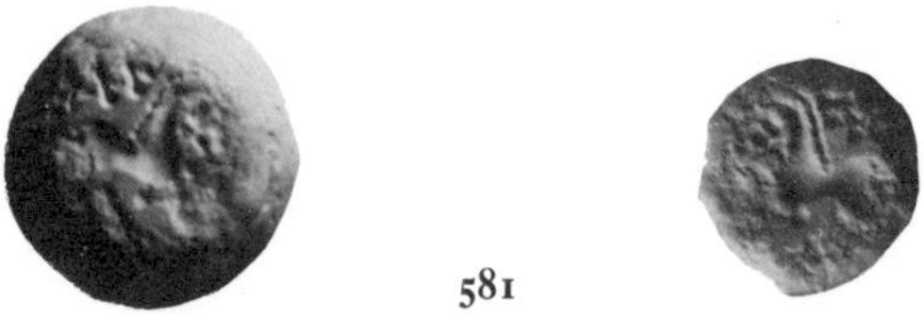

581

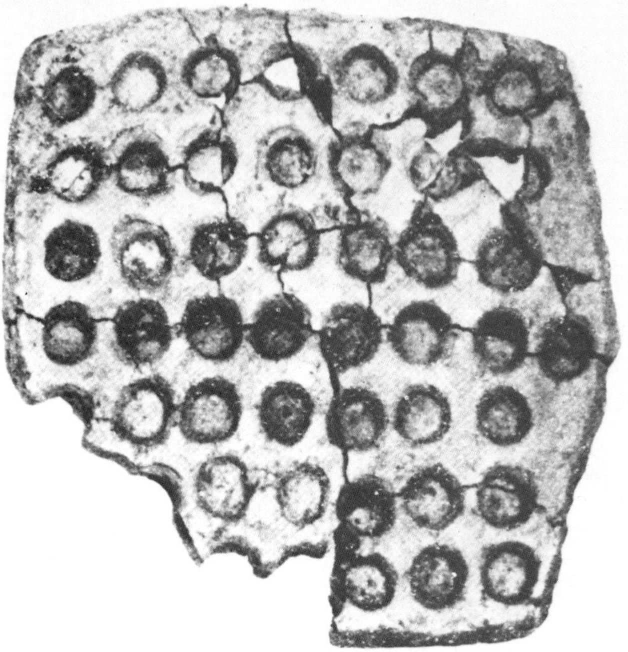

a

b

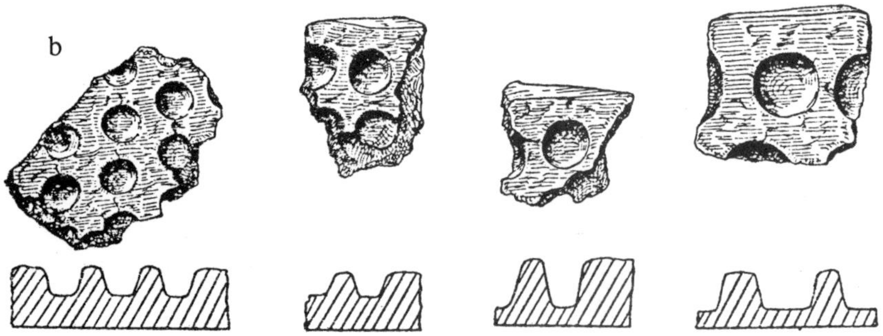

PLATE 40. COIN MOULDS FROM VERULAMIUM

PLATE 41. THE GUNDESTRUP CAULDRON

Index

References to figures and maps are shown in italic